THE EVERYTHING. CIVIL WAR BOOK

Dear Reader,

In this boc is the story of the American Civil War, the defining tragedy in our natic history ory. Indeed, the story of the Civil War has been said to be the Ar an Ilic d, a terrible struggle of will and blood that set the tone for a civili that grew to be a world power. No one who wants to understand the American story, indeed America today, can ignore the story of America's Civil War.

This is a story of more than four bloody years. The war was a long time coming and a long, long time leaving. There is heartbreak, courage, daring, honor, dishonor, disaster, cravenness, and genius to fill volumes—and it has. Here, in this single volume, we try not only to tell the struggle of the battles but also the causes of the conflict, the nature of the societies that fostered those causes, and the effects of the terrible calamity on the reunited nation. This book is rich in explanation and fact. Read through to the end and you will learn the essentials of America's greatest trial.

Brooke C. Stoddard
& Daniel P. Murphy

Welcome to the EVERYTHING Series!

These handy, accessible books give you all you need to tackle a difficult project, gain a new hobby, comprehend a fascinating topic, prepare for an exam, or even brush up on something you learned back in school but have since forgotten.

You can choose to read an *Everything®* book from cover to cover or just pick out the information you want from our four useful boxes: e-questions, e-facts, e-alerts, and e-ssentials.

We give you everything you need to know on the subject, but throw in a lot of fun stuff along the way, too.

We now have more than 400 *Everything®* books in print, spanning such wide-ranging categories as weddings, pregnancy, cooking, music instruction, foreign language, crafts, pets, New Age, and so much more. When you're done reading them all, you can finally say you know *Everything®*!

Key statistics

Important snippets of information

Memorable words

Quick handy tips

PUBLISHER Karen Cooper

DIRECTOR OF ACQUISITIONS AND INNOVATION Paula Munier

MANAGING EDITOR, EVERYTHING SERIES Lisa Laing

COPY CHIEF Casey Ebert

ACQUISITIONS EDITOR Lisa Laing

DEVELOPMENT EDITOR Elizabeth Kassab

EDITORIAL ASSISTANT Hillary Thompson

Visit the entire Everything® series at *www.everything.com*

THE
EVERYTHING®
CIVIL WAR
BOOK

2ND EDITION

Everything you need to know about the
conflict that divided a nation

Brooke C. Stoddard and Daniel P. Murphy, PhD
First edition by Donald Vaughn

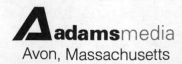
Avon, Massachusetts

Copyright © 2009, 2000 by F+W Media, Inc. All rights reserved.
This book, or parts thereof, may not be reproduced
in any form without permission from the publisher; exceptions
are made for brief excerpts used in published reviews.

An Everything® Series Book.
Everything® and everything.com® are registered trademarks of F+W Media, Inc.

Published by Adams Media, a division of F+W Media, Inc.
57 Littlefield Street, Avon, MA 02322 U.S.A.
www.adamsmedia.com

ISBN 10: 1-59869-922-9
ISBN 13: 978-1-59869-922-7

Printed in the United States of America.

J   I   H   G   F   E   D   C   B   A

Library of Congress Cataloging-in-Publication Data
is available from the publisher.

Contents

The Top Ten Facts about the American Civil War

1. Abraham Lincoln was elected on a platform not to end slavery but to deny its spread into the territories.

2. Before Robert E. Lee decided to defend his native state of Virginia, he was offered command of the Northern armies.

3. The struggle between the North and the South took place on thousands of battlefields from Ohio to the New Mexico Territory.

4. Many of the generals on either side of any given battle knew one another. Many were former roommates or friends from their years at West Point.

5. The elimination of slavery became a Northern goal only midway through the war. Lincoln had said the war was for restoring the Union; he included eliminating slavery only when he thought doing so might help the sagging war effort.

6. The high water mark of the Confederacy was likely not at Gettysburg but in early September 1862 when its armies were on the march north and England and France were seriously considering recognizing it.

7. A soldier had more to fear from disease than bullets. Twice as many soldiers on both sides died of sickness than of wounds suffered in battle.

8. Prosperous before the war, the Southern states suffered a ruined economy by war's end. The war helped spur industrialism in the North.

9. At the end of the struggle, Robert E. Lee was the most respected man in the South. He urged all Southerners to accept the verdict of the battlefield and to work as good citizens of the reunited nation.

10. The assassination of Abraham Lincoln was a disaster for the country; had the president lived, Reconstruction likely would have been less traumatic for both the North and the South.

Introduction

▶THE CIVIL WAR WAS the most severe disaster the United States has ever faced; it tore the young nation in two. The struggle was not only a constitutional crisis, it also doomed more than 600,000 Americans to their deaths and wounded an additional 400,000. It ravaged a generation of the South, and it crushed the Southern economy so badly that its recovery took half a century. It is important, therefore, to understand the Civil War, its causes, its course, its dominant personalities, its outcome, and its lasting effects.

The Civil War had many aspects. Most often remembered are the land battles, namely the thrust and parry of warfare in Virginia and the inexorable press of Union armies down the Mississippi and into Georgia. However, the land battles compose only one aspect of the conflict. There was also the naval aspect of the war, most notably the Union blockade as the Union navy worked to hamper New Orleans and other vital ports of the Southern states, and there were struggles between armed boats on the Southern rivers, which were critical to Southern transportation and trade.

And there was the war on the home front, the struggle not only to raise the armies by recruiting the young men but also to supply them with uniforms, food, ammunition, and medical care. There was the struggle to maintain the morale of the families who sent their loved ones to dangerous duties and unmarked graves. There was the struggle to win—or deny—recognition of the Confederacy by the major European powers. Economic matters were also an important part of the war, something both sides understood from the start. If the North could cripple the Southern economy, the South would not be able to support its armies in the field and thus would not survive as a nation. The blockade was meant to deny the South cash from cotton that it could use to equip its armies. As the war went on, the North used increasingly brutal means to devastate the Confederacy's farming potential. William Sherman's March to the Sea and Philip Sheridan's depredations in the Shenandoah Valley in 1864 were meant in part to cripple the supply of food to Southern armies.

And, of course, there was the aspect of slavery. Slavery was introduced to the American continent in the seventeenth century. Over the next 200 years, it became so ingrained in American culture that the South believed it could not exist without it. The North largely tolerated it, though abolitionists grew stronger and more vocal as the conflict approached, calling for full and swift emancipation, a call that itself embittered Southerners and hardened their hearts against sharing a country with their Northern cousins. Millions of African Americans lived in the South. Some were already freed and others were willing enough to work for whites with whom they had grown up, but far more were thirsting for freedom from lives of remorseless toil and corporal punishment. All across the South their lot was crushing labor and legal subjugation, yet they knew they toiled without liberty in a land whose people had themselves rebelled against legal subjugation by extolling liberty and declaring "all men are created equal."

As Abraham Lincoln said in his second inaugural address, "slavery was somehow the cause of the war." How America would struggle over and resolve the terrible institution of slavery is the principal story of the Civil War. Tragic it is, but there is more than a streak of triumph. The nation, as Lincoln foretold at Gettysburg in 1863, did "have a new birth in freedom" at war's end and started on its way to something new, a nation of different races, all free—something novel on the face of the earth.

CHAPTER 1

Causes of the Civil War

It's impossible to narrow the cause of the Civil War to a single issue or act. It's true that slavery was one of the most important contributing factors to the conflict, but it was not the singular cause. In truth, the war was the result of myriad cultural and political issues that perniciously set the North and the South against each other for decades before the first shots of the war were fired.

Regional Differences

To understand why the Civil War occurred, it is important to know what the United States was like in the mid-1800s. Unlike the fifty states we have today, the United States in the years preceding the Civil War comprised two regions that grew increasingly dissimilar. The differences between North and South escalated until they simply couldn't live as one anymore.

A short ten years before the war began, the vast majority of Americans in both the North and the South lived in rural areas rather than cities. Agriculture remained the biggest contributor to the nation's economy, and in this way the two regions were very much alike. But between 1850 and 1860, the nation's burgeoning cities—particularly in the North—received a massive influx of rural people and immigrants from other countries.

Economic Differences

The years before the war's onset saw some dramatic and fundamental changes in the nation. The North quickly took advantage of the Industrial Revolution's amazing new products, such as Cyrus McCormick's mechanical reaper, and great factories sprang up almost overnight as huge deposits of iron, coal, copper, and other important manufacturing basics were discovered and made available. It would be this industrial power, this ability to produce weapons and other goods, that would give the North a decided edge as the Civil War progressed.

In the 1850s the number of farm dwellers increased by 25 percent while urban populations rose by a remarkable 75 percent. New York City, for example, reached a population of nearly 800,000 by 1860, making it the greatest city in the Western Hemisphere. Most were immigrants, primarily from Ireland and Germany.

The Industrial Revolution did not have as profound an impact on the South. In 1852, a mere tenth of the goods manufactured in America came from Southern factories and mills. The Southern states' economy remained based primarily on agriculture, with England and the Northern states being its biggest customers. Cotton, in particular, was a huge cash crop that brought large amounts of money to the region. Tobacco, rice, indigo, and other products were also widely grown. By 1860, the South produced nearly three-fourths of the raw cotton used throughout the world, but it lacked the manufacturing capability of the North. As a result, the region was forced to buy back the goods that were created from the products it grew, placing it at an economic disadvantage and angering many Southerners.

Expansion and States' Rights

As the United States thrived and flourished during the early nineteenth century, the demand for territorial expansion grew increasingly loud. A growing number of Americans felt the nation's borders were ordained by God to extend from the Atlantic Ocean to the Pacific, a philosophy known as Manifest Destiny. If regions owned by other countries could be purchased, so be it. If not, they were more than likely to be taken by force. The Mexican War (1846–48), for example, was little more than a trumped-up conflict designed by the United States to wrest large tracts of western territory from Mexico when that country refused to sell the desired lands. On February 2, 1848, the Treaty of Guadalupe Hidalgo turned over to the United States 525,000 square miles of territory that would eventually become California, Nevada, Utah, most of Arizona and New Mexico, and parts of Colorado and Wyoming.

Manifest Destiny and the Question of Slavery

The acquisition of this western territory, as well as other tracts that had been acquired earlier, created a growing rift between the North and the South in regard to the issue of slavery and, at the same time, states' rights. The South, naturally, wanted the new territories to allow slavery, but the North did not. The Northwest Ordinance, enacted in 1787, stated that all territories north of the Ohio River were to be free; until 1819, the two regions were equally divided, with eleven states each. However, pending growth required new action.

The first solution was the 1820 Missouri Compromise, legislation that was specifically designed to keep both sides happy. Missouri entered the Union as a slave state and Maine entered as a free state.

FACT

By 1850, only a third of Americans lived in the South, compared to half at the beginning of the century. Of the nation's ten largest cities, only New Orleans was located in the South.

The territory acquired as a result of the Mexican War would require another compromise thirty years later. The Compromise of 1850, brokered by Henry Clay with Daniel Webster of Massachusetts, did little to affect the institution of slavery in the United States aside from officially prohibiting it in the District of Columbia. It admitted California into the union as a free state but allowed newly acquired territories to decide for themselves whether slavery should be permitted. Neither side was particularly satisfied with the legislation.

The Debate over States' Rights

The Missouri Compromise and the Compromise of 1850 both dealt in part with an issue of particular sensitivity to the South—states' rights. Many people, especially in the South, felt the federal government had no right to decide important issues within a state, and the shifting balance of power between the federal government and individual states remained a hot-button issue that contributed strongly to the beginning of the Civil War.

The Tenth Amendment states, "the powers not delegated to the United States by the Constitution, nor prohibited by it to the States, are reserved to the states respectively, or to the people." To most citizens of the South, this amendment clearly prevented the federal government from interfering in a state's individual affairs—such as the institution of slavery. If changes were to be made, only the population of a given state could make them. In short, the proud Southern states didn't like being told what to do and begged simply to be left alone.

An example of how strongly the Southern states felt about Northern intrusion can be found in South Carolina's 1832 suspension of a heavy 1828 tariff placed on imports at the insistence of Northern merchants. When a South Carolina state convention issued an ordinance nullifying the tariff, it brought the nation to the brink of war. President Andrew Jackson threatened to send federal troops to the port of Charleston to enforce the tariff, and the governor of South Carolina threatened to meet them with an armed militia. War was only averted with the Compromise Tariff of 1833, which gradually reduced tariffs until 1842. As a result, the South Carolina convention voted to repeal the Ordinance of Nullification, ending the crisis.

The Issue of Slavery

Without question, the issue of slavery was one of the most volatile in the smoldering enmity between the North and the South. In the decade prior to the onset of hostilities, the voice of abolition grew steadily louder in the North, forcing the South into an increasingly uncompromising defensive position. The more the North insisted that slavery was morally wrong and should be abolished, the more the South resisted. But it would take the 1860 presidential election of Abraham Lincoln—and the South's perception that his administration was going to push for the abolition of slavery nationwide—to cause eleven Southern states to secede.

Slavery in America's History

Though the imprisonment of another human being for forced labor is unimaginable today, the institution of slavery has a long history in this country. Slaves were used for labor in the original thirteen colonies. The first shipment of Africans was brought to this country in August 1619, arriving at Jamestown, Virginia, on a Dutch ship; they were sold as indentured servants, though their plight was little different from that of outright slaves. Some of the United States' most revered figures, including George Washington and Thomas Jefferson, were slave owners. Washington freed his slaves in his will; Jefferson, his finances shaky, had to rely on his creditors to grant his five favorite slaves their freedom. By the time of the Revolutionary War, slavery was legal in all thirteen colonies, though those in the Northern regions were beginning to realize that the institution simply wasn't profitable. The five Northern colonies eventually banned slavery outright, but it continued to flourish in the South, where slaves were used to work plantations and large farms.

Between 1510 and 1870, millions of Africans were captured from their homeland and taken around the world and sold into a life of slavery. Nearly half of them were brought to the Western Hemisphere, where the climate encouraged large-scale agriculture. Outlawed in all Northern states by 1846, slavery quickly became the backbone of the Southern agricultural economy. In particular, the growing global demand for cotton gave the institution new life at a time when many people in both the North and the South were starting to believe it would disappear by itself if it were left alone.

The Tragedy of Human Cargo

The import of slaves to the United States from West Africa was barbarism in its rawest form. Commonly known as the Triangle Trade, it involved exchanging rum, cotton, and other goods with Arab traders for West African slaves, selling the slaves to plantation owners in the West Indies, and returning to America with profits from the sale of goods and slaves who had been "broken in" on the Caribbean islands.

The voyage from Africa to the West Indies was the most harrowing and brutal portion of the trip. Slaves, having first been fattened up like cattle, were placed in a ship's hold with little room to sit up, much less stand. They were painfully shackled together, poorly fed, given impure water to drink, and lacked any type of sanitary facilities. The voyage from Africa to the West Indies could take from six to ten weeks, and many slaves died during the trip from a wide range of diseases. Their bodies were simply tossed overboard.

The Life of a Slave

The life of a slave in the South was exhausting, degrading, and filled with violence. Those employed as farmhands faced backbreaking labor and grueling hours. Farmhands were to be in the fields at daybreak and were forced to work almost nonstop until the sun went down. Most farmhands worked six days a week, with Sunday off if they were lucky.

Slaves were expected to obey their masters without question and to always show great humility by lowering their gaze and speaking softly whenever they were in the company of whites. Dissent was met with harsh punishment, including vicious beatings with whips. Slaves who tried to escape were sometimes hobbled with a spike through the ankle or placed in iron fetters. Some slaves were forced to wear slave collars that had bells on them; a more punishing version had lengthy prongs sticking out on four sides that prevented its wearer from lying down. Minor offenses such as drunkenness or simple disobedience were often punished by a day in wooden stocks, which clamped tightly around the slave's neck and wrists.

Since slaves seldom benefited from their labor, most worked as slowly and poorly as they could get away with without being punished, contributing to the inherent inefficiency of the system as a whole. They had little to live for—nothing to look forward to except hard labor until the day they died—and many took their own lives. Dead slaves were often buried at night because their families and friends had to work all day. In the eyes of many slave owners, a slave's death wasn't sufficient cause to lose even an hour of work time. Plantation and farm owners worked hard to keep their slaves subservient, but rebellion was more common than many people realize.

Slave Revolts

Many slaves revolted by working slowly, poorly, and inefficiently, or by quietly sabotaging tools and farm equipment. There were violent and armed insurrections as well.

Probably the most violent mass slave uprising was the Stono Rebellion of 1739, in Stono, South Carolina. In that incident, a slave named Jemmy led approximately twenty other slaves in an attack on a store that resulted in the death of two white shopkeepers. Taking what weapons they could find, including guns and powder, the small group quickly grew to nearly 100 slaves. With Saint Augustine, Florida—and supposed freedom—their destination, the gang went on a killing spree that resulted in the deaths of more than thirty whites. An armed militia eventually cornered the group in a field, slaughtering forty-four of them. Two other violent slave revolts occurred in

South Carolina that same year, resulting in even more brutal laws for the control of slaves.

Nat Turner's Rebellion in 1831 was the largest and one of the most famous slave uprisings. Turner, a slave who became a Baptist preacher, organized a revolt in Southampton County, Virginia, after receiving divine instructions. He and seven companions killed their master and his family and took weapons and other supplies. They swept through the county, killing whites and attracting slaves. In the end, fifty-five whites were murdered, including twenty-four children. Turner and nineteen other slaves were hanged; twelve others were banished from Virginia.

The Fugitive Slave Act and the Underground Railroad

The Fugitive Slave Act required federal marshals and deputies to aid in the capture and return of escaped slaves throughout the United States. It was included in the Compromise of 1850 as a way of appeasing the South, but it served only to inflame the angry passions of abolitionists in the North. Antislavery and anti-Southern sentiment skyrocketed in the Northern states as a result of the Fugitive Slave Act, and moderate abolitionists joined their more militant brothers in protesting what they saw as federally subsidized kidnapping.

Abolitionists feared the new law would lead to terrible abuses against Negroes living in the North, and they were right. There are reports of Southern bounty hunters arresting and sometimes kidnapping blacks who had lived in the North as free people or claiming children born in freedom to escaped slaves as "property" of their parents' original owners. As a result, efforts on the part of abolitionists to protect blacks living in the North increased dramatically.

The Underground Railroad was a loose system of safe havens that helped slaves escape to the North. Runaway slaves usually traveled the Underground Railroad by night, walking or riding from one safe house, or "station," to another until they were able to cross the border into a free state. The most frequently traveled routes ran through Ohio, Indiana, and western

Pennsylvania. Many slaves continued on until they were safely in Canada, which refused to deport escaped slaves.

A black family entering Union lines with a loaded cart *Photo courtesy of the National Archives (200-CC-657)*

Abolitionists participating in the Underground Railroad were subject to harassment and even imprisonment. But as the issue of slavery became increasingly important, more and more abolitionists volunteered their time and homes.

The Many Voices of Abolition

The call for the end of slavery could be heard as far back as Colonial days, but the abolitionist movement didn't become a serious force in the North until the 1830s. Driven primarily by religious fundamentalism, early abolitionists felt that slavery was a moral abomination. Not surprisingly, Southerners felt otherwise and viewed the growing abolitionist movement as just another Northern force trying to encroach on their lifestyle and economy.

The first official abolitionist organization, the American Anti-Slavery Society, was founded in 1833 and called for the complete eradication of slavery. Members also wanted full political rights for freed blacks. The abolitionist movement spread quickly, and soon there were more than 1,000 chapters in the Northern states, boasting a membership of nearly a quarter of a million people.

Abraham Lincoln was once rumored to have greeted Harriet Beecher Stowe as "the little lady who started this great war." Stowe's *Uncle Tom's Cabin*, published in 1852, explored slavery from a slave's perspective. Only the Bible outsold *Uncle Tom's Cabin* in the nineteenth century, and it sparked both action from abolitionists and protest from proponents of slavery.

Many abolitionists faced violent reaction in both the North and the South, and it wasn't uncommon for abolitionist newspaper offices to be ransacked. Sometimes the violence went even further. In 1837, Reverend Elijah Lovejoy, the editor of an antislavery newspaper in Illinois, was killed by an angry proslavery mob enraged by his advocacy.

The Fugitive Slave Law of 1850 and the publication of *Uncle Tom's Cabin* in 1852 gave the abolitionist movement renewed strength in the North as more and more whites came to realize the inherent evil, violence, and degradation of slavery.

Northern Abolitionists

William Lloyd Garrison was one prominent abolitionist. Born in 1805, Garrison grew up in a poor but religious family in Newburyport, Massachusetts. He is best known as the publisher of the leading abolitionist newspaper of its time, the Boston-based *Liberator*, which he began publishing in 1831. It was a leading voice in the New England abolitionist movement and carried wide influence.

Charles Calistus Burleigh was an attorney who became a lecturer for the Middlesex Anti-Slavery Society in Massachusetts at the young age of twenty-four. A gifted speaker, Burleigh countered the common fear that freed blacks would undercut the wages of whites in the North with the argument that blacks would stop fleeing to the North once they were free in the South.

African-American Abolitionists

A powerful speaker and writer, Frederick Douglass edited and published the influential abolitionist newspaper *The North Star* for nearly seventeen years and spoke out against the evils of slavery in numerous speeches throughout the North. Born the son of slave mother and an unknown white man in 1817, Douglass was sent to Baltimore at age eight to work as a house servant. He was taught to read and write by the mistress of the house, escaped north, and found work in Massachusetts. At age twenty-four, Douglass attended a meeting of the Massachusetts Anti-Slavery Society, where he spoke about his life as a slave and his escape. William Lloyd Garrison was taken with Douglass's speaking skills and immediately hired him as a full-time abolitionist lecturer.

Frederick Douglass
Photo courtesy of the National Archives (200-FL-22)

THE EVERYTHING CIVIL WAR BOOK

Sojourner Truth was an illiterate slave who fled her New York owner in the 1820s and spent most of the rest of her life lecturing on the horrors of slavery. She was a deeply religious woman who captivated audiences with her arguments for women's rights and abolition.

Harriet Tubman was a small yet scrappy Maryland slave who ran away from her master in 1849 and spent the better part of her life helping other slaves reach freedom through the Underground Railroad. Tubman, who had a flair for disguise, was never apprehended during her forays into the South. Slave owners in the South came to loathe Tubman for her emancipation activities, and a hefty reward was offered for her capture.

Charles Lenox Remond was the first black man to speak at public meetings on behalf of abolition. Born a free man in Salem, Massachusetts, Remond became an agent of the Massachusetts chapter of the American Anti-Slavery Society, and in 1840 he represented the organization at the first World Anti-Slavery Convention in London.

Abolition in the South

Interestingly, the South had its share of abolitionist activity too. In the late 1820s, Southern abolitionist groups actually outnumbered Northern groups, with many important Southerners freeing their slaves and assisting colonization efforts. In 1832, the Virginia legislature debated a proposal for gradual, compensatory emancipation that would have become effective in 1861. Obviously, the legislation didn't succeed, and the Southern abolitionist movement slowly died.

The Dred Scott Decision

Dred Scott was a slave who was owned by John Emerson, an army doctor from Missouri. Emerson traveled frequently as part of his job, and between 1834 and 1838 he took Scott with him to army posts throughout the United States and the western territories, including Illinois and the Minnesota Territory, where slavery had been outlawed by the Missouri Compromise. After Emerson's death in 1843, Scott sued in the Missouri courts for his freedom and that of his family, arguing that his stay in a free state and free territory had made him a free man.

The case was heard in the Supreme Court in 1856. It ruled against Dred Scott, dashing his hopes for freedom. When the Dred Scott ruling became public, Southern slave owners celebrated, confident that the issue had finally been laid to rest.

In the North, people were outraged. Many saw the decision as a call to arms; others who had tried to remain neutral on the subject of slavery found themselves compelled to join the abolitionist cause. The ruling also helped Abraham Lincoln become the first Republican president because it widened the divisions over slavery within the Democratic Party.

Bleeding Kansas

The North and the South managed an uneasy but peaceful coexistence on the issue of slavery for a long time, but as the nineteenth century progressed and the nation began to expand westward, slavery became an increasingly sensitive topic, with Northern abolitionists pushing harder and harder for slavery's elimination. The issue reached the boiling point in 1854, when part of the land acquired in the Louisiana Purchase was divided into two territories, Kansas and Nebraska, along the fortieth parallel. The Kansas-Nebraska Act, written by Illinois Senator Stephen Douglas, who had a vested financial interest in opening up the territory to Chicago-based railroads, all but voided the Missouri Compromise of 1820 and introduced the concept of popular sovereignty—the right of a people organizing as a state to decide by popular vote whether to allow slavery.

Kansas was the first to test the concept, voting overwhelmingly to become a free state. Proslavery advocates, however, refused to accept the popular vote and poured into the territory from nearby slave states such as Missouri in an attempt to shift the balance. In the North, these proslavery troublemakers gave Free State settlers no end of grief. Violence and bloodshed became common as proslavery and antislavery factions battled throughout the Kansas wilderness, earning the region the nickname "Bleeding Kansas."

More than 200 people died in the vicious guerrilla warfare. In one of the most horrifying acts of mayhem, radical abolitionist John Brown, four of his sons, and two comrades shot and hacked to death five proslavery settlers near Pottawatomie Creek on May 24, 1856, in retaliation for a raid by proslavery forces in the town of Lawrence.

John Brown's Harpers Ferry Raid

John Brown was a vociferous opponent of slavery. Unfortunately, he was also more than willing to use violence and bloodshed to further the cause he so fervently believed in. As a result, Brown is best remembered today as the radical abolitionist who fomented a slave rebellion and tried to capture the armory at Harpers Ferry, Virginia.

Brown was born in Torrington, Connecticut, in 1800 to poor Calvinist parents. Though he received little schooling as a child, Brown would grow up to be a powerful and charismatic speaker who drew the attention of many prominent abolitionists, including Frederick Douglass

John Brown *Photo courtesy of the National Archives (11-SC-101021)*

Brown found his true calling as a radical abolitionist. In 1855, he joined five of his sons in the Kansas Territory to aid Free Soilers in their fight against proslavery factions. His most notorious contribution to the battle was the Pottawatomie Massacre. Brown and his sons were never arrested for the killings.

The Revolt

Brown later conceived a plan to lead a slave insurrection in the South and start a republic of free blacks in Virginia's Appalachian Mountains. The scheme was doomed from the beginning, but Brown was able to persuade a number of prominent abolitionists to back it. On October 16, 1859, he and twenty-two followers rode into Harpers Ferry. They planned to take the federal arsenal and armory there and use the weapons to arm slaves in a rebellion they hoped would spread throughout the South.

The group seized the buildings and hoped slaves would rally to them from the surrounding area. Instead, residents surrounded the abolitionist group and began shooting. By the following afternoon, Brown had barricaded what remained of his band in a fire engine house next to the armory. A company of marines, led by Lt. Col. Robert E. Lee, soon arrived to put down the insurrection. Lee captured the hapless Brown, who was found guilty under Virginia law of murder, treason, and inciting insurrection. He was hanged on December 2, 1859.

Secession

Though the Southern states had threatened to secede from the Union over various issues for many years, it caught the world by surprise when they actually did so.

The South's Threat to Secede

As the presidential election of 1860 grew nearer, the warning bell of Southern secession rang louder and louder. Southern newspapers increasingly advocated withdrawal from the Union as it became clear that Lincoln was the front-runner, but most Northern leaders failed to heed these omens, having heard them often in the past. Lincoln refused to issue any kind of statement that might appease the frightened South during his campaign, though his opponent, Stephen Douglas, took the threats seriously. When Republicans overwhelmingly won October state elections in Pennsylvania, Ohio, and Indiana, Douglas realized that Lincoln's presidential victory was a foregone conclusion, so he immediately traveled to the South in a desperate attempt to prevent the destruction of the nation. The majority of Northerners, on the other hand, believed that the South was simply beating its chest and would fall back in line once the presidential election was over.

A Union Dissolved

The straw that broke the Southern camel's back was the election of Abraham Lincoln, a Republican and avowed opponent of slavery who was supported by many vocal abolitionists. Fearful that the North, which was richer, more populous, and industrial, would even more insistently impose its will against them, the Southern states felt they had no recourse but to pull away from the Union and form their own nation. They had the right to do so, many felt, because sovereign states had formed the Union, and thus any state that felt oppressed by the federal government could justly withdraw rather than submit to laws it deemed harmful.

"We but tread the paths of our fathers when we proclaim our independence and take the hazard . . . from the high and solemn motive of defending and protecting the rights we inherited, and which it is our duty to transmit unshorn to our children."—Jefferson Davis, January 21, 1861, upon resigning from the U. S. Senate.

The federal government felt otherwise, deeming secession a treasonous act. But President James Buchanan was loathe to do anything about it. Buchanan did say he felt the Southern states had no legal right to secede, but he also claimed he lacked the authority to stop them. One of his last acts as president was to call for a national referendum—a time-killer guaranteed to stave off the whole mess until Lincoln could take office—on whether force should be used to preserve the Union.

On December 20, 1860, South Carolina became the first state to secede. The ordinance to secede simply stated: "We, the people of the State of South Carolina, in Convention assembled, do declare and ordain that the union now subsisting between South Carolina and other States under the name 'The United States of America' is hereby dissolved."

Six states followed South Carolina's lead: Mississippi, on January 9, 1861; Florida, on January 10; Alabama, on January 11; Georgia, on January 19; Louisiana, on January 26; and Texas, on February 1. Following the fall of Fort Sumter on April 14, 1861, four more states left the Union to join the Confederacy: Virginia, on April 17; Arkansas, on May 6; North Carolina, on May 20; and Tennessee, on June 8. Together, these eleven states would make up the Confederate States of America.

Continued Dissent

Reaction to Southern secession was mixed on both sides. The overwhelming percentage of Southerners favored the move because they were tired of what they saw as growing interference in their culture, lifestyle, and economy from Northern politicians, industry, and bankers. But there were dissenting voices as well. Many Southerners felt that secession was too strong and volatile an act and that the differences between the two regions could be amicably worked out without resorting to the destruction of the Union.

In the North, opinion ran the gamut. Many felt that Southern secession was a good thing and the Union should simply let the rebellious states go. But the majority agreed that secession was treason, that it very well might destroy the republic, and that force should be used if necessary to bring the Southern states back into the Union.

CHAPTER 2

On the Eve of War

Neither the North nor the South was ready for pro-tracted hostilities. The U.S. Army was small and scat-tered, and state militias were untrained. Nor were the economies geared for war. The Southern economy was based on cotton and slave labor, and there were scarce facilities for making war equipment. The North was emerging from a financial panic and ensuing depression that had begun in 1857. Both sides hoped war would not come, but Northern leaders felt they had to fight to preserve the country they had inher-ited from their grandfathers who had forged it only eighty-odd years before.

The Nation Splits

Just before the secession of the eleven Southern states that would make up the Confederate States of America, the United States of America comprised thirty-four states and eight organized territories. Two states—Nevada and West Virginia—would be admitted to the Union during the war, and several others would be admitted shortly after. West Virginia was a particularly unexpected surprise. Though technically in the South, fifty western counties decided to break away from Virginia and remain in the Union at the onset of the war. The Union welcomed the region warmly, happy to have yet another ally.

The North and the South were decidedly different in a great many ways, but the secession of the Southern states crystallized the rift between the two regions by dividing the nation in half. A handful of slave states with at least some Union loyalties, such as Kentucky and Delaware, helped separate the North from the Deep South, but otherwise the two regions rubbed shoulders. When Virginia left the Union on April 17, 1861, it meant that Confederate forces were practically on the White House doorstep. In fact, once the war began in earnest, Lincoln could look out the windows on the second floor of the White House and see fluttering Confederate flags over Arlington Heights, Virginia, and, at night, light from Confederate campfires south of the Potomac River. As a result, the protection of the District of Columbia—the very seat of Union government—became a priority.

FACT

The Mason-Dixon Line was named for Charles Mason and Jeremiah Dixon, two British astronomers who surveyed it between 1763 and 1767. Generally composing the border between Pennsylvania and Maryland, the line today is generally regarded as the demarcation point between the Northern states and the Southern states of the Civil War.

Even after secession, neither side was particularly anxious to go to battle. Both regions had relatively small armies and neither was prepared for any type of lengthy engagement. Southern leaders said they simply wanted to be left alone, though they did identify the expansion of the borders of the

Confederate States of America—perhaps in the Caribbean and Latin America—as a long-range goal. In the North, the biggest issue was the preservation of the Union, which meant bringing the Southern states back into the fold—through military force if necessary. The common thinking was that individual states may have had certain inalienable rights, but those rights did not extend to the dissolution of the Union. The future of the nation depended on putting an end to Southern secession.

The Union

The United States of America found itself a much smaller nation than it had been just six months earlier on June 8, 1861. On that date, Tennessee—the last state to secede—broke Union ranks and joined its Southern sisters. On that date, the Union consisted of only twenty-three states and eight territories, including the Indian Territory between Texas and Kansas. Generally, these states were all or mostly north of the Mason-Dixon Line, but they also included Kansas, California, and Oregon.

"We are not enemies, but friends. We must not be enemies. Though passion may have strained, it must not break our bonds of affection."
—Abraham Lincoln, first inaugural address, March 4, 1861

Even without the Southern states, the Union made up nearly three-fourths of the area of the previous United States of America. Its chances of victory in the event of war were considerable, at least on paper. According to the census of 1860, the population of the Northern states was nearly 22 million. Of that number, an estimated 4 million were men old enough to fight in combat if called. Even more impressive, the North had nearly 100,000 factories employing more than a million workers, and nearly 20,000 miles of railroad—more than the rest of the world combined—and 96 percent of the nation's railroad equipment. On the economic front, Union banks held 81 percent of the nation's bank deposits and nearly $56 million in gold. All of this strongly suggested that the South would be at a severe disadvantage should war break out. The North may have held the advantage in every conceivable way, but the Civil War was far from an easy triumph.

Union Politics

Partisan rancor over the Kansas-Nebraska Act of 1854 plunged Union politics into turmoil. The Republican Party rose out of the carnage. The party's key platform was an economic policy that benefited the North more than the South, but what truly aggravated the South was the party's aim to halt the expansion of slavery.

The Republican Party itself was torn over the course of the war, dividing itself into three distinct splinters. Conservative Republicans favored the gradual emancipation of slaves and kindness toward the South. Moderate Republicans urged faster emancipation and some punitive economic and political sanctions. Radical Republicans sought immediate emancipation and harsh punishment against the South.

In the Democratic Party, Peace Democrats considered the war unconstitutional and supported the Southern cause. Their position was that the Republican Party caused the Civil War by forcing the South to secede and did so only to strengthen its own power base and force racial equality, a phrase intended to frighten racists who might otherwise support the Union cause. War Democrats believed strongly in the Union cause and supported the Lincoln administration on most issues. Most War Democrats had no strong feelings regarding the institution of slavery in the South and felt no compunction about restoring the Union without emancipation if necessary.

Proslavery Voices in the Union

Slavery was not the most important issue at the very onset of hostilities; the real issue was Southern independence. The Confederacy was fighting for its very existence, while the North's biggest war aim was the preservation of the Union.

Indeed, the issue of slavery was not universally condemned in the North. A good share of Northerners didn't really care if the institution continued in the South or not, and many hoped that it would. In many cases, Northern advocacy for Southern slavery stemmed from fears that an influx of newly freed Southern blacks would flood the North, take jobs from whites, and drive down wages.

The issue of slavery forced Lincoln to walk a thin line as war became imminent. Though morally opposed to slavery himself, Lincoln needed the congressional support of Northern Democrats, most of whom had little objection to the continuation of slavery in the South, so both he and Congress went out of their way to stress that they wanted to preserve the Union without interfering with the unique institutions of any state. It was hoped that this tact would also help appease the slaveholding border states of Maryland, Kentucky, and Missouri, which wavered dangerously on which side to support.

Though he greatly opposed slavery, Lincoln's greatest concern as president was keeping the nation together at any cost, and he was willing to compromise greatly to do it. Only later in the conflict would the elimination of slavery in the South become a primary aim of the Union's war effort.

The Confederate States of America

The eleven Confederate states may have appeared small and weak in comparison to the far more industrial Union states, but what they lacked in size and population they more than made up with guts and willpower. Together, the states had a total population of about 9 million people—a figure that included 4 million slaves, who certainly could not be expected to fight on the South's behalf should war break out. Because its economy was almost entirely based on agriculture—primarily cotton—the South had only 20,000 factories employing an estimated 100,000 workers. The South's railroad system was also underdeveloped compared to the North's; it was comprised of less than 9,000 miles of track.

The Formation of the Confederate States of America

As the Southern states began to secede, their leaders in the U.S. Congress resigned their positions and headed home, both eager and anxious. Their home states had done a mighty and wondrous thing, but the chore of government was only just beginning.

During the first week of February 1861, delegates from six of the original seceded states (the delegates from Texas were still in transit) met in Montgomery, Alabama, to discuss the formation of a new republic and the form of government to lead it. Montgomery was an odd choice for a provisional capital; it was little more than a tiny backwater town with unpaved streets and a population of just 8,000. By May the capital would be moved to Richmond, Virginia.

FACT

In mountainous western Virginia, farming, mining, and manufacturing were more important than large plantations. By June 1861, the people of this region were well organized and enthusiastically embraced by the Lincoln administration. A constitutional convention was held the following January, and four months later, West Virginia formally requested statehood. West Virginia officially joined the Union on June 20, 1863.

On February 8, the convention announced the establishment of the Confederate States of America and made itself the provisional Congress. With that, the delegates faced a bizarre paradox—establishing a centralized government for a collection of states that had pulled away from the Union because of their distaste for federal authority. It was a difficult job, but the delegates worked quickly. They unanimously selected Jefferson Davis as the Confederacy's provisional president and Alexander Hamilton Stephens of Georgia as its vice president.

Governing the CSA

The constitution of the CSA, approved on March 11, sounded quite a bit like the one the states had just abandoned but with some very important differences. Cabinet members were allowed to participate in legislative debates, and the president was limited to a single six-year term and given power to disapprove specific appropriations in any bill he signed. The "sovereign and independent character" of each state was made clear; the new constitution prevented the federal government from levying protective tariffs, making internal improvements, or overruling state court decisions.

The individual states were also free to create their own armies and could enter into separate agreements with each other if they so desired. While it remained illegal to import slaves from outside the nation, the central government was constitutionally prohibited from passing any laws denying the right to own slaves. Thus it was hoped that the leadership of the Confederate States of America would avoid the issues and problems that had forced them to secede from the Union in the first place.

Southerners owed Northerners $300 million when secession took place. Northerners could not collect this money and their economy suffered for it. But as the war effort continued, the government spent a huge amount of money to keep its war machine marching, and Northern industry and businesses benefited greatly.

Jefferson Davis seemed to be a good choice for president in that he was generally regarded as a moderate on most issues, a fact that made him appealing to a variety of diverse voices. William Lowndes Yancey, a vocal champion of secession, introduced Davis to the cheering throngs with the words, "The man and the hour have met. Prosperity, honor, and victory await his administration." Davis's inauguration was cause for celebration, and the event turned into a huge party with thunderous applause, clanging church bells, cannon fire, and countless renditions of "Dixie," which quickly became the new nation's unofficial anthem. Actress Maggie Smith demonstrated what the South thought of the North by dancing on an American flag, an act that outraged Northern Unionists.

Problems for the CSA

While secession and the formation of a new republic may have been what the majority of Southerners wanted, neither issue was put to a popular vote in the Southern states. Their withdrawal from the Union was decided at state conventions by a total of 854 men selected by their legislatures. Of that number, 157 voted against secession. In fact, Tennessee left the Union by an act of its governor, following the public defeat of a secession proposal.

Nonetheless, the act was done and the South's destiny set. The region had proved that its threat of secession was not merely a bluff, leaving a stunned North to decide how to react. Bringing the South back into the Union by whatever means necessary would be one of Abraham Lincoln's first and most important acts as president and would set the course of his administration, and indeed the entire nation, for the next four years.

Ugly Economics

Slavery, the backbone of the Southern agricultural economy, was also one of the region's greatest hindrances in its fight with the North. When fighting commenced in earnest, the Confederacy found it lacked the manufacturing power necessary to maintain an effective war effort. As the North forged ahead, the South remained pretty much the way it had been during Thomas Jefferson's time. A dependence on slavery had prevented the region from developing a class of skilled workers, and this would cost the South greatly in its struggle to maintain its independence. The Confederacy had plenty of men willing to fight, but it lacked all of the basic resources to help them. Slavery made the South, and it would help bring it down in a way no one had ever foreseen.

The Border States

Not all slave-owning states immediately leaped on the secession bandwagon. Four border states in the upper portion of the region—Maryland, Kentucky, Missouri, and Delaware—were cautious in determining how to proceed after the first Southern states withdrew from the Union.

Even though slavery was legal in all four border states, the proportion of slaves and slave owners was less than half of that in the states that had already pulled away from the Union. Delaware was the first to act, quickly rejecting a Southern request to join the new Confederacy.

The Confederacy had a lot to gain by way of population, industry, and defense in getting the border states to join. Between them, the states would have added 45 percent to the white population (meaning more able-bodied soldiers), as well as more industrial output and military supplies. Their locations, especially those of Kentucky and Maryland, would also have had tremendous strategic value should the Union army invade. Maryland, in particular, was vitally important because if it joined the Confederacy, the Northern capital would have been surrounded. But despite the pleas of Confederate leaders and more than a few battles, all four of the border states remained in the Union.

The Struggle for Maryland

At first, it seemed that Maryland might do otherwise. A strong pro-Confederacy attitude developed there shortly after the fall of Fort Sumter when, on April 19, 1861, a Massachusetts regiment passing through on its way to Washington, D.C., shot several civilians after being attacked by an angry mob in Baltimore. Four soldiers and twelve civilians died.

Maryland officials were outraged at the carnage and demanded that no more Federal troops be sent through the state. Just to make sure their message was clear, the mayor and police chief of Baltimore approved the destruction of key rail bridges to prevent Union troops from entering the metropolis. At the same time, secessionist sympathizers tore down telegraph wires to Washington, cutting off communication to the nation's capital for a couple of anxious days.

Despite technically being a Union state, Missouri troops fought on both sides of the war, with more than 100,000 fighting for the Union and nearly 40,000 taking up arms on behalf of the Confederacy. Over the course of the conflict, about 75,000 Kentuckians fought for the Union, and 25,000 fought for the Confederacy.

On May 13, Federal troops—including members of the Massachusetts regiment that had been attacked the previous month—occupied Baltimore and declared martial law. Several prominent citizens, including the chief of police and a number of city commissioners, were arrested for their alleged role in the riot, and suspected secessionists were held without formal charges ever being brought against them. Federal forces would present an occupying presence in Baltimore for the duration of the war. Meanwhile, Governor Thomas Hicks and the state legislature voted against secession, declaring Maryland neutral in the rift between the North and the South, an obviously difficult position to maintain. When state elections were held in November 1861, the Union Party won a stunning victory, and Maryland remained pro-Union for the rest of the war, though there were continuous grumblings from pro-Confederacy factions.

Missouri's Divided Citizenry

Missouri also had a hard time deciding where its allegiance lay. On one side was Governor Claiborne Fox Jackson, a former "border ruffian" who advocated secession; on the other was pro-Union congressman Francis P. Blair, who happened to be the brother of Lincoln's postmaster, Montgomery Blair. Many of the residents of Missouri were slave owners, but the overall makeup of the population was decidedly different from that of the states in the Deep South. A large number of German immigrants had settled throughout Missouri, with the greatest concentration around St. Louis, and they had little interest in or regard for most Southern traditions—especially slavery.

Kentucky: Requiring Great Care

Kentucky, the birth state of both Abraham Lincoln and Jefferson Davis, was even more divided on the issue of which side to join in the conflict between the North and the South. Bordered by three free states and three slave states, its sympathies were fairly evenly split between the Union and the Confederacy. Like Maryland, the state legislature voted to remain neutral, an act that was considered very close to secession, since neutrality was based on the doctrine of state sovereignty, or independence from the decisions of a central government.

Lincoln was torn over what to do about Kentucky. Because it was neutral, many goods were being forwarded through it to the seceded states, which certainly didn't help the Union cause. But Lincoln decided to treat Kentucky with a gentle hand rather than force the issue, and in the end his plan paid off: state elections in June and August 1861 saw tremendous Unionist victories. The state's official stance of neutrality came to an end when Confederate troops under Major General Leonidas Polk invaded Kentucky from Tennessee to take the strategically important city of Columbus.

The population of the Confederacy at the start of the war was 9 million (5.5 million whites and 3.5 million slaves), with nearly 1.14 million men of combat age. It had 20,000 factories employing nearly 100,000 workers, 9,000 miles of railroad, $47 million in bank deposits, and $37 million in gold.

Even though the Confederacy would have benefited from the strategic location of the border states, it wasn't shedding many tears over its loss. Instead, it concentrated on what it had rather than what it lacked, bolstering its borders on land and sea, gathering supplies, enlisting soldiers, and generally gearing up for a war that seemed inevitable. Now that the new nation had been formed, it was time to protect itself.

Making Armies and Officers

At the onset of the Civil War, the North's army was small, consisting of just 16,000 men scattered as far as Oregon and California. The newborn Confederacy had no ready army at all. As the inevitability of war became clear, both sides set about bolstering their military might, forming armies made up primarily of volunteer state militia and selecting officers to lead them.

Following the bombardment of Fort Sumter, Abraham Lincoln, believing the conflict would be over fairly quickly, called on the states to provide 75,000 militia at the government's service for a ninety-day enlistment. The call brought a rush of eager young recruits anxious for a little excitement. It also forced the remaining Southern states—Virginia, North Carolina, Tennessee, and Arkansas—to leave the Union and join the Confederacy. Though their sympathies were with the South, all four states had hoped until the very last moment that the situation could be settled without the risk of bloodshed. That hope was dashed with Lincoln's call to arms.

The Untrained State Militias

The state militias that made up the Northern army at the beginning of the conflict were an interesting but often motley group. Very few of them had received any type of combat training, and most of their drill instruction had been solely for show. In other words, they were civilians playing soldier who had been asked to become the real thing.

The typical militia regiment was made up of companies from neighboring towns, and many of the groups had never even met, much less trained together. This proved to be a serious hindrance because warfare in the mid-1800s required soldiers to engage in highly intricate movements as they went from marching formation to fighting formation. Coordination was essential and could be instilled only through numerous and lengthy drills, something the majority of militiamen had never done.

The population of the Union states at the start of the war was 22 million, with 4 million men of combat age. It had 100,000 factories employing more than 1 million workers, 20,000 miles of railroad, 96 percent of the combined nations' railroad equipment, the majority of coal mines and canals, $189 million in bank deposits, and $56 million in gold.

The individual companies were often led by men with little or no military experience or background. Instead, they were chosen as leaders by popular vote or because they were of higher social status than the others. Field experience would quickly eliminate leaders who were unfit, but in the beginning, the armies of both the North and the South were composed primarily of amateurs leading amateurs.

Career Soldiers

There were plenty of career soldiers on both sides, though the North had a difficult time deciding how best to use them. Lieutenant General Winfield Scott commanded the Union army at the beginning of the war. Though battle experienced and an able strategist, he was seventy-five years old and in poor health. After a few Union defeats and growing public dissatisfaction, Scott was retired and replaced by George B. McClellan. Lincoln would spend a lot of time shuffling his officers around.

A great many of the Union's best military minds, most of them West Pointers, defected to the South. As a result, Jefferson Davis, himself a West Point graduate with some field experience, planned to use trained soldiers for his general officers as often as he could. One of his first appointees was Robert E. Lee, who had rejected command of the Union's principle army after Virginia seceded. Davis made him a full general in the Confederate army. Other bold Confederate officers included Pierre Gustave Toutant Beauregard, appointed to command the chief Confederate army in Virginia, General Albert Sidney Johnston, and General Joseph E. Johnston. Both Beauregard and Joseph E. Johnston would find their military skills hampered by a rancorous relationship with Davis.

Union and Confederate Cabinet Officers

During the early days of the Civil War, the Union and the Confederacy were governed by an intriguing collection of men.

Secretary of State William Henry Seward (Union)

Seward believed that the many compromises that had held the nation together would eventually fail, and in 1858 he warned that the bitter fighting over slavery would result in an "irrepressible conflict" between the North and the South.

Secretary of the Treasury Salmon P. Chase (Union)

One of the most radical and controversial members of Lincoln's cabinet, Chase served three years before conflict with Lincoln forced his resignation. Chase came to prominence in Ohio as an abolitionist lawyer who specialized in defending runaway slaves and entered the Senate in 1848. He later served two terms as governor of Ohio and became a prominent member of the newly formed Republican Party. Like Seward, Chase hoped to be the Republican candidate in the 1860 presidential election but accepted Lincoln's invitation to join his cabinet. Though he had little experience in finance, Chase was able to contain a mounting budget deficit and effectively finance the Union's war effort.

Secretary of the Navy Gideon Welles (Union)

Welles, a noted Connecticut journalist and politician, was chosen by Lincoln as secretary of the Navy so that New England would have a voice in the cabinet. With no prior experience, he proved quite adept at the job, preparing the strategy for and overseeing the execution of the Union blockade of Southern ports and promoting the construction of ironclad ships.

"The mystic chords of memory, stretching from every battlefield and patriot grave to every living heart and hearthstone all over this broad land, will yet swell the chorus of the Union when again touched, as surely they will be, by the better angels of our nature."—Abraham Lincoln, first inaugural address, March 4, 1861

Secretary of War Simon Cameron (Union)

Cameron achieved his cabinet position as a result of a convention agreement that Lincoln knew nothing about and proved so corrupt and generally inept that Lincoln shipped him off to be minister to Russia within a year of his appointment. Cameron was replaced by Edwin M. Stanton, a vocal Unionist who had served as attorney general under James Buchanan.

Postmaster General Montgomery Blair (Union)

Blair was the only member of Lincoln's cabinet to advise sending provisions to Fort Sumter and threatened to resign, just two weeks after taking office, if Lincoln did not act on the issue.

Secretary of State Robert Toombs (Confederate)

A rich and powerful Georgia plantation owner, Toombs resigned his United States Senate seat following the election of Abraham Lincoln and returned to his home state to assist its secession. Toombs hoped to be the first president of the Confederacy and was disappointed when he was passed over in favor of Jefferson Davis. Davis offered Toombs the position of secretary of state, but Toombs quickly became bored. Since the Confederacy had not been recognized by any foreign powers, there was little for the secretary of state to do. He remained in the position only five months before resigning to become commander of a Georgia brigade on the Virginia front—despite the fact that he had no military training.

FACT

The delegates of the Confederate provisional congress constructed and ratified their new nation's constitution in a matter of weeks. It took the U.S. Continental Congress two years from draft to ratification (1787–89) to achieve a similar feat. Of course, the U.S. Continental Congress was starting from scratch, whereas the Confederate provisional congress at least had a template from which to work.

Secretary of the Navy Stephen R. Mallory (Confederate)

Prior to secession, Mallory was a senator from Florida and served as Naval Affairs Committee chairman. When he first took office, the Confederate navy consisted of just ten ships mounting fifteen guns and no organizational framework. But Mallory managed to create an imposing naval force despite limited resources and scant support from his government. Mallory encouraged innovation and strongly supported the development of ironclad ships, torpedoes, and even submarines.

Attorney General Judah P. Benjamin (Confederate)

Benjamin was one of the most prominent and influential Jewish-American statesmen of the nineteenth century. He was also a brilliant legal mind, attending Yale University at age fourteen. He became a successful attorney in New Orleans and owned a sizable plantation with several slaves. In 1852, Benjamin was elected to the U.S. Senate and remained in office until Louisiana seceded from the Union. He was appointed attorney general by Jefferson Davis, then secretary of war in 1861. Benjamin was transferred to the State Department a year later and was influential in securing some much-needed foreign loans for the Confederacy.

Secretary of War Leroy P. Walker (Confederate)

An Alabama native, Walker was offered the position of secretary of war primarily to give his home state a voice in the Confederate cabinet. However, he quickly proved himself inept and resigned after just seven months. Walker was replaced by Judah P. Benjamin, but four others would also hold the difficult post over the course of the Civil War.

Secretary of the Treasury C. G. Memminger (Confederate)

As the Confederacy's first secretary of the treasury, Memminger instituted a financial policy based on paper money that did little to help the new republic; Confederate money became nearly worthless.

CHAPTER 3

Lincoln and Davis: Leaders of the North and South

The terrible sundering of the nation during the 1770s and 1780s presented political leaders with entirely new problems, and they struggled to find solutions. The main work fell to two men, both born in Kentucky only a year apart. The family of one went north to Indiana and Illinois, the other south to Louisiana and Mississippi. Both grew up on small farms; neither could be said to have grown up privileged or well-connected. Yet fate and their own talents would set them to lead the North and the South.

Abraham Lincoln and Jefferson Davis

The Civil War presented the greatest challenge an American president had ever faced up to that time. The fact that Americans were forced to do battle against each other is the most tragic feature of the Civil War and just one of many factors that made the conflict unique in the course of American history. The Civil War truly was a war that pitted brother against brother and friend against friend, and this horrible aspect took an agonizing toll on the two men in charge—U.S. president Abraham Lincoln and Confederate president Jefferson Davis.

Abraham Lincoln *Photo courtesy of the National Archives (111-B-3656)*

Jefferson Davis *Photo courtesy of the National Archives (111-B-4146)*

Lincoln and Davis shared more similarities than differences. Both men were born not far apart and within a year of each other in Kentucky. Both men were relatively unpopular leaders, especially during those times when their side experienced devastating losses on the battlefield. Both men experienced serious problems with their military leaders. Both men suffered the loss of dear friends and loved ones over the course of the war.

At the end of the Civil War, Abraham Lincoln was declared a hero and Jefferson Davis a scoundrel. Yet both men were merely following their hearts and did what they considered best for their countries, as any good leader would.

Abraham Lincoln's Childhood Years

Abraham Lincoln was born on February 12, 1809, to Thomas and Nancy Lincoln on the family farm near Hogdenville, Kentucky. The Lincoln family members, including Abraham's younger sister Sarah, were hardworking farmers who toiled the land, planting corn and other crops. Thomas Lincoln was a simple, uneducated man who was known for his honesty and affable personality. He worked hard to support his family, and everyone pitched in as best they could. It was from his parents that Abraham Lincoln learned the value of hard work, diligence, and strength of character. They also instilled in him a dislike for the institution of slavery, which they found morally objectionable.

Tragedy and a New Family

When Lincoln was seven years old, his family moved from Kentucky to Indiana and started another farm. Two years later, Lincoln's beloved mother passed away. Her death hit Lincoln hard, and some speculate that his deep sorrow may have been the basis for the depression that would afflict him for most of his adult life. Less than a year after Nancy's death, Thomas traveled back to Kentucky to find another wife to help him support his farm and children. In Elizabethtown, he became reacquainted with Sarah Bush Johnston, a widow whom he had courted prior to meeting Nancy. They wed quickly, more out of convenience than romantic love; Thomas needed a wife and Sarah needed a husband to help her support her three small children. Thomas paid Sarah's outstanding debts, and they returned to Indiana.

Sarah brought tremendous love to the Lincoln household. Sarah and Thomas embraced each other's children as their own, and Abraham quickly came to accept her as his mother. He never forgot his birth mother, however, and differentiated the two women by referring to Nancy in later years as his "angel mother."

Overcoming Adversity

Lincoln received only a few years of formal schooling as a youngster, but he was a very bright student. He wrote well, became proficient at basic mathematics, and excelled at spelling, often stumping his fellow classmates in school spelling bees. Lincoln was also a voracious reader and frequently memorized entire passages from the limited number of books that were available to him in his younger years. Lincoln made the best of what was available to him and used it to further himself personally and professionally for the rest of his life.

Europeans—mainly English, Irish, and Germans—continued to move to America during the Civil War. In the five years between 1861 and 1865, 800,000 Europeans immigrated to America despite the war. The immigration and a healthy birthrate was the reason the population of the Northern states was greater after the war than it had been at the beginning.

Lincoln worked hard to be successful, but most of his early ventures didn't pan out. He became a shopkeeper in New Salem, Illinois, when he was twenty-one, but the business didn't flourish as he had anticipated. When Lincoln's partner died, Lincoln was left with a heavy debt. He worked a variety of jobs, including surveyor and postmaster, to pay off his creditors, and such endeavors only helped to strengthen his reputation as a man of honesty and integrity. While he was certainly not averse to hard physical labor, Lincoln soon realized that being a lawyer would be a good way to maintain financial stability, and he started reading law books as a path toward that goal. Two documents that impressed him greatly were the Declaration of Independence and the U.S. Constitution. The men who wrote them became Lincoln's personal heroes.

Lincoln's Early Politics

Illinois was a state in the throes of change, and Lincoln was driven to make his mark in state politics. His first political position was a seat in the state legislature, which he won when he was just twenty-three. He would spend four terms in office, from 1832 to 1838, and it was there that his reputation as a man of principle and idealism was forged.

An Adept Statesman

Lincoln was especially adept at managing people and calming conflict, and he was selected Whig floor leader at the beginning of his second term. He was a leader in the establishment of the Bank of Illinois and led the campaign to move the state capital from Vandalia to Springfield. Lincoln made his first stand on the issue of slavery in 1837, when he protested a number of resolutions passed by the Illinois legislature condemning abolitionist societies. Lincoln admitted that he felt Congress could not interfere with slavery in the states in which it already existed, but he personally felt that the institution was founded on "both injustice and bad policy" and that steps should be taken to prevent its spread into new territories. This would be Lincoln's personal policy regarding the institution of slavery right up to the issuance of the Emancipation Proclamation in 1862.

Lincoln passed the state bar in 1836 and set up a law practice in Springfield a year later. As a circuit lawyer, Lincoln traveled through fifteen counties for six months of the year, a situation that allowed him to meet the populace and hear their thoughts on the most important issues of the day. Such folksy socializing enabled Lincoln to understand the common man and helped him in his capacity as a state legislator.

On the Campaign Trail

In 1840, Lincoln did some political stumping for the Whig presidential candidate and used the platform to promote a central banking system. After two unsuccessful bids, he was elected to the U.S. House of Representatives in 1846. In Congress, Lincoln came out against the Mexican War and for the Wilmot Proviso, a piece of legislation that would have banned slavery in any territory acquired from Mexico. His term ended in 1849, and Lincoln returned to his law practice in Springfield.

Lincoln managed to avoid politics for four years, but the Kansas-Nebraska Act pushed him back into the political arena. Lincoln actively campaigned against the act throughout Illinois and was elected to the state legislature as the leader of the Illinois factions opposing the spread of slavery into the territories. However, Lincoln quit the state legislature after just a few months to run for the U.S. Senate, a bid he lost. In 1856, Lincoln joined the Republican Party, which advocated the end of slavery, and he made numerous speeches on behalf of John C. Fremont, the first Republican presidential candidate. Fremont lost the 1856 election to James Buchanan, but he set the stage for Lincoln's presidential run four years later.

The Lincoln-Douglas Debates

Abraham Lincoln was a gifted public speaker, but he found his talents put to the test in the now famous Lincoln-Douglas debates of 1858. Lincoln had been chosen by the Republican Party to run against Stephen Douglas for the U.S. Senate that year. In an attempt to get his name out there and generate some much needed publicity, he quietly challenged Douglas—one of the most famous political figures of his time—to a series of seven debates on various issues, primarily the extension of slavery into the territories. Douglas accepted, but he knew he was taking a big chance in doing so. The result was a confrontation between two well-spoken, outspoken men that is still remembered today as one of the most thrilling examples of American politics in action.

The Question of Slavery

Slavery immediately became the hottest issue in the debates, and the verbal sparring often got extremely ugly by contemporary standards. Rather than fielding questions from journalists, as is the case today, the candidates themselves decided the tone and content of the debates.

Douglas tried to discredit Lincoln on the issue of slavery by painting him as a rabid abolitionist who wished to put blacks on equal footing with whites. He also suggested that Lincoln was advocating interracial marriage and hinted that if emancipation were to occur, the Illinois Territory would be overrun with freed blacks who would take jobs away from whites. Lincoln countered by calling Douglas's claims "counterfeit logic." He tried to explain his position as rationally as he could, noting that his call to halt the spread of slavery did not mean he was advocating any type of amalgamation of the races. He also reiterated his long-held belief that slavery was "a moral, social, and political evil" but that the federal government had no right to interfere in the rights of states in which slavery already existed.

Shared Respect

Douglas knew Lincoln was no backwoods bumpkin, and he would have to be in top form in order to win the debates and then the election. Though they were fierce opponents, each man respected the other. Douglas described Lincoln as "the strong man of his party—full of wit, facts, dates—and the best stump speaker in the West. If I beat him, my victory will be hardly won." Said Lincoln of Douglas: "Senator Douglas is of worldwide renown. All the anxious politicians of his party . . . have been looking upon him . . . to be President. Nobody has ever expected me to be President."

"A house divided against itself cannot endure, permanently half slave and half free. I do not expect the Union to dissolve—I do not expect the house to fall—but I do expect it will cease to be divided. It will become all one thing or all the other."—Abraham Lincoln, Lincoln-Douglas debates, December 1858

Lincoln ultimately lost the Senate race to Douglas, who was elected by state legislators, not a popular vote as is the case today. But Lincoln ended up a bigger winner in the long run. His excellent showing in the debates and the fact that he provided Douglas with challenging competition made him a national figure and greatly increased his popularity within the Republican

Party, which found his moderate stand on the issues a pleasant change from more radical Republicans like William Seward and Salmon Chase. Party officials would demonstrate their approval just two years later by selecting Lincoln as the Republican presidential candidate.

Lincoln's First Presidential Election

The presidential election of 1860 was one of the most raucous in American history. The Democratic Party convened in Charleston, South Carolina, in April, to select a suitable candidate. It adjourned without doing so after fifty delegates from the Southern states stormed out when the party refused to include a platform that guaranteed the constitutional protection of slave owners. The Democrats reconvened the following month in Baltimore but were again unable to reach a suitable compromise on the slavery issue, and, once more, the Southern delegates walked out, taking the majority of the upper Southern delegates with them. The remaining Democratic delegates selected Senator Stephen Douglas as their presidential candidate, based on a platform of popular sovereignty, once again pitting Douglas against Abraham Lincoln.

FACT

Abraham Lincoln was the first American president to wear a beard. The look set a precedent, and of the next nine men to hold the high office, only William McKinley was clean shaven.

The more than 100 Southern Democrats who had walked out of the Baltimore convention gathered elsewhere in the city and nominated John Breckinridge of Kentucky as their candidate of choice. Their platform called for the federal government to protect the rights of persons and property in the territories and wherever else its constitutional authority extended. Breckinridge was endorsed by incumbent president James Buchanan and former presidents John Tyler and Franklin Pierce.

The Republican Candidates

Meanwhile, the Republican Party held its convention in Chicago and established a platform that, among other things, opposed the spread of slavery into the territories. Contenders for the nomination included William Seward of New York, who was popularly viewed as a radical abolitionist; Salmon Chase of Ohio; and Edward Cameron of Pennsylvania. Lincoln wasn't the first choice of most of the delegates, but he was the second choice for many of them because of his relatively moderate stand on the important issues. The Pennsylvania delegation switched to Lincoln on the second ballot, and Lincoln took the nomination on the third ballot. Part of his victory may have resulted from a backroom deal that promised Cameron a cabinet post should Lincoln win, and Cameron became Lincoln's first secretary of war.

In the election of 1860, Abraham Lincoln won 1,866,000 popular votes for 180 electoral votes; Stephen Douglas won 1,375,000 votes for 12 electoral votes; John Breckinridge won 846,000 popular votes for 72 electoral votes; and John Bell won 560,000 popular votes for 39 electoral votes.

The Do-Nothing Party

A contentious faction of the Whig party calling themselves the Constitutional Union Party also met in Baltimore. They selected John Bell of Tennessee as their preferred candidate; however, neither the party nor Bell had much to offer voters. Their platform addressed none of the important issues, such as slavery, and merely vowed to uphold the Constitution. As a result, the party came to be jokingly known as the Do-Nothing and Old Man's Party.

The Election Results

When election day rolled around, the race for president had been regionally divided into two specific contests: Lincoln and Douglas in the North (Lincoln wasn't even on the ballot in the Southern states), and Bell and Breckinridge in the South. The candidates campaigned vigorously, and the races contained more than their share of mud slinging and rumor mongering. But in the end, the sharp division within the Democratic Party guaranteed a victory for Abraham Lincoln, who won almost 40 percent of the popular vote and, more importantly, the electoral votes of the largest states in the North and the West.

Jefferson Davis: A Short Biography

Jefferson Finis Davis faced a long, arduous, and ultimately losing battle almost from the day he was selected provisional president of the infant Confederate States of America. The position called for a man of tremendous character, well accomplished in both governing politics and military strategy, and Davis was lacking in both areas. Although his military and political background was less than stellar, his dedication to the Southern states made him the ideal candidate among the members of the provisional congress, who saw in Davis a more moderate leader than many other aspirants. Davis did his best to establish the Confederacy as a self-sufficient, independent nation, but mercurial public opinion, infighting within his administration and military, his own personality quirks, and a war the South could hardly win would prevent him from achieving his goals.

Early Life

Davis was born in Christian County, Kentucky, on June 3, 1808, the youngest of ten children. Though he would become a devout Confederate patriot, he was only a second-generation Southerner; his grandfather had moved from Pennsylvania to Georgia, where Davis's father was born. When Davis was a child, his family moved to Mississippi, where his father owned a small farm. Though a practicing Baptist, Davis attended a Catholic seminary back in Kentucky and entered West Point in 1823. A mediocre student, he graduated in the last third of his class.

Upon graduating from West Point, Davis served as an officer in a number of distant posts in Illinois and Wisconsin and saw a little military action during the Black Hawk Indian War, though the conflict did little to enhance Davis's military skills. Davis fell in love with the daughter of one of his post commandants, Colonel Zachary Taylor, who would go on to become the twelfth president of the United States. Davis and Sarah Knox Taylor married against the colonel's wishes after Davis resigned from the army. The newlyweds both contracted malaria; Sarah died within three months of their marriage and her widower would suffer from bouts of malarial fever for the rest of his life. Davis spent the next ten years working on his plantation in Mississippi. It was during this period that Davis really came to identify with the Southern mentality and lifestyle, including the institution of slavery. He became a proud Southerner and states' rights advocate and, like most of his countrymen, bristled at the thought of any sort of Northern intrusion.

Davis in the Political Sphere

Davis eventually became involved in politics and won a seat in the House of Representatives in 1845. He was supported and encouraged by his brother Joseph, a man of wealth and national influence. In that same year, Davis fell in love with and married Varina Howell, the pretty and personable daughter of a local landowner.

FACT

"Dixie" may be primarily associated with the Confederacy today, but it was such a popular song in the 1860s that it was played at the inaugurations of both Abraham Lincoln and Jefferson Davis. It was treated as the national anthem of the Confederacy during the Civil War, and it became emblematic of the Old South.

Davis was in office just a few months before resigning his seat to participate in the Mexican War, where he saw just enough action on the battlefield to convince himself that he was an accomplished military man. Sadly, such was not the case, and Davis's own inflated self-image would spark numerous conflicts with his more battled-seasoned military leaders during the Civil War.

Davis re-entered national politics as a senator from Mississippi and made a name for himself by strongly supporting Southern causes, including states' rights and slavery, which he thought should be expanded into the territories. In 1853, President Franklin Pierce appointed Davis secretary of war. During his three years in office, Davis assumed an expansionist stance in foreign affairs, a position that reflected his position regarding the expansion of slavery. When his term was completed, Davis returned to the Senate, where he continued his vocal advocacy of slavery.

"You are the last best hope of liberty . . . The country relies upon you. Upon you rest the hopes of our people; and I have only to say, my friends, that to the last breath of my life I am wholly your own."—Jefferson Davis to a crowd in Richmond, Virginia, 1861

Despite Davis's unwavering support of Southern causes and his deep love of the South, he did not endorse secession and struggled throughout the Democratic conventions of 1860 to encourage some sort of compromise that would keep the Union whole. But with the election of Abraham Lincoln and the new president's statement that he would not tolerate the spread of slavery into any more territories, Davis knew that the line had been drawn. With a heavy heart, he resigned his Senate seat on January 21, 1861, and joined his fellow Southerners in seceding from the Union.

Presidential Responsibilities

Davis had hoped to become commander of the Confederate army and was surprised when he was made provisional president—a position he assumed primarily because the bickering delegates could not agree on any other choice. Davis took the reins of the new republic with an eye toward total independence and international recognition, but he faced many obstacles.

His biggest problem was that he headed the central government of a new nation whose states were suspicious of concentrated power and preferred to retain as many rights for themselves as possible. The states recognized the need for a central government but didn't want to give it any power. Issues such as taxation, conscription of troops, currency, and the suspension of civil laws in the face of a war were a source of constant debate as the states tried to decide just how much authority their new government should have.

All of this, of course, made preparing for a war with the North all the more difficult for Davis, a man who lacked many of the basic leadership skills that made Abraham Lincoln the best man to lead the Union during this troubling period. By comparison, Davis was easily distracted, too confident of his own limited abilities, unwilling to compromise on important issues, lacking in people skills, and fragile in health. Though his heart was in the right place, Davis was a man in over his head from the very beginning.

Facing a War of Attrition

The South started with no army, lacked the manufacturing capability to produce sufficient arms and other necessary goods, and soon suffered from a Northern blockade of its most important ports. Its greatest advantage was its military leadership. Left alone, they very well might have been able to resist the North until both sides were ready to talk peace, but Davis wouldn't let them do their jobs. He constantly fought with his commanding officers, who grew increasingly weary of his nonstop meddling. The only officer in whom Davis expressed complete confidence was Robert E. Lee. As a result, Davis's reputation within the Confederacy suffered greatly over the course of the war, as did the reputations of those who were closest to him.

FACT

Jefferson Davis never sought the restoration of his American citizenship following the Civil War, although he was elected to the U.S. Senate in 1874. Davis was not allowed to serve as a senator because the Fourteenth Amendment barred from office anyone who had "engaged in insurrection or rebellion against the United States, or given comfort to the enemies thereof." Davis's American citizenship was restored posthumously by President Jimmy Carter.

Up until the very end of the war, Jefferson Davis was confident that he could broker peace with the Union and save his beloved Confederacy. In February 1865, Davis bragged from the Confederate capital of Richmond, Virginia: "We may well believe that before another summer solstice falls upon us it will be the enemy who will be asking us for conferences."

CHAPTER 4

Military Leaders of the North and South

What sets the Civil War apart from all other American military conflicts is that many of the opposing officers knew each other. They had studied together at West Point, fought side by side in the Mexican War, and had even been friends. At the First Battle of Manassas, for example, Pierre G. T. Beauregard, who was second in the class of 1838 at West Point, battled Irvin McDowell, who had graduated twenty-third in the same class.

Politics and Generals

In today's U.S. Army, rank is determined by experience and expertise, but things were a little different during the Civil War. It was an era in which political favors were often repaid with military appointments, and, as the war began to heat up, President Abraham Lincoln found himself under constant pressure to appoint men with little or no military experience. Many of the Union's early military officers were loyal Republicans, influential War Democrats, or everyday people demanding payback for some earlier favor. As might be expected, the majority of officers so appointed had no right to lead men into battle, and during their relatively brief command they only served to embarrass themselves and their respective War Departments. The First Battle of Manassas resulted in a humiliating Union rout when inexperienced officers panicked and ran in the face of the enemy, abandoning their men.

Civil War armies were largely organized as follows: four infantry regiments formed a brigade, commanded by a brigadier general; three brigades composed a division, commanded by a brigadier or major general; two or more divisions formed an army corps, commanded by a major general in the Union and by a major or lieutenant general in the Confederacy.

General Benjamin Franklin Butler is a prime example of wartime incompetence. A prominent Boston attorney and influential Democrat, Butler used his influence to grab a military appointment. He managed some early successes but embarrassed himself mightily when, as military governor of New Orleans, he ordered the confiscation of Confederate property and was accused of stealing silverware from area homes and churches. Butler also succeeded in angering the entire population of New Orleans with his controversial "Woman Order," which stated that any woman who insulted or berated a Union soldier would be treated like a common prostitute. Butler was recalled by his superiors in Washington in December 1862 after corruption and bribery by Northern speculators became commonplace in the city under his administration. Butler was later given a field command in Virginia, and his embarrassments continued to mount throughout the rest of the war.

Ideally, the full strength of an infantry regiment was 1,000 men, 4,000 men for a brigade, 12,000 men for a division, and 24,000 or more men for a corps. Confederate divisions and corps were typically larger than those in the Union army because a Southern division often contained four brigades and a Southern corps contained four divisions.

Not surprisingly, the incompetence demonstrated by many appointed officers did little to instill pride or confidence in the men who served under them, and morale in such units was often very low. In many cases, the battle experience of common soldiers far exceeded that of their commanders. Personal behavior was also an issue. Many officers drank heavily, frequented prostitutes, and generally behaved quite badly, setting a horrible example for their men.

Winfield Scott

General Winfield Scott was a lifelong soldier with an illustrious career when the Civil War broke out in 1861. He had served as general-in-chief for nearly twenty years and, at age seventy-five, was nearing the end of his ability to lead effectively. He advised Lincoln to spend time training an army while a blockade strangled the South economically, a strategy that became known as the Anaconda Plan.

Scott recommended Robert E. Lee as field commander of the U.S. armies, but Lee turned it down to join the Confederacy. The job instead went to George McClellan, who resented and snubbed Scott.

The early days of the war took the shine off of Scott's armor. The press and the public blamed him for the Union's early losses. Scott resigned as the head of the Union army and McClellan replaced him. Scott died in 1866, having watched his much-ridiculed Anaconda Plan play an integral role in the Union's final victory against the Confederacy.

George B. McClellan

Had George Brinton McClellan been as good a soldier as he thought he was, the Civil War might have come to a much faster conclusion. Unfortunately, the cocky and arrogant general was prone to chronic hesitancy, allowing the enemy to retreat and rebuild time after time. President Lincoln became so frustrated by McClellan's failure to follow through on the battlefield that he eventually removed him from command of the Union army.

Major General George B. McClellan *Photo courtesy of the National Archives (111-B-4624)*

McClellan was born in Philadelphia in 1826, the scion of a wealthy family. He entered West Point at age sixteen and graduated second in his class. His classmates saw great things in McClellan, and he was voted most likely to succeed. Upon graduation, McClellan was appointed brevet second lieutenant in the engineer corps and shipped off to hone his military skills in the Mexican War. He fought well and received commendations for his performance in several important battles. He taught at West Point, then worked as a civilian in the railroad industry.

In 1861, McClellan was made major general of the Ohio Volunteers, then routed a Confederate army in western Virginia. After the disaster at the First Battle of Manassas, Lincoln appointed McClellan commander of the Army of the Potomac. He was well respected by the soldiers, but he was openly disdainful of Lincoln and stalled when the president urged action. Ultimately, McClellan set the Union army in motion toward Richmond via ship, beginning the Peninsular Campaign.

Approximately 80 percent of the Union fighting forces was infantry, 14 percent was cavalry, and 6 percent was artillery. The Confederate army had a similar proportion of artillery but a slightly higher proportion of cavalry.

McClellan was never able to shake his poor reputation for caution. Yet he was an excellent organizer and is generally credited with shaping the Army of the Potomac into the fighting force that eventually defeated Robert E. Lee's Army of Northern Virginia.

Ulysses S. Grant

Grant was born Hiram Ulysses Grant in Georgetown, Ohio, in 1822. His father was a hardworking tanner and his mother a devoutly religious woman who had great hopes for her son. As a child, Grant preferred horses to studying. He proved a skilled rider but did poorly in school.

At West Point and Beyond

Despite his poor grades, Grant managed to make it into West Point thanks to a recommendation from his local congressman, who mistakenly referred to him as Ulysses Simpson Grant in his letter to the academy. Grant continued his tradition of mediocrity at West Point, graduating twenty-first in a class of thirty-nine. At Jefferson Barracks near St. Louis, he met his future bride, Julia Dent. He disagreed with the Mexican War but fought bravely and learned much about handling soldiers and supplies.

Lieutenant General Ulysses S. Grant *Photo courtesy of the National Archives (200-CA-38)*

Following the Mexican War, Grant was assigned to a variety of distant posts. He missed Julia and began drinking, but being short and slight (he weighed 135 pounds), alcohol sometimes got the better of him. Reprimanded, he resigned from the army.

Grant moved with his family back to St. Louis, where he tried a number of occupations with little success. Finally, his two brothers hired him as a clerk at their leather store, and there he stayed until the beginning of the Civil War.

The Civil War

When the first shots were fired on Fort Sumter, Grant eagerly volunteered for the Union army but had great difficulty getting someone to assign him to a true command. Finally, in June 1861, he was made colonel of a regiment of volunteers from Illinois. Three months later, Grant was promoted to brigadier general and assigned to a command in Illinois.

One of his first tasks was to attack a small force of Confederates in Missouri. He set out with his troops and later admitted that he became quite nervous as he approached the enemy camp. But he discovered the camp had recently been abandoned. The lesson he learned from this, he recounted, was that the enemy was just as likely to be scared of you as you were to be scared of him. The lesson prompted an aggressiveness that never left him, and he eventually won complete victory for the Union armies.

William Tecumseh Sherman

Sherman was born in Ohio in 1820. He graduated from West Point and served in the Mexican War.

The Union army consisted of approximately 2.2 million men. They ranged in age from eighteen to forty-six, the average age being in the midtwenties. The majority had been farmers, and very few had any previous military experience. The average Union soldier was 5 feet 8 inches tall and weighed 145 pounds. About 75 percent were born in the United States, and nearly all were volunteers.

Sherman's affection for the South didn't stop him from rejecting a commission in the Confederate army when the Civil War broke. A Unionist, he joined the Federal army and was appointed a colonel in the infantry. Sherman saw combat in the first Manassas campaign in July 1861. A month later, he was promoted to brigadier general and assigned to Kentucky. In October, Sherman was made commander of the Department of the Cumberland, but he found himself in constant fights with his commanding officers and the press. After he was accused of being unstable, Sherman's command was severely restricted and he even contemplated suicide. However, he was able to overcome his depression and was given a new chance as commander of the Fifth Division, Army of the Tennessee, in March 1862.

Sherman participated in the Battle of Shiloh, during which he was wounded and had three horses shot out from under him. Some newspapers criticized Sherman's command in this battle, but General Grant and General Halleck had only praise for Sherman's bravery and quick thinking. From that time forward, Grant and Sherman became a remarkable team, pressing their commands through some of the hardest fighting of the war until the North finally prevailed.

FACT

Ely Parker, a full-blooded Seneca, was the highest ranking Native American officer in the Union army. Grant made Parker his military secretary with a rank of lieutenant colonel. He suffered prejudice during the war but was with Grant when Lee surrendered. Upon learning that Parker was a Seneca, Lee is reported to have remarked, "I am glad to see one real American here." Parker replied, "We are all Americans."

David Farragut

David G. Farragut is one of the few genuine naval heroes to come out of the Civil War. He is probably best remembered for a statement he made during the Battle of Mobile Bay: "Damn the torpedoes! Full speed ahead!"

Farragut was born in Tennessee in 1801 and was taken in as a foster child by Commodore David Porter, a respected naval hero. Farragut fought in the War of 1812 and was a prisoner of the British for a time.

When the Civil War broke out, Farragut's duties were light at first, but in January 1862 he was appointed commander of the squadron ordered to break down the naval defenses guarding New Orleans and take the city. It was a formidable task; the river approach to New Orleans was guarded by two forts and numerous Confederate gunships. But Farragut was confident the city could be captured, and he succeeded. He also played an important role at Vicksburg and most famously at the Battle of Mobile Bay.

Robert E. Lee

Robert Edward Lee stands out as one of the most conflicted commanding officers of the Civil War. A dedicated Southerner who turned down command of the Union army to remain faithful to his home state of Virginia, he emerged from the war a hero to the South despite numerous losses and near escapes on the battlefield. Lee managed to rally his army again and again in the face of heavy odds. His remarkable dedication to the war effort typifies everything that made the South such a formidable foe during the four-year conflict.

FACT

One of Robert E. Lee's most trusted companions was his horse, Traveller. Lee bought the Confederate-gray stallion during his 1861 western Virginia campaign and rode him in almost every important battle, often relieving stress by taking his horse for an evening ride. He once wrote his wife, "Traveller is my only companion; I may say my only pleasure."

Born in Virginia in 1807, Lee was descended from a family that had more than its share of influential statesmen and soldiers. His father, Henry "Light Horse Harry" Lee, was a former governor of Virginia and a cavalry officer during the Revolutionary War. However, Henry Lee died when Robert was only eleven years old, leaving the family somewhat impoverished. Robert was raised by his mother, Anne, to whom he was extremely close.

Early Military Career

A good student, Lee entered West Point in 1825, his admittance all but guaranteed by a testimonial letter signed by five senators and three representatives. Lee studied hard and graduated second in his class in 1829. Because of his high grades, he was assigned to the corps of engineers and traveled to a number of different posts over the next seventeen years. During this time, he married Mary Ann Randolph Custis and started a family.

During the Mexican War, Lee was commended for his commitment to the various combat assignments to which he was appointed. In 1852, he was made superintendent of West Point. It was a highly coveted assignment, but Lee found the work unexciting and was transferred to the Second Cavalry Division in 1855, spending much of his time in Texas.

As the tension between the North and South began to heat up, Lee realized that although he wasn't an advocate of either slavery or states' rights, he had to follow his heart and remain faithful to his home state of Virginia. His superiors in Washington tried desperately to keep him as the Southern states began to secede, even offering Lee the command of the Union army, but he refused and resigned his commission. By June 1861, Lee was appointed a general in the Confederate army and advisor to President Jefferson Davis.

General Robert E. Lee *Photo courtesy of the National Archives (111-B-1564)*

At the beginning of the war, Lee worked hard to bolster the Confederate army. He stopped a Union advance from western Virginia and organized defenses along the coasts of Georgia and South Carolina.

Lee's Service as Confederate General

On May 31, 1861, Lee took command of the Confederate army defending Richmond after General Joseph Johnston was wounded in the Battle of Seven Pines. He renamed the force the Army of Northern Virginia, which is how it is remembered.

Jeb Stuart

James Ewell Brown Stuart became renowned for his leadership and daring as one of the Confederate army's most skilled cavalry commanders. Stuart was born in Virginia in 1833. His father was a wealthy lawyer, and Stuart received a good education. He entered West Point in 1850 and graduated thirteenth in his class. He was made a second lieutenant in the Mounted Rifles and was assigned to the Texas frontier, where he was wounded by Cheyenne.

FACT

Lee was in Alexandria, Virginia, when radical abolitionist John Brown and his followers captured the federal arsenal at Harpers Ferry, Virginia, on October 16, 1859. Lee was assigned to lead the troops against Brown. Helping him was Jeb Stuart. Thomas "Stonewall" Jackson was sent to witness Brown's execution. Less than two years later, all three men were fighting against the Union.

In 1859, he volunteered to serve with Lee to bring radical abolitionist John Brown into custody at Harpers Ferry, Virginia. In 1861, he was made a lieutenant colonel in the First Virginia Cavalry. Like many soldiers in the war, Stuart had family members on the other side; his father-in-law was a general in the Union army.

Stuart was in the fighting from the beginning, taking part in the first Manassas campaign. He was promoted to brigadier general in September 1861. During the Peninsular Campaign, Stuart and his cavalry troops provided Lee with invaluable information regarding McClellan's troops by making a complete circuit of the Union forces over a three-day period, capturing numerous prisoners, arms, and equipment along the way. The information he obtained helped the Confederates win the Battle of Gaines's Mill.

Stuart's reputation continued to strengthen, and he was promoted to major general in July 1862. He was also placed in command of all cavalry forces in the Confederate's Army of Northern Virginia, which he led through a number of important battles.

Thomas "Stonewall" Jackson

Thomas Jonathan Jackson was one of the finest officers in the Confederate army, a consummate professional who earned the respect and loyalty of all who served with him. So famous are his exploits on the battlefield that his name is practically synonymous with the Civil War, even though he died in battle midway through the conflict.

FACT

Though he was a superb soldier, Stonewall Jackson was also a hypochondriac and was prone to eccentric behavior. He often held his right arm in the air for several minutes at a time, habitually sucked lemons, napped before battle, believed Northerners were devils, and refused to write a letter that would be in the mail on a Sunday.

Jackson was born in what is now West Virginia in 1824; he was orphaned as a youngster and raised by an uncle. Though he received little education as a child, Jackson managed to secure a spot at West Point and studied with such vigor and determination that he graduated seventeenth in a class of fifty-nine.

During the Mexican War, Jackson fought in the battles of Vera Cruz, Contreras, and Chapultepec. He showed exemplary skills and was promoted to major within eighteen months. After the Mexican War, Jackson was transferred to a number of different posts, including Florida, where he helped quell the Seminole uprising. In 1852, he resigned his commission to become a professor of military tactics and natural philosophy at the Virginia Military Institute.

Lieutenant General "Stonewall" Jackson
Photo courtesy of the National Archives (111-B-1867)

A religious man with strong convictions and few bad habits, Jackson enjoyed a number of quiet personal pursuits, including travel, until the Civil War started in 1861. When his home state of Virginia seceded, Jackson went with it and joined the Confederate army. One of his first tasks was to train infantry at Harpers Ferry, and by June 1861 he was promoted to brigadier general.

The Legend of "Stonewall"

Jackson received his now famous nickname at the First Battle of Manassas. According to reports, Jackson and his men fought off a Union advance with such courage that General Barnard Bee supposedly called out to his troops, "Oh men, there are Jackson and his Virginians, standing behind you like a stone wall! Let us determine to die here, and we shall conquer. Follow me." Jackson immediately became known as "Stonewall," a name that followed him for the rest of his life.

THE EVERYTHING CIVIL WAR BOOK

In October 1861, Jackson was promoted to major general and placed in command of the Army of the Shenandoah Valley. He played a vital role in the Second Battle of Manassas, Antietam, and Fredericksburg before being mortally wounded by his own men at Chancellorsville.

Pierre G. T. Beauregard

Pierre Gustave Toutant Beauregard was one of the Confederate army's best officers and one of its first heroes, but a rancorous relationship with President Davis kept him from achieving the fame—and commands—that went to many of his associates. Beauregard was born in Louisiana in 1818 to a wealthy and prosperous Creole family. A gifted student, he attended West Point and graduated second in his class. Like most of his contemporaries, he honed his military skills during the Mexican War and spent many years with the corps of engineers. As the army's chief engineer in New Orleans, he supervised the dredging of the mouth of the Mississippi.

Beauregard commanded the Confederate troops that captured Fort Sumter and, as a result, became the South's first war hero. He was also a commander at the First Battle of Manassas and helped achieve the Confederate army's first battlefield victory, though Jefferson Davis berated Beauregard for not pursuing the panic-stricken Union soldiers all the way into Washington. He would go on to command assignments at Shiloh and Corinth, but the cantankerous Davis accused Beauregard of being too elaborate in his military strategy and relieved him of duty.

Beauregard was reassigned to Charleston, South Carolina, where Jefferson felt he could do no harm. However, Charleston became a frequent target of attack by Union forces, and Beauregard fought valiantly to protect it. In April 1864, Beauregard was sent back to Virginia, where he played a crucial role in stopping two potentially devastating Union attacks around Richmond.

Joseph E. Johnston

Joseph Eggleston Johnston was another talented Confederate officer who had recurrent problems with Jefferson Davis. However, he was a very effective, well-liked leader who held important commands in the eastern and western theaters throughout the war and did his very best against long odds.

Johnston was born in Virginia in 1807. He attended West Point and saw quite a bit of combat following graduation, including service in the Seminole War and the Mexican War. In the 1850s, he saw duty in the Kansas Territory during the bloody conflict there and was made quartermaster general of the U.S. Army in June 1860. He resigned his commission in April 1861, when Virginia seceded from the Union.

Johnston was made a brigadier general in the Confederate army in May 1861 and was the commander of the Confederate troops that won the First Battle of Manassas, though he deferred the planning of strategy to Beauregard, who had a greater knowledge of the battlefield. It was the first military victory for the Confederate army and a stunning and unexpected blow against the overly confident Union.

The following month Johnston was named a full general and appointed to command the Department of the Potomac. He was wounded in the Battle of Seven Pines in May 1862 and temporarily relieved of duty while he recuperated. In November, Johnston was appointed commander of the Department of the West, but Jefferson Davis refused to support his battle strategy, and Johnston suffered humiliating defeats. As a result of these losses, Johnston's reputation among Confederate leaders in Richmond suffered greatly. Eventually, Johnston was brought back east to command the Army of Tennessee and ordered to stop Sherman's march toward Atlanta in 1864.

Other Important Military Figures

The armies of the Union and the Confederacy were commanded by a large number of men.

The Union

Joseph Hooker (1814–79) was known by the nickname "Fighting Joe" Hooker, which he greatly disliked. He led the Union attack at Antietam and was wounded, but he recovered to command a corps in the Battle of Fredericksburg just three months later. He was appointed to command the Army of the Potomac in January 1863. Hooker lost to Lee in the Battle of Chancellorsville in May 1863. He was removed from the Army of the Potomac in June 1863 just before the Battle of Gettysburg. Hooker saw combat in the Battle of Chattanooga and the siege of Atlanta.

FACT

Contrary to legend, the word "hooker" as slang for prostitute was not derived from General Joseph Hooker, who was known for his many vices. The word "hooker" was in common usage long before the Civil War began.

George G. Meade (1815–77) saw action at Mechanicsville, Gaines's Mills, and White Oak Swamp, where he was badly wounded. He returned to lead his brigade in the Second Battle of Manassas and the Battle of Antietam. Meade replaced Hooker as commander of the Army of the Potomac on June 28, 1863—just in time to lead it during the Battle of Gettysburg.

George Henry Halleck (1815–72) was appointed major general in charge of the newly formed Military Department of Missouri and was later placed in command of the Departments of Kansas and Ohio. He took command of Union forces after the Battle of Shiloh, with instructions to crush Beauregard's army but acted with such hesitancy that Beauregard was able to retreat. Lincoln appointed Halleck general-in-chief of all the armies of the North, where he proved more skilled as an administrator than commander.

Philip Sheridan (1831–88) was one of the youngest commanders to serve in the Civil War. He fought in numerous battles in both the east and the west but was most famous for his scorched earth policy during his Shenandoah Valley Campaign of 1864–65.

Ambrose Everett Burnside (1824–81) raised a brigade that fought well at the First Battle of Manassas and was instrumental in the capture of several vital Southern coastal positions some months later. Promoted to major general, Burnside twice refused offers to take over the Army of the Potomac from McClellan, with whom he was friends, but he finally accepted when Lincoln offered him the position in 1862. His tenure there proved short-lived, if bloody and demoralizing for the North.

George Custer (1839–76) is remembered more for his last stand at Little Bighorn in 1876 than his participation in the Civil War. At twenty-three, he became the youngest general in the Union army. He distinguished himself at Gettysburg with a series of daring frontal attacks that held back Jeb Stuart's advance on the Union flank and rear. Custer and Stuart met again at the Battle of Yellow Tavern in 1864.

FACT

The word "sideburns" was derived from Union general Ambrose Burnside, who was renowned more for his impressive muttonchops than his skill as a field commander. After the Civil War, Burnside went on to serve as governor of Rhode Island and U.S. senator.

Custer was present during Lee's surrender to Grant at the Appomattox Court House, Virginia. Custer and his cavalry had played an important role in forcing Lee's retreat to Appomattox, and Philip Sheridan thanked Custer by giving him the table upon which the surrender had been signed.

The Confederacy

Nathan Bedford Forrest (1821–77) rose from private to lieutenant general in the Confederate army and became one of the war's most feared cavalry commanders because of his lightning raids on enemy camps. His cavalry successfully covered the Confederate withdrawal following the Battle of Shiloh, even though Forrest was seriously wounded. He saw combat at the battles of Murfreesboro and Chickamauga, among many others. Forrest led the extremely controversial capture of Fort Pillow, Tennessee, in which his men were accused of slaughtering more than 200 unarmed troops, primarily black soldiers who had already surrendered.

Albert Sidney Johnston (1803–62) was a skilled commander who was considered the equal or superior of Lee early in the war. He commanded in the west and managed to establish a bridgehead in Kentucky to protect Tennessee from a Union offensive. This line broke when Grant captured Fort Donelson in February 1862. Johnston was killed two months later at the Battle of Shiloh.

John Bell Hood (1831–79) fought well in a number of battles, including the Seven Days Battles, Second Manassas, and Antietam. He was wounded at Gettysburg and lost his right leg in the Battle of Chickamauga. Eventually he took over the Army of the Tennessee from Johnston in an attempt to force back Sherman's thrust into Georgia.

Braxton Bragg (1817–76) commanded the coast between Pensacola and Mobile during the first summer of the war and was promoted to major general of the regular army in September 1861. Bragg served under Johnston as chief of staff at the Battle of Shiloh. He was promoted to commander of the Army of the Mississippi in June 1862, replacing Beauregard. Bragg had initial successes in Kentucky but lost the opportunity for more gains by wasting time trying to set up a secessionist government in Frankfort. He commanded at the battles of Murfreesboro, Chickamauga, and Missionary Ridge. He was favored by Jefferson Davis, which explains why he lasted so long in command, but he was generally disliked by his superiors as well as those who served under him. Bragg showed flair as a military tactician but also demonstrated potentially fatal indecision on the battlefield.

James Longstreet (1821–1904) graduated from West Point in 1842. Joining the Confederate army in 1861, he rose quickly and served mainly under Lee, who called Longstreet his "warhorse." Longstreet rose to the position of lieutenant general by 1862. He commanded a corps at Second Manassas, the right wing of Lee's army at Antietam, and a corps again at Gettysburg. He led his corps west in late summer 1863 to lend weight to the Confederates during the Battle of Chickamauga. By spring of 1864, he was with Lee again fighting Grant's army and was wounded at the Battle of the Wilderness.

CHAPTER 5

The Course of the War: 1861

The year 1861 opened under a dark cloud; the nation had been split into two parts. Lincoln had first to worry about Federal property besieged by Southerners. South Carolina fired on Fort Sumter before supplies arrived, and the war was on. The North responded with an "On to Richmond" campaign, the beginnings of a naval blockade, and strikes at Southern forces along their northern borders.

Besieging Fort Sumter

South Carolina seceded in December 1861, followed by the other states of the Deep South in January and February. United States property remained within the boundaries of the Southern states. The most problematic of these were military stores and installations. Obviously the Southern states did not want islands of Federal control within their borders; they felt they were entitled to these arms and supplies themselves.

Geoffrey Ward explains in *The Civil War* that many Federal installations quickly concluded it was folly to hold out as Union-controlled blips deep within Confederate territory, and they turned over their materials and fortifications without a shot. The soldiers who were loyal to the Union then traveled north; soldiers in the Federal army with Southern sympathies often chose to leave the ranks of the Federal army and cast their lot with the Confederacy.

Most troublesome to the Federal troops were the fortifications at Charleston. The harbor was protected on either side by mainland Forts Moultrie and Johnson and by pentagon-shaped Fort Sumter on a small island in between, smack in the path of any ship wishing to reach or depart Charleston city. Federal troops at the garrison quickly understood they could not defend Forts Johnson and Moultrie from land attack, so they were abandoned to South Carolinians, who moved in with large numbers to man the batteries. The Federals under Major Robert Anderson withdrew to the relative isolation and safety of water-surrounded Fort Sumter.

FACT

Montgomery Meigs was appointed quartermaster general of the U.S. army in June 1861. A graduate of West Point, Meigs had a remarkable flair for efficiency and was responsible for supplying the army with almost everything it needed. As a result, the average Union soldier was better equipped than his Confederate counterpart.

Anderson was a veteran of the Mexican War and had strong Southern ties, yet he was loyal to the Union. Anderson settled into Fort Sumter with sixty-eight men to await orders from Washington. South Carolinians saw the fort as an insult to their sovereignty. They could not abide a Federal fort commanding Charleston, the most important city in their state and one of the most important in the seceded states. They demanded it be turned over to them, and negotiations began almost as soon as South Carolina seceded.

Buchanan's Dilemma

President Buchanan was stymied. As the leader of the U.S. government he believed the Constitution did not allow secession, but neither did it offer a way to prevent or reverse it. He also felt he could not readily surrender an important fort. Anderson reported that Fort Sumter could be defended, but he would need reinforcements and additional supplies.

FACT

Josiah Gorgas
Josiah Gorgas is a little-known hero of the Confederacy. A West Pointer from Pennsylvania, Gorgas was made the Confederate head of ordnance. He organized new arsenals throughout the South, used a corps of agents who purchased weapons, and fostered plans for capturing weapons from the enemy. His efforts were so successful that Confederate soldiers never lacked weapons and ammunition.

According to Shelby Foote's *Civil War: A Narrative*, Buchanan decided to send reinforcements and supplies. A merchant steamer called *Star of the West* carried them, but as it approached Charleston harbor on January 9, Confederate gunners fired on it. Although the ship sustained no damage, her captain turned and abandoned the relief expedition. President Buchanan did not consider this an act of war because no blood had been shed.

Lincoln Addresses the Conflict

At Lincoln's inauguration on March 4, Lincoln vowed that the U.S. government would not start a war with the South, nor would it try to take back Federal facilities held at that point by Confederate forces. He did promise, however, to "hold, occupy, and possess" forts and other installations still under Federal control within the Confederacy, and that included Fort Sumter.

Lincoln was thrown into the first serious crisis of his presidency the day after his inauguration, when he received a frantic wire from Anderson at Fort Sumter, reporting that the facility had less than a six-week supply of food. The fort would be impossible to hold if new supplies were not sent immediately.

General-in-Chief Winfield Scott told Lincoln that resupplying the fort was impossible, and Secretary of State William Seward advised that the fort simply be evacuated in an attempt to cool growing agitation in Charleston. Lincoln chose an option he hoped would appease both sides: he would resupply the fort but not reinforce its defenses. He then sent a message to Francis Pickens, the governor of South Carolina, telling him of his decision and began to organize the relief fleet.

The Fall of Fort Sumter

Despite Lincoln's seemingly peaceful hand, Jefferson Davis, the newly sworn president of the Confederacy, was not in a conciliatory mood. He wanted nothing less than the surrender of the fort, and he ordered Brigadier General Pierre G. T. Beauregard to take the fort by force if necessary. Beauregard sent Anderson a message informing him of his intent to bombard the fort if it were not evacuated. A pragmatic Anderson replied, "Gentlemen, I will await the first shot and if you do not batter the fort to pieces about us, we shall be starved out in a few days." Anderson then informed Beauregard's emissary that he would evacuate the fort by noon on April 15 if he did not receive additional orders or supplies by that time. Anderson was told the terms were not acceptable, and the Southerners prepared to fire on the fort before Lincoln's relief fleet could reach them.

C. Brian Kelly reports in his *Best Little Stories from the Civil War* that at the beginning of the Civil War the population of the Northern states was 31.4 million and the population of the Southern states was 12.3 million.

At 4:30 A.M. on April 12, a single mortar was fired to signal the forty-three Confederate guns around Fort Sumter to begin their bombardment. The shelling continued all through Friday, April 12, and into Saturday, April 13. In all, more than 4,000 explosives were hurled at the fort. Anderson fired guns, but holding the fort was never a serious consideration. On the second day of the bombardment, hot shells set portions of the fort on fire. Realizing there was no way he could mount any type of reasonable defense, Anderson ordered the American flag lowered and replaced with a white flag of surrender. None of his men had been injured.

Fort Sumter, South Carolina, April 4, 1861, under the Confederate flag *Photo courtesy of the National Archives (121-BA-914A)*

During the fort's evacuation the next day, Anderson ordered a cannon salute to the United States flag. One of the big guns exploded, killing Private Daniel Hough. Another soldier, Private Edward Galloway, was gravely injured and died a few days later. They were the war's first military casualties, victims of an accident.

On April 15, Abraham Lincoln proclaimed a state of insurrection—not a state of war—and issued a call for 75,000 volunteers to quell the rebellion. The Civil War had officially begun.

The Anaconda Plan and the Beginning of the Blockade

General Winfield Scott, presiding at secession over the Union armies, saw the war was likely to be a long one. The South was a vast territory, and the Union would have to invade the South and crush the Confederacy's ability to defend itself. The deeper the Union armies penetrated into the South, the longer its supply lines would have to be and the more vulnerable they would be to Confederate attack.

Though it was a slave state, Kentucky, in June 1861, showed a strong sentiment for the Union. In a congressional election that month Unionists outpolled Southern sympathizers by 97,000 to 37,000 votes.

Scott felt the armies needed for such work would have to be large and highly professional. The Northern armies at the time were neither. Accordingly, Scott suggested that the North spend time recruiting and training large armies, which would take considerable time. In the meantime, he proposed a naval blockade of the Southern ports in order to prevent the Confederates from purchasing war materiel from abroad or shipping out cotton for cash that could be exchanged for war goods. He also recommended sealing off the land borders, a sort of blockade on land. He then suggested moving down the Mississippi River to cut the Confederacy in two. This would prevent economic and military exchange east and west of the river and deprive the Southerners of the economic benefit of the Mississippi River and valley.

As it turned out, this was very close to the strategy the North followed, but at the time the press and political critics thought Scott's plan would be far too slow in bringing the Confederacy to its knees. They dubbed the strategy the Anaconda Plan for its aim of strangling the Southern republic into submission. They put pressure on the Lincoln administration to hurl an army south toward Richmond, whip the Southerners in a single blow, and end the insurrection once and for all.

Naval Blockades

As Scott would have been the first to admit, the Union did not have a navy close to being large enough to strangle Southern trade, even though the South did not have a navy at all. The Southern coastline was so long that blockade runners could slip in and out almost at will. They did so for years, though the task became increasingly difficult as the Union navy grew and as the Union captured more Southern ports.

King Cotton

The Confederate nation unwittingly bolstered the Anaconda concept from the very beginning. A major goal of Confederate diplomacy at the beginning of the war was to convince England to declare the Northern blockade illegal so that the Royal Navy could intervene and protect British trade with Southern merchants.

In 1861, the Confederacy hoped to force England's hand through an unofficial policy that became known as cotton diplomacy. Knowing that England imported nearly three-fourths of its cotton from the South, the Confederacy began withholding cotton supplies from British textile manufacturers. Their goal was to use economic extortion to compel England (and to a lesser degree, France) to recognize the new Confederate republic as an independent nation. It made sense in theory: no cotton meant no textile production, thereby bringing the British textile industry and thus the government to its knees.

There was just one flaw with the plan: England and France both had more cotton than they knew what to do with. A bumper crop just prior to the war pushed prices down and allowed the two nations to stockpile almost two years' worth. In fact, as late as 1862, England was able to ship some of its cotton back to mills in New England. In addition, England had found ample new sources of cotton in Egypt and India. British leaders contemplated the situation and finally decided that the loss of Southern cotton was less of a problem than the loss of the more lucrative Northern industrial markets, especially during wartime. Ultimately, cotton diplomacy netted the Confederacy almost nothing.

The First Battle of Manassas

The First Battle of Manassas, also known as the First Battle of Bull Run, was the first large battle of the war. Union officials looked to an easy victory that would crumble the South's willingness to resist; Southerners looked to show that they could defend their vast territory. The Confederate forces dug in along a small stream called Bull Run near the town of Manassas, Virginia, protecting a vital rail connection there.

FACT

Confederate general Pierre G. T. Beauregard, in addition to being a skilled military tactician and soldier, designed the Confederate army's "Southern Cross" battle flag. Beauregard proposed the flag after the First Battle of Manassas, arguing that the flags of the Union and the Confederacy were easy to confuse in the chaos of battle.

The battle was set more for political than military reasons. Confederate leaders, eager to prove their mettle against the more industrial North, had moved the capital of the Confederacy to Richmond, Virginia, greatly angering Northern politicians. Meanwhile, the press and the public were loudly pushing for the Union to move "on to Richmond." More importantly, by the time the battle was set, many of the 75,000 Northern volunteer recruits were nearing the end of their ninety-day enlistment and were getting ready to go home.

Battle Plans

Union general Irvin McDowell's strategy was simple: approach the Confederate forces, crush them, and push on to Richmond. Opposing him was Confederate general Beauregard, already a Southern war hero for his role in the fall of Fort Sumter. Beauregard reasoned that a Confederate victory might impress upon the Union the strength and fortitude of the Confederate army and result in a truce and an early peace.

Both the North and the South had three armies in the area. McDowell had 30,600 troops along the Potomac facing 20,000 Confederate soldiers under Beauregard. Union general Robert Patterson had 18,000 men facing 12,000 Confederates under Joseph E. Johnston near Harpers Ferry. And Union general Benjamin Butler commanded 10,000 men in Fort Monroe at the tip of the Virginia peninsula, guarded by a small unit of Confederates under John B. Magruder, although neither Butler nor Magruder would play a role in Manassas.

McDowell left Washington for Manassas Junction on July 16, 1861, but did not arrive until July 18. His large army was slowed by a huge number of supply wagons and the carefree attitude of the neophyte soldiers, who often broke rank to gather berries or rest in the shade. Union reconnaissance troops sent to feel out the enemy were met and driven back by Confederate forces at Blackburn's Ford, a small Confederate victory that demoralized the green Union troops.

The Fighting Commences

McDowell meant to drive Beauregard from Manassas Junction by feigning an attack on the Confederate center, then clobbering the Confederate left. Patterson was to keep Johnston from joining Beauregard, giving McDowell a decided advantage in numbers. However, Johnston gave Patterson the slip and was able to come to Beauregard's aid.

"Steady, men. Hold your fire until they're on you. Then fire and give them the bayonet. And when you charge, yell like furies!"—Colonel Thomas "Stonewall" Jackson to his men at the First Battle of Manassas

The battle itself began on July 21. Beauregard's grand plan to attack McDowell, based on Napoleon's strategy at Austerlitz, was a dismal and immediate failure. His troops were simply too inexperienced. McDowell's army gained an early advantage thanks to its greater numbers, and it appeared the Union would win; several Confederate units were defeated as Union infantry advanced on a small plateau called Henry House Hill. It was here that "Stonewall" Jackson earned his nickname.

Just when a Union victory seemed assured, Johnston's army arrived from Harpers Ferry to reinforce Beauregard. Fighting aggressively, the Confederate forces caused the Union line to crumble. Retreat was called, and the Union soldiers, most of whom had never been in battle before, began to race to the rear as the Confederates shot at them. The retreat turned into a rout as officers abandoned their troops, terrified soldiers fled in panic, and the entire Union supply train became a horrible, tangled mess of carts, trucks, and ambulances. Chaos reigned, and the situation was made worse by the presence of hundreds of sightseers, many with picnic baskets in hand, who had arrived from Washington in carriages and buggies to watch from a grassy slope a few miles away. Federal losses totaled 2,896 men dead, wounded, or missing. Confederate losses totaled 1,982.

The First Battle of Manassas would foreshadow a great many other battles in which outmanned and outgunned Confederate forces would defeat the Union army through skill, bravery, and sheer battlefield tenacity. It also proved to Lincoln and others that the short, clean war they had hoped for was not going to happen.

Attacking Port Royal Sound and the Outer Banks

In order to make the blockade as effective as they could, the Northern navy would require harbors where it could station and supply ships. The navy already had Fortress Monroe in Chesapeake Bay at the southern tip of the peninsula between the York and the James rivers. But in hopes of cutting off more Southern cities and securing places of refuge for its ships, the navy looked to sanctuaries south.

A tempting prospect was the sheltered waters of Pamlico and Albemarle sounds off the North Carolina coast. In August 1861, the Union navy seized Hatteras Inlet, a passage from the Atlantic into Pamlico Sound, by bombarding two strongholds on either side for two days. The Confederates could not resist such a display of force, and the Northerners had a foothold on North Carolina's Outer Banks. If they could gain complete control of both these sounds, they could cut off the ports of New Bern and Beaufort—both with rail facilities—and Plymouth and Elizabeth City. The Union navy began to plan an expedition that would expand its reach beyond Hatteras Inlet to the sounds themselves.

FACT

General Joseph E. Johnston moved his Confederate troops by railroad to Manassas Junction for the First Battle of Manassas in July 1861. It was the first time in history that soldiers were transported to a battle via train.

Another objective was the good anchoring at Port Royal Sound bounded at the southern side by Hilton Head between the cities of Savannah, Georgia, and Charleston, South Carolina. In November, Captain Samuel Du Pont headed a naval expedition of seventy-four ships to the sound. The Confederates were ready with prepared forts and more than forty guns, but the Union navy won gunfire duel and battered the protecting forts into submission.

Ball's Bluff and Belmont

Still relishing in its victory at Manassas, the Confederates maintained scattered forces not far south of the Potomac River, some in sight of Washington's Capitol building itself. One such was a signal station with a cannon at Munson's Hill, about ten miles from the Capitol. In late summer, a Union colonel attacked up the hill and withdrew after taking a few casualties. In late September the Confederates themselves withdrew, believing the position untenable. When the Federals advanced they found that the "cannon" was really a log painted black, and the story of the earlier repulse at the hands of a "Quaker gun" made it into the newspapers.

Defeat

One result of this discovery was renewed congressional and civilian pressure on the Federal army to press the Confederates with more vigor. When reports arrived at Union army headquarters that it seemed Southerners were about to abandon Leesburg, about two-thirds of the way up the Potomac River toward Harper's Ferry from Washington, D.C., senior officers gave orders to allow for army units to press where feasible. On the Virginia side, Federal troops marched upriver to Dranesville, then stopped. On the opposite side of the river, Federal troops prepared to cross.

FACT

The fight at Ball's Bluff did not amount to much of a battle compared to the one at Manassas or the many to come, but it was notable for its casualties. Not only was a U.S. senator killed, among the Federal soldiers captured were a grandson of Paul Revere, a son of the writer Oliver Wendell Holmes Sr., and a nephew of poet James Russell Lowell.

These troops were under the command of Colonel Edward Baker, a U.S. senator from Oregon and a good friend of Lincoln. On October 21, Baker crossed the Potomac with several regiments and climbed a 100-foot bluff— Ball's Bluff—to press the Confederates. Upon encountering Rebels, the Federals regrouped in a field backing up to the steep bluff itself. Confederates concealed in the edge of the field fired at them, killing Baker. The Confederates charged and the Union men scrambled down the slope in an attempt to escape. A hundred were shot and 700 captured. Lincoln wept when he learned his good friend Baker had been killed.

The War in the West

Despite political pressure and a good deal of concentration and effort, the Union was getting nowhere pressing Confederate forces southward in Virginia. But in the west, the war became more fluid. It was obvious to both sides that rivers were gateways to the Deep South. The Mississippi, of course, flowed through the heart of the South, and the Tennessee and Cumberland rivers were watery highways to Tennessee, Mississippi, and

Alabama. Ulysses S. Grant would first try to crack the Southern defenses along the Mississippi River at Columbus, Kentucky, at the lower point of Illinois.

"We cut our way in and we can cut our way out."—General Ulysses S. Grant to his regimental commanders after being surrounded by Confederate counterattackers at the Battle of Belmont

Grant led an expedition south on the Missouri side of the river to the Confederate encampment of Belmont, across the river from the heavily gunned fort at Columbus. At first the attack was successful, but the Northern soldiers stopped to celebrate in the Confederate camp. The Southerners rallied, took advantage, counterattacked, and surrounded the undisciplined Union men. Grant turned cannons on the Confederate lines and blasted a gap through which his soldiers could escape.

Grant withdrew, but he learned lessons that would benefit him in the future: condition the men for any eventuality and follow up diligently when the enemy is on the defensive. The western war was about to break loose.

CHAPTER 6

The Course of the War: 1862 Part I

The Confederacy had constructed itself into a credible nation. The armies it had raised had repulsed large Federal forces, but few could doubt that the full power of the North had yet been organized to move against Southern armies and Southern territories. Northerners hoped a Federal general would emerge to crack Southern military skills. That man turned out to be Ulysses S. Grant. In the first part of the year, another military star began to shine very brightly as well: Robert E. Lee.

Fort Henry

As 1862 opened, the Confederacy had reason for optimism. After almost nine months of war, it was holding its own. True, it had lost most of northwestern Virginia and some of its coastal areas were occupied or threatened, but it had repelled an attack in northern Virginia and it was holding a line there close to that of the previous summer.

In the west, the Southerners had turned back Grant's raid against the stronghold of Columbus, Kentucky, on the Mississippi River. It was holding a line that stretched from there through Forts Henry and Donelson near where the Tennessee and Columbia rivers flowed into the Ohio and up into central Kentucky, a line that sheltered all of Tennessee. In central Kentucky the Confederate and Union armies were more or less on equal terms. But to the west, the Union would likely have an advantage: it could build steamships with armor and guns that could control rivers, and rivers could take them into the Deep South. The principal river, of course, was the Mississippi, and if the North could control this north-south waterway, the Confederacy would be grievously wounded. But Columbus was a very tough stronghold. Grant would try something else instead: Fort Henry on the Tennessee River.

The Appeal of Fort Henry

Fort Henry was especially tempting because if it fell, Union gunboats—the general name given to the Northern river-cruising warships—could cruise directly south through the width of Tennessee into northern Mississippi and Alabama. Columbus would have to be abandoned or its garrison cut off. In January, Grant devised a plan with Navy Flag Officer Andrew Foote to capture Fort Henry. Grant and Foote steamed up the Tennessee River from Paducah, Kentucky, and disembarked short of the fort. The plan was for Foote's gunboats to soften up the defenses with a barrage and then storm them with the soldiers, but luck tilted toward the Union men. When they reached the fort, they found that much of it was inundated because the Tennessee River was in a flood stage. On February 6, Foote unleashed his barrage on the hapless Confederates, who realized resistance was pointless and escaped as quickly as they could to Fort Donelson on the Cumberland River twelve miles away. Of all the significant Union victories of the war, this was the easiest. It laid open western Tennessee all the way into the Deep South, and it opened the way to Fort Donelson

Fort Donelson

Grant's orders concerned only Fort Henry, but he quickly saw his opportunity for opening two rivers rather than one to Union forces. He immediately pressed his soldiers for the short march to Donelson. Unfortunately, Donelson was not as vulnerable as Fort Henry, and it now had a reinforced garrison. The Confederate commander of the whole Kentucky line, Albert Sydney Johnston—considered by many to be the best general the South had—faced a grim choice. Losing Fort Donelson would be disastrous for the Southern cause, but sending additional troops to the fort would remove them from elsewhere. Johnston decided to send some reinforcements to the fort; it would have 16,000 men to Grant's 15,000, though Grant was looking for reinforcements.

FACT

At Fort Donelson, Grant commanded fifty-four-year-old Brigadier General Charles F. Smith, who had been commandant of West Point when Grant was a cadet. They worked very well together, however, and Grant sought the older man's advice. It was Smith who first received the letter about surrender from Donelson and told Grant, "No terms for the damned rebels."

Fort Donelson was really a formal fort plus a fortified area that embraced the small town of Dover. The Confederates had made lines of defenses outside both, and they had heavy guns to battle any gunboats coming at them. Shortly, Foote tested these riverside defenses in the hope that he could batter the fort into submission just as he had Fort Henry, without the help of the army. But here the Southern gunners had high ground, and they repulsed Foote's gunboats with significant loss. If the fort were to be taken, Grant's ring of besieging soldiers would have to do the work.

They did, but with the help of a tremendous Confederate error. Three generals were in charge of the defense of Donelson: John Floyd, who had served as secretary of war to President Buchanan but had little military training; Gideon Pillow; and Simon Bolivar Buckner, a West Pointer and a friend of Grant's. The three Confederates realized that Grant's strength meant he would capture the fort, and they determined that their best course was to break out of Grant's besieging ring and retreat toward Nashville.

"Sir: Yours of this date proposing . . . terms of capitulation is just received. No terms except unconditional and immediate surrender can be accepted. I proposed to move immediately on your works. I am sir, very respectfully your obedient servant, U. S. Grant."—Ulysses S. Grant, responding to Confederate general Simon Bolivar Buckner's terms of surrender at Fort Donelson

On February 15, the Southerners opened the road that would allow them a retreat toward Nashville. But rather than hasten along it, by order of General Pillow they turned back to their old quarters to fetch their belongings. Grant, somewhat surprised by the Confederate breakout attempt, was hard pressed to close the gap. But he also realized that if the Southerners were trying to break out to the south, they were probably weak along the northern trenches. Grant ordered an attack there, and Union men captured some of the fortifications in this sector.

Unconditional Surrender

Floyd, Pillow, and Buckner realized they were hemmed in for good. Floyd passed command to Pillow and escaped; Pillow passed command to Buckner and escaped. Nathan Bedford Forrest broke out with some of his horsemen, but Buckner was left to perform the odious job of surrender. He sent a letter through the lines asking his old friend Grant for terms. Grant, thinking Floyd or Pillow in command, wrote one of the most famous letters in military history and certainly one of the shortest. Buckner, irritated and distressed, nevertheless surrendered unconditionally. When the press learned the details of the siege they dubbed U. S. Grant "Unconditional Surrender" Grant.

On February 16, General Buckner surrendered 13,000 prisoners at Fort Donelson. To that time, according to Bruce Catton's *Terrible Swift Sword*, it was the largest prize of prisoners ever won by the U.S. Army

The North could finally celebrate its first important victory against a substantial Confederate land force with a great deal at stake. Grant became a hero. Johnston's line was now broken in the middle. He had to abandon the stronghold of Columbus, Kentucky, on the Mississippi River, and he had to retreat from central Kentucky. He also could not hold Nashville because its location on the Columbia River left it vulnerable to attack by Union gunboats. The greater part of Tennessee now lay open to the North, which also gained the psychological victory of capturing the capital of a seceded state.

Peninsular Campaign Begins

In Washington, General George McClellan, then in charge of all Union armies, looked at his maps and decided there was a better way of capturing the Confederate capital—Richmond—and thus ending the war. Instead of marching against a sizeable Rebel army in northern Virginia, roughly seventy miles from Richmond, he would transport the Union Army of the Potomac down Chesapeake Bay to near the mouth of the James River, on which Richmond was situated. He would then proceed up the north bank of the James River, past the Revolutionary War battlefield of Yorktown and the old Virginia capital at Williamsburg to Richmond. There, with superior numbers, he planned to besiege and capture the Confederate capital.

This plan won begrudging approval in Washington. President Lincoln and Secretary of War Edwin Stanton were fearful that with the Army of the Potomac gone, a swift Confederate army could overrun Washington, a triumph that might well lead to the ultimate victory of separation the

Confederacy wanted. Lincoln and Stanton gave approval to McClellan's plan only if he left enough troops in front of and around Washington to protect the city.

Additionally, McClellan's duties were rearranged. He would no longer be in charge of all Federal armies, only its largest, the Army of the Potomac. In the west, Lincoln and Stanton put General Henry Halleck in charge.

The Start of the Campaign

McClellan began his campaign to the southern end of Chesapeake Bay in good form. He was disgruntled that the Army of the Potomac would have only 90,000 soldiers for the job, not the 130,000 he had planned on; much of the remainder was left guarding the capital under the command of General McDowell, leader of Union forces at the First Battle of Manassas. He landed his army at Fort Monroe on the tip of the peninsula between the York and the James rivers. At the same time, Confederate president Davis and his chief commander in the region, Joseph Johnston, concluded that they were spread too thin in northern Virginia and should pull Johnston's army back to Richmond.

McClellan's Methods

McClellan was a methodical commander. He did not like to move before all his preparations were made and all of his supplies and soldiers on hand. Eventually he got his men moving up the peninsula—in what later would be known as the Peninsula Campaign—toward Yorktown where the Southerners were establishing defensive lines. When McClellan saw these lines he stopped. In reality, there were not many Confederates there, but they all fell under the command of General John Magruder, who had had some theatrical experience before the war. Magruder marched his men in and out of trees and made such a fuss that McClellan believed he was facing a far larger force than he was. He stopped his march and called for heavy siege guns to be brought up. All of this and other preparations would take a month, until early April.

The Battle of Shiloh

Grant's victories at Forts Henry and Donelson opened the Tennessee and Columbia rivers to Union gunboats and control. Grant made swift use of his advantage, sending Federal troops to take Nashville on the Columbia. He also sent Foote's gunboats up the Tennessee River. Confederate general Albert Sydney Johnston saw no alternative but to retreat to the important rail junction of Corinth, Mississippi, where the railroad running from Memphis to the eastern Confederacy crossed the railroad running north-south between Mobile, Alabama, and the Ohio River valley. There he would collect as many Southern soldiers as he could and stop Grant's drive south.

FACT

Brigadier General Charles F. Smith served under Grant, his former pupil, at Forts Henry and Donelson. Grant held him in the highest regard. Smith died of an infection in 1862, and Grant's biographer Jean E. Smith reports that William Sherman later wrote that had Smith lived and remained a general "no one would have ever heard of Grant or myself."

Grant, too, was eager for a fight. If he could defeat the Southerners in Corinth, Memphis would likely fall into Union hands, an important goal in winning the Mississippi River from the north all the way to the Gulf of Mexico. Grant advanced with 42,000 troops to a place called Pittsburg Landing on the west side of the Tennessee River near the Mississippi border. He remained there for nearly a month, waiting for the arrival of Don Carlos Buell's army, which had been in central Kentucky and then Tennessee. Once Buell's men arrived, Grant planned to advance on Corinth and defeat the Rebels there.

Southerners Strike First

Johnston saw the danger of Grant reinforced with Buell, however, and decided to strike secretly and swiftly. Johnston's second in command, Pierre G. T. Beauregard, liked the idea at first but then changed his mind; he felt that marching 20,000 Confederate soldiers twenty miles from Corinth to

Pittsburg Landing would be too easily detected and that Grant would be reinforced before they arrived.

But Johnston persisted and when his army arrived on the outskirts of Pittsburg Landing on April 6, they found no signs of Buell's arrival. Nor was there much awareness that a large force of Rebels was so close by. The Confederate forces had succeeded in catching the Union troops off guard, and after three hours of brutal, bloody fighting, they managed to overrun divisions commanded by William T. Sherman and Benjamin Prentiss near Shiloh Church. The battle could have turned into a rout, but Johnston's army lost its momentum when his soldiers started rummaging through the overrun Union camps looking for food and supplies.

The Confusion of Battle

The battle became increasingly disorganized, and soldiers on both sides scrambled to find their correct units. One major battle turned into numerous smaller skirmishes, with both sides taking heavy casualties. In many cases, confused Confederate troops dressed in both blue and gray fired on their own men, and hundreds of panic-stricken soldiers on both sides ran from the battlefield in terror.

When Grant arrived on the scene, he ordered his remaining men to hold their positions in a dense thicket at all costs. With Grant barking orders and doing his best to rally them, the Union soldiers managed to repel more than a dozen hard Confederate charges. Johnston, who was directing the assaults, took a bullet in the thigh and bled to death. In the early evening, the 2,200 defenders of the thicket—which came to be known as "the Hornet's Nest" because of the constant gunfire—were ordered to surrender as they came under attack by Confederate artillery. But it was growing dark and had started to rain, so Beauregard, who assumed command upon Johnston's death, decided to delay a final assault until the next morning. The decision cost him greatly.

Grant Fights Back

During the night, Buell's army began to arrive and Grant positioned them for a morning attack. Beauregard awakened the following morning to face an army nearly twice as strong as before. Fighting resumed around 7:30 A.M., and the Union forces were able to recapture almost all of the ground they had lost the previous day. The Confederates made one counterattack but were pushed back. Late in the afternoon, Beauregard ordered a withdrawal back to Corinth, covered by Nathan Forrest's cavalry.

Thus Grant's army won the battle, but Grant was strongly rebuked for being caught off guard. Halleck, Grant's superior officer, accused Grant of being drunk at the time. It was a false accusation—Grant had been away from the front to have a leg injury treated—but it was typical of Halleck. Halleck also blamed Grant for the large number of Union casualties. In fact, the casualties for these armies—still full of untested volunteers—were horrendous.

More than 13,000 Union soldiers were killed, wounded, or missing in the battle, compared to 10,694 on the Confederate side. This loss included more than twice the number of dead than all previous the engagements of the war combined.

Shiloh crushed any hope that the Confederacy could reverse the losses of territory inflicted by the defeats at Forts Henry and Donelson any time soon. And it inflicted cruel casualties that the South would have difficulty making up. The battle also shocked Northerners. It was the largest, bloodiest battle ever fought in America, and it was clear that the Confederacy was not going to give up its struggle for independence with a few simple setbacks; rather, it was going to commit its young men to fighting no matter the cost in lives and money until they won or were decidedly crushed.

The Valley Campaign

Before the war, Thomas "Stonewall" Jackson had been an eccentric instructor at the Virginia Military Institute in the upper part of the Shenandoah Valley. Jackson was given command of a force in the Shenandoah Valley with the object of keeping it clear of Union forces. In late March, he attacked Federal troops at Kernstown, believing they were heading out of the valley to reinforce General McDowell closer to Fredericksburg. Jackson misjudged the number of Union men against him and he was repulsed. Washington figured that if Jackson could attack at Kernstown, he must be stronger than they had supposed and they had better keep even more men in northern Virginia to protect the capital. Lincoln and Stanton shuffled troops accordingly, depriving McClellan of troops he was counting on. Both Stonewall Jackson and Robert E. Lee took note.

When McClellan began building up his army on the peninsula throughout April, Lee and Jackson devised a plan by which Jackson would wreak as much havoc as he could in the valley, tying up Federal forces there so they could not reinforce McClellan.

Throughout the Valley Campaign, Jackson had control of at most about 17,000 troops, but he faced and tied up about 50,000 Federal soldiers.

In early May, just as McClellan was finally moving past the Yorktown lines, Jackson and his small force faced three larger Federal forces in or near the Shenandoah Valley. Union general John Fremont was just to the west in the West Virginia mountains. General Nathaniel Banks was at the lower part of the valley, and McDowell was to the east of the valley with various divisions he could send to the valley as reinforcements.

Jackson on the Loose

As McClellan advanced toward Richmond, Jackson got under way. He marched slightly out of the valley near Staunton and defeated an advance guard of Fremont's, effectively ending advancement by Fremont from this area. Then he re-entered the valley, ducked behind Massanutten Mountain, which bisects much of the lower valley, and struck a portion of Banks's command at Front Royal. Banks then had to retreat to Winchester, where Jackson attacked and defeated him on May 25. Panicked, Banks retreated all the way north of the Potomac, and the politicians in Washington grew exceptionally worried.

Jackson made a bold pursuit but then turned back toward the valley once Banks had crossed the Potomac. Jackson then outraced Federal forces trying to cut him off at Strasburg by coming from both the east and west. The Federals pursued the numerically inferior Confederate force south along the valley until in early June Jackson turned and struck again, first at Cross Keys and then at Port Republic. This halted two Federal armies out to defeat him.

Jackson's men soon became hardened to long and difficult marches. Their general would have them up early and press them continuously, but the conditioning paid off. Soon Jackson's men were known as "foot cavalry," and they could see that speed and position could win them victories at far less cost in blood.

Having tied up all of these Union troops—many of whom had been slated to reinforce McClellan—Jackson took his small army through Brown's Gap in the Blue Ridge Mountains to join the Confederate forces guarding Richmond.

The Seven Days Battles

By late May, McClellan had managed to march his host of Federal soldiers up the peninsula between the York and James rivers to the gates of Richmond. He sent a portion of his army north of the Chickahominy River, the better to link up with portions of McDowell's army. The Chickahominy River parallels the James for a way before flowing into it and was a difficult barrier for infantry and cannon to cross when flooded.

Confederate general Joe Johnston saw an opportunity to raise the Union siege on Richmond. On May 31, he took many of his troops out of their defenses and trenches guarding Richmond and struck that part of the Federal host south of the river. However, subordinates misunderstood their orders or did things their own way, and the ensuing fight, called Fair Oaks or Seven Pines, was basically a draw. Very significantly, however, Johnston was seriously wounded in the fight. President Davis replaced him with his military advisor, Robert E. Lee, who began calling his command the Army of Northern Virginia.

Lee's New Plan

After the Battle of Seven Pines, the Southerners withdrew again into their Richmond defenses, but both Davis and Lee could see that the Union stranglehold would eventually capture Richmond. Like Johnston before him, Lee decided to take a huge risk by taking his men out of their defenses and attempting to defeat the Federal troops in open battle.

When Lee withdrew men from Richmond defenses south of the Chickahominy River, only 25,000 Southerners remained to face about 75,000 Federal troops south of the river. McClellan, however, did not understand his overwhelming superiority of numbers in this area.

Lee conferred with Stonewall Jackson, then finishing his astonishing work in the Shenandoah Valley. The plan was to have Jackson slip away from the Union armies there, march to Richmond's north side, join with Lee's men coming out of their defenses, and fall upon the northern flank of McClellan's army. Done precisely, the attack would crumple McClellan's army from one wing to the other.

A Week of Fighting

It did not go exactly according to plan. Two of Lee's subordinate commanders, Generals James Longstreet and D. H. Hill, withdrew their troops from their entrenchments and marched them in stealth north of the Chickahominy. Jackson, however, was late. His tardiness was uncharacteristic and is sometimes blamed on exhaustion owing to his fevered Valley Campaign, but Longstreet and Hill went into battle without him on June 26. This became known as the Battle of Mechanicsville, the first of the so-called Seven Days Battles, a week of fighting that wrecked McClellan's hopes for capturing Richmond.

On this and the next day, McClellan might easily have battled his way into Richmond south of the Chickahominy River, but he severely overestimated the number of Confederates he faced. Instead, he pulled his right wing down toward the remainder of his army. The next day, Jackson still wasn't in position, but Lee kept pounding, a battle that became known as Gaines' Mill. The following day, McClellan continued his retreat south toward Harrison's Landing on the James River, where Union gunboats could use their considerable artillery if need be to fire over the Union army in its defense.

QUESTION?

When Robert E. Lee took over the Confederate army protecting Richmond, why did he name it the Army of Northern Virginia?
Lee understood that most of the troops had come down from northern Virginia and felt he should lead the army back there to fight the Federals further north and away from Richmond, which was in southern Virginia.

Lee continued the offensive on June 29 in a battle called Savage Station and again on June 30, a battle called Fraser's Farm. Throughout the Seven Days, Confederate forces were smaller than Union ones, but McClellan always thought the opposite. He retreated to a prominence called Malvern Hill near Harrison's Landing. On July 1, Lee, believing one last blow would crush the Union host, sent his soldiers up Malvern Hill. But here Union artillery cut them down in large numbers. Lee had to stop, and the Federals were safe alongside their powerful gunboats.

Richmond was liberated and McClellan's army was clearly beaten and demoralized. The Southerners had taken a terrible risk, but they had won and gained what turned out to be almost three more years of life for the Confederacy.

CHAPTER 7

The Course of the War: 1862 Part II

Lee's repulse of McClellan at Richmond gave the Southern armies new opportunities. Lee moved north, crushed a Federal army at Manassas again, and crossed north of the Potomac River. Southern armies also broke out of Tennessee to invade Kentucky. Now it was the South that looked to have victory within its grasp, but it was not to be. McClellan turned back Lee at Antietam, and Buell stopped the main Confederate army in Kentucky at Perryville in October. A wearisome stalemate prevailed.

Jackson Versus Pope in Virginia

Lee's repulse of McClellan's army in late June and early July considerably changed the tenor of the war in the east. Through the spring McClellan had rolled his mighty army irrepressibly toward Richmond. This, combined with the defeat of Johnston's army at Shiloh in April, made the outlook for an overall Union victory look good, even imminent. But by early July, it was clear that McClellan's army was not much of a threat to Richmond. Indeed, it was unfit for offensive action any time soon.

Lee felt so anyway, and he began to look north, where a new threat was forming. This was an army under the command of John Pope, growing stronger in the vicinity of Fredericksburg. Pope's army was made up of parts of McDowell's army and elements of the Federal armies that had been fighting against Stonewall Jackson in the Shenandoah Valley. Pope called his force the Army of Virginia. The idea was that he would move south to press the Confederate Army of Northern Virginia between it and McClellan's Army of the Potomac. Meanwhile, Lincoln had placed General Halleck in charge of all Union armies and brought him to Washington from his pervious command in the west. It was hoped this new arrangement would help coordinate moves between the various Union forces, especially between Pope's army and McClellan's.

"Always mystify, mislead, and surprise the enemy, if possible; and when you strike and overcome him, never let up in the pursuit so long as your men have strength to follow; for an army routed, if hotly pursued, becomes panic-stricken, and can then be destroyed by half their number."—Stonewall Jackson

However, in 1862, the Union was not quite up to the task. Halleck visited McClellan on the James River but could not get him moving to again threaten Lee. Lee sensed this and knew it gave him an opportunity. He must deal with Pope before McClellan stirred again. With this in mind, Lee sent Stonewall Jackson and 25,000 men north toward Pope's army. In short order, Halleck, seeing that McClellan would not move against Richmond, ordered

McClellan to return the Army of the Potomac to northern Virginia in order to reinforce Pope. This, of course, would take some time.

Lee again took a large gamble, dividing his army a second time and sending Jackson west toward the Shenandoah Valley. Jackson disappeared behind the Bull Run Mountains just shy of the valley, then swung north and east again, marching to the rear of Pope's army. Jackson seized the huge concentration of Union army supplies at Manassas Junction, burning what his men could not eat or carry. Pope set off in pursuit, but Jackson was nowhere in sight, having hidden along a wooded ridge near the battlefield where First Manassas had been fought the previous July. As Pope attempted to find Jackson's force, Jackson pounced on one of Pope's divisions, setting up the battle of Second Manassas.

Second Manassas

Pope had located Jackson at last. He understood that Jackson's force was considerably smaller than his own and he was determined to smash it. He marched his men toward Jackson's position as fast as he could. But in this haste and desire to crush Jackson's men, Pope neglected to consider the rest of Lee's army, the segment under Lee and his chief subordinate James Longstreet that had also moved north from Richmond. Lee and Longstreet were following Jackson's route behind the Bull Run Mountains and out of sight of Pope's main force.

Pope hurled his men at Jackson's position, but the Southerners were lodged on good ground. Through the day of August 29 they held off the Union charges. Near the end of the day, Jackson pulled back some of his exhausted men. Pope took this to be the beginning of a retreat and determined he would smash the retiring Rebels in the morning. On August 30, Pope attacked again, but by this time Lee and Longstreet emerged from behind the mountains and marched on the field with 30,000 fresh Confederates.

Turning the Tables on Pope

As Pope tried to overrun the Confederate "retreat," he was met with a tremendous assault from Longstreet on his left flank. This virtually rolled up that half of Pope's army, and the Northern general had to beat a hasty retreat toward Washington. Important reinforcements from McClellan's Army of the Potomac were arriving just then, but they could do little to reverse Pope's fortunes.

"The news just reaches me from the front that the enemy is retreating toward the mountains. I go forward at once to see."—General John Pope on the morning just before being crushed by advancing Confederates at the Second Battle of Manassas

The Federals retired to the fortifications around the Union capital, giving the Confederacy a much-needed victory. This marked the latest in a string of remarkable accomplishments for Robert E. Lee since June. He had lifted the siege of Richmond and moved the Union forces all the way back to the fortifi-cations of their own capital city. He had also demoralized the Federal forces and demonstrated to the world that the Army of Northern Virginia was one of the great military forces in recent history. However, it came with a heavy price: a combined total of more than 14,500 men were killed or wounded in the fighting between August 16 and September 2.

Antietam

With the Federal forces around Washington demoralized, Lee realized he could march the Army of Northern Virginia north into Maryland and Penn-sylvania. If he could defeat a major Union army on its own territory, the North would become even further discouraged about an eventual victory, and England and France might well recognize the Confederacy as a new nation, which would be a big boost to the Confederate cause.

Lee's immediate goal was the capture of the Union railroad center in Harrisburg, Pennsylvania, also the state capital. He hoped to take the small city by dividing his army. While Lee moved into Pennsylvania, Stonewall Jackson would capture the Union garrison at Harpers Ferry, then hook up with Longstreet's three divisions and join Lee near Harrisburg.

The plan might have worked, considering the lackluster and sluggish history of the Union Army of the Potomac. Moreover, Pope had been reassigned and McClellan placed in charge of the now united Federal armies in and around Washington. McClellan was known to be a slow mover and very cautious. But, through an incredible quirk of fate, McClellan came into possession of a copy of Lee's plans, which had been found wrapped around some cigars near an abandoned Confederate camp. At first McClellan thought the orders might be a trap and failed to act on them for nearly sixteen hours. Lee, meanwhile, was told that his plans were in the hands of the enemy and worked hard to protect his three vulnerable flanks.

Antietam Bridge, Maryland *Photo courtesy of the National Archives (165-SB-19)*

Fighting broke out in a number of locations along the planned route, and the Confederates experienced heavy casualties. On September 15, Lee was planning a retreat back into Virginia when he learned that Jackson had taken Harpers Ferry and collected some much-needed supplies. Lee quickly changed his mind and ordered all of his divisions to meet in Sharpsburg, Maryland. McClellan, again overly cautious, allowed Lee's forces to converge. On September 17, he finally attacked; 75,000 Union troops faced just 40,000 Confederates.

The Bloodiest Day

Lee's left flank, led by Stonewall Jackson, was almost annihilated during the Union onslaught, led by Joseph Hooker, Joseph Mansfield, and Edwin Sumner. The Rebel soldiers took a horrible pounding until they were reinforced by two fresh Confederate divisions, who fought back with amazing vigor. Within just twenty minutes, an astounding 2,200 Union soldiers were killed or wounded in an area known as the West Woods, and Sumner was forced to retreat.

FACT

General Ambrose Burnside attempted for hours to get his men across a stone bridge over Antietam Creek. Georgians on heights beyond the bridge kept the Federals at bay until a swift rush got the first men across. The bridge is still intact and known as Burnside's Bridge.

Later in the day, the Union army focused on decimating the Confederate center, led by Major General Daniel Hill. Sumner's remaining divisions attacked Hill's line for three brutal hours, resulting in such carnage that the narrow road on which it occurred became known as Bloody Lane. The assault broke the Confederate center, and Union forces under the command of Burnside crossed Antietam Creek to attack Lee's right flank. Lee's army probably would have been destroyed during the ensuing battle if it hadn't been reinforced by a division led by A. P. Hill, which arrived after a grueling thirty-mile march from Harpers Ferry. Upon arrival, Hill's men launched a blistering counterattack that helped keep the Union forces at bay.

Had McClellan continued his assault, it's very likely he could have completely devastated Lee's army. But instead of making one final push, he let his troops rest, as did Lee. Then Lee retreated back to Virginia on the evening of September 18, having lost nearly a quarter of his army at Antietam.

The Aftermath

The Battle of Antietam was the single bloodiest day of fighting in the Civil War, with a combined total of more than 27,000 casualties. It was also a decisive victory for the Union and gave Abraham Lincoln the confidence he needed to issue his Emancipation Proclamation, which effectively changed the Union's war aims to include the abolition of slavery. The Emancipation Proclamation also paved the way for increased Union manpower by allowing African Americans to be become soldiers.

The Invasion of Kentucky

While Lee was leading the Army of Northern Virginia from Richmond up through central Virginia and toward victory at Second Manassas, Southerners were turning the tide in the west, too. And, as in the east, Union blunders helped the South's cause. After Grant's hard-fought victory against the Confederates at Shiloh in April, General Halleck—then still in the west—ordered a very slow advance toward Corinth. The advance was so slow that it allowed Southerners some time for rest and refitting.

Of 583 generals serving for the North, forty-seven were killed in battle or died of wounds; eighteen died of sickness or accident, according to *Civil War Day by Day*. Of 425 generals serving for the South, seventy-seven were killed in battle or died of wounds; fifteen died of sickness or accident.

When Halleck's army did reach the Southern stronghold at Corinth, the Confederates simply let him have it and retreated further south into Mississippi. Halleck then dispersed his troops to various strategic points. Grant believed this a large mistake, arguing that the Union armies should hotly pursue the Southerners and try for a knockout blow in an attempt to win the war in the west. Halleck held firm and then headed to Washington for his new job as commander of all Federal armies.

These developments allowed the South to take the initiative in the west. It had an army under Braxton Bragg at Chattanooga and another under Kirby Smith at Knoxville. Bragg was in overall command. He decided his army and Smith's would slice up through eastern Tennessee into Kentucky, heading for the Ohio River. With luck, they could rally Kentuckians to the Confederate colors, induce Kentucky into formally joining the Confederacy, win back all of Tennessee, and extend the border of the Southern nation to the environs of Cincinnati, Ohio, and Cairo, Illinois.

FACT

In a fight between a portion of Bragg's force and a Union stronghold at Munfordville, Kentucky, Union commander John Wilder found himself outnumbered and surrounded. A former businessman rather than a military professional, he came through the lines to respectfully ask the Confederate commander what he should do. Confederate general Simon Buckner was amazed but acted every bit the gentleman and explained to Wilder his options. Wilder surrendered.

Bragg and Smith started off in August in good fashion. They stole north of the Union forces before the Union could react. Union general Don Carlos Buell and his armies were forced to give up what they were doing and hasten north in an attempt to restrain them. Smith and Bragg marched into Lexington, Kentucky, early in September. At no other time did the Confederacy's chances of success seem brighter. Bragg and Smith were north of Buell in Kentucky; Lee was north of the Potomac. But Lee's offensive was blocked at Antietam, and the offensive near the Ohio River turned to disappointment.

Late in the month and early in October, Union armies defeated Rebels at Iuka and Corinth, Mississippi, denying any reinforcing support for Bragg and Smith by a drive north into western Tennessee.

Moreover, Bragg unaccountably seemed to have lost his nerve after a sterling campaign during which he had returned Southern control to previously surrendered territory. Buell managed to march north of Bragg and into Louisville, which was Buell's base of supplies. Buell finally forced Bragg to battle in the town of Perryville on October 8. The contest was a hard-fought draw, but it spelled the end of the invasion of Kentucky by the

Southern armies. As in the east after Antietam, the Confederates retreated back into safer territories.

Target Vicksburg

After the battle of Shiloh in early April, Union forces made relentless, if slow, progress toward the important rail junction of Corinth, Mississippi. In addition, the Southern stronghold of Island No. 10 on the Mississippi River in northwestern Tennessee fell to Northern troops. At the end of April, flag officer David Farragut captured New Orleans, the largest city in the Confederacy. In early June, the Federals won a naval battle on the Mississippi at Memphis and then occupied that city. It looked as if the Federal forces could control all of the Mississippi River, in effect cutting Texas, Arkansas, and Louisiana away from the Confederate nation.

General Ulysses S. Grant wanted to go faster during this period, but he was overruled. Once Corinth was taken, he wanted to continue with a large force to plunge further south in pursuit of the main Confederate army in the region, but he was ordered to disperse the main Union force into virtual garrison groups so the captured territory could be controlled.

When Halleck left for Washington, Grant hoped to move south but was occupied with the threats at Iuka and Corinth. Once these had been handled, he set his eyes on the stronghold that kept the last section of the Mississippi River in Confederate hands.

"We—even we here—hold the power, and bear the responsibility. In giving freedom to the slave, we assure freedom to the free—honorable alike in what we give, and what we preserve. We shall nobly save, or meanly lose, the last best hope of earth."—Abraham Lincoln, report to the Congress, December 1, 1862

In the late fall, Grant set out down the railroad in central Mississippi in an attempt to march far enough before turning west to capture Vicksburg from the land side. Generals McClernand and Sherman set out with Federal troops down the Mississippi River from Memphis to see what they could do from the river side. Grant's campaign ran into trouble when Confederate cavalry under Earl Van Dorn and Nathan Bedford Forrest wreaked havoc along Grant's line of supply in northern Mississippi and western Tennessee, with Van Dorn capturing a great deal of Grant's war materiel at Holly Springs on the railroad far in Grant's rear. Grant conceded that getting at Vicksburg from the eastern or land side was going to be too impractical, and he gave it up.

Meanwhile, Sherman and McClernand were no more successful. An attack by Sherman up the bluffs north of the city was bloodily repulsed. Vicksburg was going to be a very difficult Confederate city to capture.

Fredericksburg

Things were not going much better for the Federals in the east. There were high hopes after Lee's Army of Northern Virginia had been turned back at Antietam. Some speculated that another battle might crush him. But as usual, McClellan was reluctant to be aggressive; he kept his army north of the Potomac for weeks while Lee rested and refitted his army back in Virginia. President Lincoln finally grew impatient and replaced McClellan with Burnside.

According to E. B. Long's *Civil War Day by Day*, at the end of 1862, the Union armies had 699,000 men present for duty. The Confederate armies had 304,000 men present for duty. One year earlier, the figures were 527,000 and 258,000 respectively.

Burnside wanted to take the Army of the Potomac directly south the 100 miles between Washington, D.C., and Richmond, Virginia. Directly on that line was the town of Fredericksburg on the southern side of the Rappahannock River, and Burnside marched the army to the north side in good order. If he had been able to cross the river then, he could have taken the town and moved on, but the pontoon bridges he needed were misplaced. While

Burnside waited, Lee moved his Army of Northern Virginia to the heights behind the town.

Burnside finally got his bridges and crossed the river in mid-December. He set out his army in full panoply and advanced on December 13, but the Confederates had built their defenses well. Although Burnside launched charge after charge and the Union men showed themselves to be as brave as any soldiers could be, they had no chance of success against the well-placed Confederate defenders. The slaughter was especially astonishing on a sloping field in front of a stone wall behind the city in an area called Marye's Heights. Burnside had to admit defeat and withdrew to the north side of the river again. Union killed, wounded, and missing totaled 12,653, while the Confederate total amounted to less than half as many—5,309. The battle ruined Burnside's effort at overall command and showed the folly of attacking uphill at well-established Confederate entrenchments.

CHAPTER 8

The Course of the War: 1863 Part I

After a year and a half of warfare, both sides were showing strain. In the North, Lincoln added the abolition of slavery to the war's objectives, hoping to rally enthusiasm. In the South, increasing hardships were being asked of the people. The South was in danger of losing control of the Mississippi River. In the east, its armies continued to hold ground, but it was not likely the Confederacy could win the war that way. Invading the North and winning a victory there or capturing a major Northern city began to look like a chance worth taking.

Murfreesboro

After Bragg and Smith retreated out of Kentucky in the late fall of 1862, they did not quite march as far south as their starting point in southeastern Tennessee. Bragg, in fact, settled a large force in Murfreesboro, not too far south of the state capital of Nashville, and there awaited developments. Union general Halleck in Washington was upset with General Buell's lackluster pursuit of the retreating Southerners and replaced him with William Rosecrans, who had showed some offensive spirit and good sense in northern Mississippi. Washington urged Rosecrans to advance against Bragg and force him out of Tennessee. Rosecrans was reluctant—it was wintertime and he felt he needed more preparation—but he moved at last in the waning days of 1862.

E. B. Long's *Civil War Day by Day Almanac* states that there were more than 10,000 military actions during the Civil War. Virginia had the most engagements at 2,154, followed by Tennessee with 1,462. Missouri had 1,162 and the New Mexico Territory seventy-five.

Rosecrans's Federals came up against Bragg's Confederates just north of Murfreesboro and spread out in order of battle. Bragg's men were similarly arrayed, the battle lines stretching across the road running to the town from Nashville, the railroad line, and Stones River, which ran generally north-south in this area. Oddly, both Rosecrans and Bragg developed the same battle plan: hold firm with the right and put as much power as possible on the left in order to crush the opponent's right. Carried out with syncopated timing, the armies would merely have looked like a dog chasing its tail. Both planned to attack on the same morning, December 31, but Bragg made the first move. Rosecrans had to abandon his own plan and wage a defensive battle instead.

Bragg's Rebels were indeed strong on Rosecrans's right and soon bent the straight Union line until it resembled a perpendicular angle. The Federals had taken a terrible beating, losing about a fourth of their army and dozens of cannon. But Rosecrans had the good fortune of having General

George Thomas just at the apex of this angle, and Thomas was a stalwart fighter. He got his soldiers to hold firm and Bragg's men ground to a halt. Nevertheless, at day's end Bragg felt he had a victory and expected Rosecrans to hasten back up the Nashville road. Instead, Rosecrans and his exhausted army stayed put.

FACT

A principal Union army in the west in 1863 was the Army of the Tennessee, named for the Tennessee River. A principal Confederate army in the same region was the Army of Tennessee, named for the state.

Bragg was astonished and dismayed but remained silent the next day. On January 2, 1863, he launched an attack against Rosecrans's left wing, but the Federal artillery broke it up. Bragg realized he could do nothing more to dislodge Rosecrans's army and called for a retreat. Rosecrans's men marched into Murfreesboro, where they were to refit for six months.

The Battle of Murfreesboro, or Stones River as it is sometimes called, could have been a Union defeat. At the end of the fighting it was a draw, but within a bit of time it looked more like a Union victory. Because Bragg could not destroy or drive away Rosecrans, the Confederacy could not count on relief from Tennessee going to Vicksburg in its struggle to defeat Grant.

Grant Maneuvers Against Vicksburg

Grant, having been thwarted in his effort to capture Vicksburg from the eastern or land side, would try to capture it by moving down the Mississippi River instead. He had to go down the Arkansas and Louisiana, or western, sides. Vicksburg was on the eastern or Mississippi side of the river, and to its north was the complex and swampy Yazoo River, which would have been a nightmare to march an army through. Grant's original hope—to follow the railroad down through central Mississippi to the state's capital at Jackson, then turn west—was the natural route, though it was now useless to him on account of the 1862 troubles.

Vicksburg was a great prize because with it came the last 150 miles of Mississippi River. The Southerners could stop any attack north from New Orleans at Port Hudson just north of Baton Rouge, but if Vicksburg fell, no one seriously believed Port Hudson could hold out. Nor would it make much difference in helping to connect the three western states of the Confederacy to the eastern ones.

Grant Faces Adversity

Vicksburg proved to be a very tough nut to crack. Owing to the Yazoo River system, Vicksburg was unlikely to be taken from the north on the Mississippi side. Nor could it successfully be assaulted in direct attack across the river from the Louisiana shore because of its high ground and strong defenses. Grant and his army could sit opposite the city on the Louisiana side and face it in frustration until and unless they could find a way to get at it.

Grant tried moving into the Yazoo River region and going south with gunboats, but this effort failed so he began to think about moving the army south, crossing the Mississippi River south of the Vicksburg onto relatively good ground and then attacking the city from the south and east. But he could not cross the wide river without transports protected by gunboats. And he could not get such boats south of the city because of the mortars and cannon aimed at the river from the city itself.

Through the early months of 1863, Grant tried various schemes of getting gunboats and transports below the city without trying to run them past the powerful city batteries. These involved digging canals or opening new channels in the swampy region on the Louisiana side of the river. If his men could make new channels wide enough, or if he could get the mighty Mississippi to carve a new course west of its main stream, the boats could be moved below the city out of range of the city's guns. But despite the efforts of masses of men digging and hauling, nothing quite worked. Grant was no closer to capturing Vicksburg in April than he had been on New Year's Day.

The Battle of Chancellorsville

Union luck was not any better in the east. Burnside had the notion in late January to dislodge the Army of Northern Virginia from Fredericksburg by marching his army up the Rappahannock to where it could ford the stream, then descend on Lee's rear. He put such a movement in motion, but then faced three days of cold rain that turned dirt roads to mud pits along which cannon could scarcely move. Burnside canceled the expedition, and the Army of the Potomac returned to its camp across the river from Fredericksburg even more discouraged than before. Because he was both uninspired and unlucky, most people agreed that Burnside had to be replaced. One of his subordinates, General Joseph Hooker, was selected to take over Burnside's command. The new Army of the Potomac commander was arrogant and vain, but he was well liked by his men, had fought well in the Peninsula Campaign and at the Battle of Antietam, and showed tremendous promise.

Hooker decided that Burnside's plan, which had the misfortune of ending in the "Mud March," had merit. He decided to attack Lee on two fronts. He left a third of his 115,000 troops near Fredericksburg to keep Lee's army busy there and took the remainder of his men up and across the Rappahannock to engage Lee's relatively unprotected left flank and rear.

Hooker Versus Lee

The first part of the plan went well. Late in April, Hooker got the Army of the Potomac up the Rappahannock and across the river without much fuss, then occupied the crossroads of Chancellorsville about eight miles from Lee's rear. He was confident that he could destroy Lee's army by pressing him from two sides with overwhelming numbers. But Hooker failed to take into consideration Lee's considerable military skills. With just 60,000 troops, Lee used the same tactic that had brought him victory at the Second Battle of Manassas: he divided his troops, leaving 10,000 men at Fredericksburg and taking the rest to meet Hooker's force behind him.

The Stealth Attack

On May 1, Stonewall Jackson surprised Hooker's men as they moved toward the Confederate line. Hooker lost his nerve and ordered a withdrawal. Major General Jeb Stuart notified Lee that Hooker's right flank was vulnerable, so Lee divided his forces a second time. Jackson and 26,000 men marched in stealth to the end of Hooker's right flank and attacked, forcing the Union soldiers into a two-mile withdrawal.

But Lee's grand victory was tempered by bad news: Jackson had been severely injured when Confederate troops mistook him and his mounted staff for Union cavalry and opened fire. He died a week later. Stuart assumed command of Jackson's infantry and launched another attack against Hooker's army on the morning of May 3.

Meanwhile, a portion of Lee's army helped defend his men at Fredericksburg, where they were being threatened by Union troops under General John Sedgwick. After a day-long battle, Sedgwick retreated, joined by Hooker the following day. The Union army suffered more than 17,000 casualties in the battle; the Confederacy lost about 13,000.

"I have the finest army on the planet. I have the finest army the sun ever shone on. . . . If the enemy does not run, God help them. May God have mercy on General Lee, for I will have none."—Union general Joseph Hooker before the Battle of Chancellorsville

Many historians consider the Battle of Chancellorsville Lee's greatest victory. Greatly outnumbered, he out-thought and outmaneuvered his opponents. His victory opened up strategic options for him and put the Army of the Potomac on the defensive.

Lee Moves North

The Army of Northern Virginia's victory in early May 1863 again opened the door for Lee to move the main Confederate army north of the Potomac River to threaten Washington, D.C. Lee's decision to take the war into the North was based on a number of factors. Lee wanted to bring some relief to Virginia, which had seen more than its share of battles and was running low on supplies. He also hoped that a solid victory in Union territory would bring the Confederacy some much needed international recognition by proving it was a force to be reckoned with. Finally, a victory in the east might cause Northern strategists to take manpower away from General Grant, who was then tightening his grip on Vicksburg.

Lee's Northward Journey

Lee got things going by advancing his 70,000 troops northeastward from Fredericksburg on June 3. Four days later, Confederate and Union cavalry engaged in a heated battle at Brandy Station, near Culpepper, Virginia. The Confederates won, but they were greatly surprised by the new skill and daring of the Union horsemen, a bad omen for the Confederates.

But on the whole Lee proceeded north unmolested. Lincoln wanted the capital protected and so required assurances the Army of the Potomac would stay between the city and the Army of Northern Virginia. This it did, moving slowly north. Lee wanted to monitor his opponent's movements and, as was usual, asked his cavalry chief Jeb Stuart to be his eyes and ears, keeping Lee informed of movements and developments.

The Army of the Potomac moved more swiftly and covered more ground than Stuart had anticipated, and he became isolated on the far side of the Union army as his own force, the Union army, and the Confederate army all moved north. This meant Lee could not get significant information from Stuart. Moreover, Hooker was replaced as head of the Army of the Potomac by General George Meade.

FACT

General Hooker had irked his superiors on more than one occasion, but the final straw came as Lee was moving north. Hooker was in pursuit when he engaged in an argument with commander-in-chief Henry Halleck over the proper use of the Harpers Ferry garrison. Hooker tendered his resignation as commander of the Army of the Potomac and Halleck took it.

Through the end of June, Lee managed to move his army into Pennsylvania, enjoying the bounty and good weather there and threatening Northern cities, including the capital of Pennsylvania, Harrisburg. But Lee was blind to the movements of the Army of the Potomac because of his lack of communication from Stuart. For all Lee knew, the Union army was still south of the Potomac River. On June 28, Lee was shocked to learn that in fact the Army of the Potomac was loosely concentrated around Fredericksburg, Maryland. His own army scattered, Lee ordered the parts of his army to assemble at the crossroads town of Gettysburg, setting up the cataclysmic battle there.

Victory on the Mississippi

Grant had tried everything he could to get at Vicksburg, and nothing was working. He had to fall back on the simplest and perhaps riskiest plan of all. He would order the river fleet to steam past the cannons on the Vicksburg bluffs in hopes of getting enough of them south of the city to escort his army from the Louisiana side of the river to the Mississippi side.

William Sherman did not like Grant's risky plan for capturing Vicksburg, but when the two of them reached the outskirts of the city from the east Sherman turned to his commander and said: "Until this moment I never thought your expedition a success. I could never see the end clearly until now. But this is a campaign. This is a success if we never take the town."

If he could accomplish this, he would be largely cut off from his base of supplies. This ran counter to established military logic. He would be out of communication with his superiors in Washington, who no doubt would be severely troubled that one of their main armies had disappeared from view. Grant would have to live off the land, maneuver in hostile territory—likely against superior numbers—and hope for the best. It was a terrible risk, and his own trusted subordinate William Sherman was against the plan, but Grant felt he had no other option.

Grant Advances

In the dead of night on April 16, Admiral David Porter sent his gunboats drifting downriver past Vicksburg. The Confederates spotted them and began their bombardment. The gunboats roared their engines to gain speed. Surprisingly, their casualties were low and the first part of Grant's plan was a success. Porter ran more boats past the batteries on succeeding nights and soon he had enough south of the city to effect Grant's amphibious operation.

Grant managed to move about 30,000 Union soldiers onto the Mississippi side of the river before the Confederates could bring much defensive power to bear. Grant marched his men north and east, the main objective being the Mississippi capital and rail junction of Jackson, through which reinforcements for the Vicksburg garrison would generally need to come. Within two weeks, Grant's army was there, having won battle after battle with Southern forces hastily sent to oppose them. Grant captured Jackson on May 14. General Joe Johnston, who was commanding Confederate armies in the region, attempted to bring in a sizeable army to oppose Grant, but he needed the Vicksburg garrison to come out of its defenses and add its weight to his own numbers. He ordered General John Pemberton, who commanded in Vicksburg, to leave the city and fight in the open. Pemberton did emerge, but he couldn't combine with Johnston's force. Instead, he fought Grant's army on May 16 at the Battle of Champion's Hill. Grant bested him, and Pemberton had to retreat with his 30,000 men back into Vicksburg.

"The Father of Waters again goes unvexed to the sea."—Abraham Lincoln during the summer of Vicksburg's surrender, an event that assured Union dominance of the Mississippi River from Illinois to New Orleans

Grant followed swiftly and tried to storm the Vicksburg defenses. He failed twice and began building his own fortifications to lay siege to the city in late May. He extended his lines north of the city, thus re-establishing communication with Union forces upriver and opening up a steady stream of supplies and reinforcements. He also sent a force east to protect his rear and keep Johnston's forces at bay. Meanwhile, Johnston failed to aggregate any army large enough to have a chance of dislodging Grant from his Vicksburg earthworks. Starved, with no hope of supplies, reinforcements, or relief, Pemberton surrendered Vicksburg and his 30,000-man army on July 4.

Cavalry Raids North and South

The Confederacy was a very large area, and both the Northern and Southern armies learned within a year or so of Fort Sumter that the war was not going to be like anything they had studied in their history books. As Northern armies advanced into the South, they left behind them vast swaths of territory peopled by Confederate guerrillas and sympathizers. This was a perfect scenario for Confederate raiding parties of swift horsemen who could disrupt the important supply lines keeping the Northern armies fed, clothed, and armed. They could rip up railroad tracks, burn bridges, raid supply depots, besiege or overrun small garrisons, and cause other sorts of damage that would have dire and sometimes crippling effects on Northern offensive campaigns into the Southern heartland. The North, too, learned that cavalry had significant uses other than acting as a screen in front of an army or a means of collecting information. Its cavalry could divert attention from the major moves of infantry and cut supplies to Southern forces.

Brigadier General Jeb Stuart *Photo courtesy of the National Archives (64-M-9)*

Much of the most effective cavalry work took place in the west beginning about a year after the war began. In the east, cavalry more or less stuck to its traditional role, though Jeb Stuart learned it could win renown for its leaders, raise morale, and humiliate the enemy. The Union cavalry was slower to gain the skills needed to run off on its own in independent command.

In the west, Union cavalry detached itself earlier from the infantry armies. Famed cavalry leader Nathan Bedford Forrest had a fierce independent streak, evidenced early by his determination to break out of the Fort Donelson siege with his horsemen. This he did through a harrowing night and set up a military career elevated into legend.

Confederate general Earl Van Dorn captured the important rail and supply depot at Holly Springs in December 1862, practically wrecking Grant's first move against Vicksburg along the line of the railroad down central Mississippi. Confederate John Hunt Morgan sliced into central Tennessee the same month.

Grant made good use of his cavalry leader Benjamin Grierson during the Vicksburg campaign. He sent Grierson off through the whole length of eastern Mississippi just as he was beginning to move his army south of the city. The point was to distract Pemberton and to disrupt his supplies and communications. The raid worked just about as Grant hoped it would.

CHAPTER 9

The Course of the War: 1863 Part II

Losing Vicksburg was more than the South could afford, and Lee's gamble to win a victory in Pennsylvania risked bigger losses. As the year progressed, most of the important military action took place in the center, in southeastern Tennessee, where Braxton Bragg nearly destroyed a Union army and bottled up the remnants in Chattanooga. The North needed someone to reverse Bragg's victory, so they called in Ulysses S. Grant.

Gettysburg

When Robert E. Lee ordered a concentration of his Army of Northern Virginia at the little town of Gettysburg, Pennsylvania, in late June, he was at a disadvantage he had never encountered before: he did not fully understand the size or the position of his opponent. Lee had been out of contact with his eyes and ears, Jeb Stuart's cavalry, for more than a week. He did know one thing for sure: George Meade had taken over command of the Army of the Potomac. Lee knew Meade, and he predicted Meade would not make the same kind of crippling errors that John Pope, Ambrose Burnside, and John Hooker had made over the past year. He could also assume that the Army of the Potomac, no matter what parts of it were nearby, would have more manpower when fully concentrated than his own Army of Northern Virginia. Lee would assemble at Gettysburg and wait until Jeb Stuart joined him. Then he hoped to make the kinds of maneuvers and flank attacks that brought him and his army victory after victory.

Gettysburg was the single bloodiest battle of the war, not counting the 1864 Wilderness and Spotsylvania fights as a single battle. The number of killed, wounded, and missing in the two armies together was 51,000 men.

Meade did not give him the chance. Despite having been repeatedly bested—even humiliated—by the Army of Northern Virginia, the Army of the Potomac marched directly toward their old foe. This was, after all, not Virginia; the Northern soldiers were defending territory in one of their own states.

Day One

On July 1, the first Confederate infantry converging on Gettysburg was spotted by Union cavalry commander General John Buford, whose troops were in advance of Meade's army camped on a hill southwest of town. Buford sent his men to engage the Confederates and called for reinforcements. The

Rebel soldiers raced back to camp with news of the Union troop movements, and a Confederate attack on the Union cavalry line was ordered. So began the Battle of Gettysburg.

The first Union infantry to arrive in support of Buford were from the First Corps, led by Major General John Reynolds. The Southerners continued to advance. Reynolds was killed in the ensuing battle, which laid waste to the Iron Brigade of the West, one of Reynolds's best fighting units. The Confederates kept pressing the Federals, though more were coming in behind them and spreading out to the right. Lee came up and was not convinced that here was a place for a general battle, but far off he could see another wing of his army advancing from the north that would outflank the growing number of Federals. He ordered these men forward.

Union and Confederate dead, Gettysburg *Photo courtesy of the National Archives (165-SB-36)*

During this first day of fighting, the Confederates outnumbered the Union forces. They drove these elements of the Army of the Potomac back through the streets of Gettysburg to what was called Cemetery Hill and Cemetery Ridge south of the town. A final attack might have pushed the Federals off of this high ground, but Lee's subordinate, General Richard Ewell, did not risk it. Both armies settled down for the night. They rested or dug entrenchments while more regiments and divisions made their way toward the little town in support of their comrades.

Day Two

When morning broke, the Union army had formed its men into the shape of a fishhook. The shank was located along Cemetery Ridge, which ran due south from the town and ended in two prominences called Little Round Top and Big Round Top. The curved part of the fishhook was at the northern part of Cemetery Ridge—Cemetery Hill—bending eastward. The barb at the end of the fishhook was a prominence called Culp's Hill.

The Confederate commanders were unsure how to attack the Union position. General Longstreet wanted to maneuver the Army of Northern Virginia to a location between the Federals and Washington, D.C., drawing them into a battle against Confederate defensive works. Lee, however, still did not have Stuart and could not be sure how such a maneuver could be successfully carried out; he overruled Longstreet and ordered an offensive against the Federals south of the town. His hope was to send Longstreet secretly to the south and come upon the open flank of the Union army just as Jackson had at Chancellorsville two months before.

"In a larger sense, we cannot dedicate, we cannot consecrate, we cannot hallow this ground. The brave men, living and dead, who struggled here, have consecrated it far above our poor power to add or detract."
—Abraham Lincoln, Gettysburg Address, November 19, 1863

The main trouble was that the Union army's southern flank had changed during the night and then again during the day. Not only had more Federal troops come up as reinforcements, but Union general Daniel Sickles decided on his own to move his corps a mile forward from the Union battle line. Moreover, Union troops were beginning to fortify Little Round Top, which had been deserted. If Longstreet obeyed Lee's orders strictly, his men would be subjected to flanking fire from Little Round Top. Longstreet had to delay and reconfigure his attack and did not get it going until about 4 P.M., but it came with terrible ferocity.

Dead Confederate sharpshooter in the Devil's Den, Gettysburg, Pennsylvania
Photo courtesy of the National Archives (165-SB-41)

The Confederates nearly conquered Little Round Top. Had they done so, they may have won the battle. They smashed Union positions in places whose names have now grown into American legend: the Peach Orchard, the Wheatfield, and Devil's Den. Longstreet's men nearly caved in this sector of the Union army, but the Federals held on and Meade deftly sent reinforcements at the right times to the right places. Lee also struck at Cemetery Hill and Culp's Hill, but he could not dislodge the Union men from their strong positions.

Day Three

Lee was now in a quandary. He did not have enough supplies for days of maneuver in Pennsylvania. He had to soundly defeat the Federal army or retreat. He chose to attack in a high-stakes gamble of smashing the Union center and sending the Federals reeling. In this endeavor he sent Jeb Stuart, who arrived at last the night before, around the rear of the Union army to descend on the back of Cemetery Ridge. At the front he would send forth 15,000 men in what has become known as Pickett's Charge.

It almost worked, but Stuart was stopped by Federal cavalry in a desperate clash, and the 15,000 who advanced a mile over farmers' fields faced such withering fire that they could not break the Union line for more than a few minutes. Thousands were captured, and only about half the men who began the charge ever got back.

Lee Versus Meade after Gettysburg

Lee's Army of Northern Virginia suffered terrible losses at Gettysburg, and its supplies were low. Retreat was its only course, but when it reached the Potomac it found the river so high it had to wait for lower water. Lincoln urged Meade to take this opportunity to crush Lee's wounded army, but Meade's Army of the Potomac was hardly in better shape than Lee's Army of Northern Virginia. Its losses had been severe as well. Meade made a slow advance against Lee's fortified position alongside the Potomac. When Meade finally did get in position and prepared for an attack, Lee managed to move his army across the river at last and into Virginia. Lincoln never quite forgave Meade for what Lincoln thought an important missed opportunity.

"No one is more aware than myself of my inability for the duties of my position. I cannot even accomplish what I myself desire. How can I fulfill the expectations of others?"—Robert E. Lee, offering his resignation to President Jefferson Davis a month after Gettysburg; Davis refused to accept it

Meade followed Lee into Virginia, but he wasn't eager to bring the Rebels to battle. Battered as it was, the Army of Northern Virginia was a very dangerous enemy; Meade wanted to avoid any repeat of the debacles that had sent the Army of the Potomac reeling back into Washington as it had on two previous occasions. Meade tried attacking a portion of Lee's army as it moved along the Blue Ridge in Virginia, but Lee quickly brought in reinforcements, making success unlikely.

Lee and President Davis sensed that Meade would not be able to make a successful assault on Lee's army for a while and so detached 12,000 men under General Longstreet, sending them to Bragg's army in Tennessee. Indeed, Meade and Lee never did come to grips during the late summer and fall of 1863. Meade tried to get an advantage over Lee that he thought would help him win a battle, but he never saw one he liked enough. Lee at one point set his smaller army north in hopes of catching Meade scattered or in an awkward position, but these maneuvers never led to a situation Lee liked enough to risk battle. At one point he considered invading the North again when he was close to the Potomac and Meade near the Washington defenses, but he concluded that his men—many of whom were shoeless—were not well enough supplied and his army too weak; he retired to a defensive line near the Rapidan River. Meade, like Lee, ultimately sent a good portion of his army to Tennessee to help Federals there after the Battle of Chickamauga.

The Battle of Chickamauga

President Lincoln had long favored eastern Tennessee as a region to be controlled by Union forces. There was a great deal of Union sympathy in the mountainous and hilly area where large slave-holding plantations did not take hold. After long months of recuperating from the Murfreesboro battle in January, General Rosecrans started a drive in August to gain control of southeastern Tennessee.

"Some of Bragg's people set up the 'rebel yell.' It was taken up successively and passed round to our front, along our right and in behind us again until it seemed almost to have got to the point whence it started. It was the ugliest sound that any mortal ever heard."—Ambrose Bierce, on Rosecrans's staff at the Battle of Chickamauga

Rosecrans did well. He maneuvered his army in swift marches that forced Bragg's Army of the Tennessee out of one position after another until Bragg had to give up the key city of Chattanooga. At the same time, Burnside moved against Knoxville and occupied that small city in early September.

FACT

Among those killed during the Battle of Chickamauga was a teenaged girl who had disguised herself as a soldier so that she could fight with the Union forces. Also killed was Confederate brigadier general Ben Hardin Helm, Mary Lincoln's brother-in-law and a good friend of President Lincoln.

Rosecrans was not content to remain the occupier of Chattanooga. He kept pressing Bragg southeast until Bragg was south of the Georgia state line. Confident of keeping Bragg on the run, Rosecrans split his army into segments and pressed down the hilly Georgia roads, but Bragg was being reinforced by Longstreet's 12,000 men from the Army of Northern Virginia. When Bragg had these men—he now outnumbered the Federals by 10,000 soldiers—he made a quick reversal and staged an attack on Rosecrans.

The three columns of Rosecrans's army would have made easy pickings for Bragg's army, but delays and poor planning kept Bragg's subordinates from launching an effective attack, and several small skirmishes alerted Rosecrans to Bragg's trap.

On September 13, Rosecrans began regrouping his troops on the west bank of Chickamauga Creek, south of the Tennessee-Georgia border. Patrols from both sides engaged in a number of small skirmishes near the creek on September 18, and the Battle of Chickamauga began with a vengeance the next day.

The Battle Begins

Bragg's strategy was to attack Rosecrans's left flank and smash the Union army by forcing it into a valley from which it could not retreat back to Chattanooga. However, assaults by Confederate troops were met with a withering response from soldiers commanded by George Henry Thomas.

The day's fighting in the area's thick woods degenerated into vicious hand-to-hand combat that brought the Confederates only very small gains and heavy casualties on both sides.

Confederate general Leonidas Polk was instructed to perform a sideways attack against Thomas early on September 20, but Polk delayed the assault. Bragg then ordered Longstreet to conduct an all-out frontal attack, which proved successful. Rosecrans, unable to see a large section of his troops, erroneously believed there was a break in his lines and sent an entire division to fill it, leaving a gap on the Union right. Longstreet's forces barreled through this gap, overrunning Rosecrans's headquarters and forcing more than half of his army into a retreat back to Chattanooga.

"The Rock of Chickamauga"

Rosecrans himself was swept up in the retreat, leaving Thomas to command what was left of the Union force. Thomas bravely refused to retreat and rallied his troops to form a defensible line on the ridge of Snodgrass Hill. For the remainder of the day, Longstreet and Polk sent wave after wave against the Union forces, but they were unable to dislodge them. As a result of his stalwart defense, Thomas received the nickname "the Rock of Chickamauga."

The casualty list for both the Union and Confederate armies in the Battle of Chickamauga was an astounding 28 percent, reports *Civil War Day by Day*. The Federals suffered a total of 16,170 dead, wounded, or missing; Confederate losses for the two-day battle totaled 18,545 men.

Thomas finally realized the futility of his position and ordered his men to withdraw to Chattanooga as night fell. The Confederates won a victory, but Thomas's bravery in the face of terrible odds helped keep the Union army from being completely destroyed as it retreated. The Confederate casualties included ten of Bragg's generals, a situation that so depressed him he failed to attack the Union forces in retreat toward Chattanooga. Bragg's inaction, which allowed the Union forces to regroup and fortify in Chattanooga, greatly angered his subordinates. Longstreet and Polk demanded that he be dismissed, and Nathan Bedford Forrest refused to serve under him any longer.

But despite Bragg's failure to strike a decisive blow against the Union army, the Confederate victory at Chickamauga did wonders to revive the flagging spirits of the South, which had suffered the twin defeats of Gettysburg and Vicksburg.

Chattanooga Besieged

The Union forces were able to hold off Confederate assaults on their fortifications in Chattanooga, which lay on the southern side of the Tennessee River, so Bragg ordered a siege. While Rosecrans's men hunkered down in the city, Bragg's men took up positions in the hills outside, notably on Missionary Ridge and Lookout Mountain, their lines of trenches and fortifications touching the river both upstream and downstream of the town. By early October Confederate artillery commanded the routes by which supplies could be brought into Chattanooga. Within weeks, the entrenched Union soldiers found themselves perilously low on food and other supplies.

FACT

While preparing his battle plans, Grant reconnoitered some of the front lines. Rebel soldiers recognized him, marched out, and gave him a formal salute. Grant also had a brief talk with a Confederate private who had come to a stream to fetch water.

The North responded by placing Grant in command of the military district of the west, and thus in command of the army in Chattanooga. Grant headed for the city to help relieve it and defeat the besieging Rebels. One of his first acts was to replace Rosecrans with Thomas. Then, with his chief engineer, William F. Smith, he developed a daring plan to break the Confederate siege. The first part of his strategy was to open a supply line across a long loop in the Tennessee River by driving away Confederate forces there. Once done, supplies could be brought in by boat, wagon, and bridge.

Grant was able to do this and put his so-called "cracker line operation" into effect on October 26. The first supply ship arrived safely on November 1. As he waited for reinforcements to arrive from Memphis and Vicksburg, Grant planned the next step of his offensive: forcing the Confederates off their dangerous position on Missionary Ridge and from Lookout Mountain.

At the same time that Grant was forming his strategy, the Confederate army underwent some dramatic changes. Generals Leonidas Polk, Daniel H. Hill, and Thomas C. Hindman, disgusted with Bragg's slowness at Chattanooga, complained to the War Department and were granted transfers. Bragg also picked this time to send several divisions and thirty-five cannon under the command of Longstreet eastward against Burnside in Knoxville. This move severely weakened Bragg's lines on Missionary Ridge just as the Union army was getting ready for a major assault.

The Battle of Chattanooga

Grant put his battle plan into action on November 23 with the arrival of fresh troops under the command of Sherman. Grant's first goal was Orchard Knob, which was the forward position in the center of the Confederate line on Missionary Ridge. The battle began with an ingenious ruse on Grant's part: he dressed his divisions as if for a military parade and had them march below the hill. When curious Confederate soldiers on the knob moved down for a closer look, the Union soldiers attacked and, following a heated battle, took control of the hill.

QUESTION?

Was Pickett's Charge the largest charge of the war?
No, the famous Confederate charge at Gettysburg was not the largest of the Civil War. The charges at Missionary Ridge during the Battle of Chattanooga, Cold Harbor, and Franklin are among the larger charges. Of these, only the charge at Missionary Ridge was successful.

Grant made Orchard Hill his headquarters for the coming fight and ordered Sherman's divisions to attack the Confederate right on the north end of Missionary Ridge. He also ordered Hooker—who arrived with his men from the Army of the Potomac—to take Lookout Mountain on the Confederate left. Early on the morning of November 24, Hooker engaged the enemy in a battle made difficult by rain and fog; hours later, he emerged the victor. Sherman, delayed by the rain, made slower progress and didn't arrive on Bragg's right until that afternoon.

The Battle of Missionary Ridge began on the morning of November 25. Sherman's forces and artillery struck repeatedly at the Confederate line along the north end, but they were repelled. To draw the Confederates away from Sherman's front, Grant ordered Thomas in the center to attack the Confederate forces at the base of Missionary Ridge. The wiser Confederate soldiers realized what was happening and withdrew immediately, but many stayed and fought, only to be overrun by Union troops. Having taken the Confederate line, the Union soldiers, acting without orders, raced up the slope in an unexpected attack that successfully drove the Rebels into a full retreat. Chattanooga was saved.

FACT

General Thomas's men ran up Missionary Ridge without orders. Many of them shouted "Chickamauga! Chickamauga!" as they charged, furious at the Rebels for having beaten them there. Many also wanted to impress Hooker's men from the Army of the Potomac and Sherman's men from Vicksburg to show that they were indeed good fighters.

The defeat at Chattanooga was an important nail in the coffin of the Confederate cause. It cost the South important communication and supply lines and opened the door for Sherman's Atlanta campaign.

Knoxville Relieved

Part of the Confederate disaster at Chattanooga owed to shifting Longstreet's men from the ring around Chattanooga to the lines around Knoxville, almost 100 miles away. Longstreet believed he should not be sent to Knoxville, but orders were orders.

When Longstreet arrived, Burnside was well entrenched in defenses around the city, especially in forts originally constructed by Confederate defenders earlier in the war. Longstreet heard a rumor that Bragg had been beaten at Chattanooga and was in retreat. Longstreet thought retreat might be the best course for him as well, preparatory to a return to Virginia, but he was also honor-bound to try to dislodge Burnside's men from the city. He called for a dawn rush against one of the forts protecting the city. His men, however, were literally tripped up. The Federals had strung telegraph wire from stake to stake and stump to stump knee-high. When they managed to fight through that they ran into a ditch protecting the fort. They had been told the ditch was five feet deep, but in fact it was nine feet deep. For a time, they tried to hoist men up on others' shoulders but the effort soon proved hopeless. The Southerners retreated.

Longstreet then heard that not only was Bragg in retreat, but also that Sherman was en route to Knoxville with six divisions. That would give Burnside far more men than the Southerners had outside. Longstreet quit the environs of Knoxville and eventually found his way back to Lee's Army of Northern Virginia.

CHAPTER 10

The Course of the War: 1864 Part I

After the Battle of Chattanooga, Grant was clearly the most victorious general in the Northern ranks. Many wanted him to have overall command of all Union armies and military affairs. Congress wanted it, and Lincoln was willing enough to remove himself from the military tinkering he had indulged in during past years. Over the winter, Grant was made general-in-chief, and Henry Halleck became his chief of staff. Grant's plan for 1864 was to press the Confederacy on as many points as he could, principally with drives on Richmond and Atlanta.

That Devil Forrest

One of the most celebrated figures of the American Civil War is Nathan Bedford Forrest, a cavalry and guerilla leader who had no military training but nevertheless demonstrated extraordinary military skill and wreaked havoc among Federal forces from the Appalachian Mountains to the Mississippi River. He led Confederate troops from 1861 to the end of the war and was never captured.

Unquestionably physically brave, he was under fire more than 150 times, wounded several times, and had twenty-nine horses shot from under him. He killed thirty men. He enlisted as a private in 1861 and left the war a lieutenant general. He fought both behind enemy lines with guerilla forces of several thousand and as the cavalry arm of the South's conventional armies in open battle with Northern ones.

"The Wizard of the Saddle"

America does not know quite what to make of Forrest, nicknamed "the Wizard of the Saddle." Born poor in 1821 in the Tennessee frontier, he was in a couple of shoot-outs while still in his twenties. He made a fortune in the 1850s as a planter, speculator, and slave trader. When the war began he was one of the richest men in the South. He was a passionate Confederate, but in the spring of 1865 he counseled his men to accept the verdict of the battlefield, return home, forget their grudges, and be good citizens of their nation. Unquestionably, Forrest was a racist; both he and his men hated the thought of African Americans taking up arms against them. He and his men had a similar hatred of Tennessee men who fought for the North. These feelings led to the controversy about the battle at Fort Pillow in April 1864 when Forrest's men killed African American and Tennessee Federals trying to surrender. Forrest could not have been said to have given orders to this effect, but nevertheless he was in command and he was present at the battle. His association with the Ku Klux Klan after the war also stained his reputation. He later denounced the organization and wanted it disbanded, though he deplored much of the federal military rule of the former Confederate states.

Sullied as Forrest is, he was unquestionably a ferocious and talented warrior. William Sherman called him "that Devil, Forrest" and "the most remarkable man our Civil War produced on either side." Celebrated Civil War historian Bruce Catton called him "one of the authentic military geniuses of the whole war." It was said that when Confederates were stirring up trouble along his lines of supply, Grant was not particularly concerned unless he learned that the leader of the raiding forces was Forrest—and then Grant was noticeably anxious.

A Force on the Battlefield

Two of Forrest's celebrated battles are Parker's Crossroads, Tennessee, in December 1862, and Brice's Crossroads, Mississippi, in June 1864. In the first, Forrest was attacked from behind when his rear guard missed an assignment, and he ordered charges in both directions to extricate his force. In the second, with little more than 3,000 men, he outfought more than 8,000 Federals led by a West Pointer.

"For the particular kind of warfare which Forrest had carried on neither army could present a more effective officer than he."—Ulysses S. Grant, in his memoirs, written after the Civil War

Forrest presaged the mobile warfare of the middle twentieth century. He moved his cavalry with energy and insight, then had them dismount to fight effectively as infantry on foot. Legend mistakenly has him spelling out his tactical genius, "Git thar fustest with the mustest." He undoubtedly agreed with the notion but more likely put it as "Git thar furst with the most men."

Up the Red River

Ever since the Union had occupied New Orleans in the spring of 1862 there had been talk of mounting an expedition up the Red River, which flowed into the Mississippi just upriver from Baton Rouge and stretched toward northern Texas. Compromising the Confederate army at Shreveport would allow the North to shield its gains on the lower Mississippi, keep Louisiana and Arkansas out of the war, and make Texas vulnerable. In addition,

France had become a power in Mexico, and a Union presence closer to the Rio Grande would discourage France from helping the Confederacy via Mexico.

General Nathaniel Banks in New Orleans started the Red River expedition in mid-March, and Northern troops occupied Alexandria, Louisiana, later in the month. However, Confederate general Sterling Price prevented Union general Frederick Steele and his 15,000 men from assisting Banks. The Federals faced stiff fighting from the Confederates at Sabine Crossroads on April 8 and at Pleasant Hill the following day. Banks turned around. The Federals dammed the abnormally low river enough to raise the water level, then broke the dam and used the descending wave to move their gunboats forward. The expedition did not accomplish anything for the Northerners.

Battles of the Wilderness and Spotsylvania

Grant felt so strongly about his drive south against the Army of Northern Virginia that he decided to position himself with the force that would do the attacking, the Army of the Potomac. He had decided earlier to allow Meade to remain the commander of this venerable army, so Grant and Meade would travel together. Grant would communicate with Sherman and his other subordinates by telegraph as Grant's headquarters moved south.

Grant pushed off on May 4, part of his grand plan to move all major Union armies against the Confederacy at once. Grant had considered trying to maneuver the Army of the Potomac around Lee's left flank, proceeding south toward Charlottesville before turning southeast toward Richmond, but he decided to move by Lee's right flank instead. Doing so would allow the Army of the Potomac to better defend Washington, D.C. Grant expected that if the Army of the Potomac set out for Richmond, Lee's army would try to defend Richmond rather than making a quick dash to Washington. To proceed past Lee's right flank, Grant would have to march through territory called the Wilderness, which was exactly what its name implied. Grant hoped he could march through this tangle with his 120,000 soldiers and battle Lee on the far side in open farm country.

The Battle of the Wilderness

But Robert E. Lee was never one to do what his opponents wanted him to do or thought he would do. Lee only had about 65,000 men in the Army of Northern Virginia. He felt that if he could attack in the Wilderness, the Federals would have a much harder time making their men and artillery work effectively than they would in open country. As soon as Lee detected that Grant had moved into the Wilderness, he set his own army in motion. The Army of Northern Virginia smashed into the Army of the Potomac broadside and launched the Battle of the Wilderness. It also launched a new kind of war—ceaseless war. For the next eleven months, the two armies were engaged almost continuously, and there were casualties practically every day.

Burying the dead at Fredericksburg, Virginia, after the Wilderness Campaign, May 1864 *Photo courtesy of the National Archives (111-B-4817)*

The Battle of the Wilderness lasted through May 5 and 6. It was a confused and bewildering fight in a dark, dry forest. Units became separated. Whole divisions became lost for hours. Units fired on other units of their own army. At the end of the first day's fighting, generally a draw, portions of the woods caught fire and burned wounded men to death. On the second day, Lee's hopes were almost realized; his smaller army took advantage of the confused terrain and began to outflank both the north and south ends of Grant's vast host. But Confederate general James Longstreet was wounded by his own men, and nightfall dampened the Confederate advantage.

The Battle of Spotsylvania Court House

By this time, Grant had had enough of the Wilderness. He wanted to get out, and he thought he saw an advantage. If he could march overnight out of the Wilderness and reach the crossroads of Spotsylvania Court House, he would be closer to Richmond than Lee's army. He then could capture Richmond or force Lee to attack the Army of the Potomac on ground of Grant's own choosing. Grant set the army in motion on May 7 but discovered on May 8 that Lee had anticipated the move and barely won the race for the crossroads. Grant attacked, but Lee's men held on. Over the course of the next couple of days the Rebels built miles of formidable log-and-earth breastworks.

Grant threw division after division against the Confederates over the next two weeks. He broke the Confederate line twice, but the Southerners managed to patch it enough to keep their army together.

"I . . . propose to fight it out on this line if it takes all summer."—General Ulysses S. Grant to his staff in Washington, D.C., from the battlefield at Spotsylvania Court House, May 11, 1864

The casualties were terrific—29,000 for the two armies together in the Wilderness, 30,000 for the two armies together at Spotsylvania. In total, almost 60,000 men were lost—a third of the 175,000 men who began the campaign. Lee could make up some of his losses by calling on troops in Richmond, but Grant had far more resources and manpower to draw on. Bloodied but not defeated, the Army of the Potomac shifted out of its battle lines again and raced toward Richmond around Lee's right flank.

The Drive on Atlanta

As winter turned to spring in 1864, William T. Sherman was in Chattanooga with 100,000 troops, mainly western veterans of the Vicksburg and Chattanooga campaigns. Grant's plan to end the war was to press the Confederate armies along all fronts at once, the main two thrusts being south toward Richmond, Virginia, and southeast from Chattanooga toward Atlanta, Georgia, along the Western & Atlantic Railroad. If Sherman could take Atlanta, an important rail and industrial hub of the Deep South, the North would deprive the Confederacy of an important transportation and industrial resource and demonstrate to its people and the world that it could not defend its principal cities.

"The W&A RR of Georgia should be the pride of every true American because by reason of its existence the Union was saved. Every foot of it should be sacred ground, because it was once moistened with patriotic blood. Over a hundred miles of it was fought in a continuous battle of 120 days, during which, night and day, were heard the continuous boom of cannon and the sharp crack of the rifle."—General William T. Sherman on the Atlanta campaign

Grant had exceptional confidence in Sherman; he had worked with the man since the early months of the war and he knew Sherman's capabilities. Moreover, Sherman had the larger army and adequate supplies. He faced an army of only 62,000 men, which the South struggled to keep in the field. Sherman, however, understood that he faced a very difficult task. President Davis had finally given up on Braxton Bragg after the Battle of Chattanooga and put Joseph Johnston in charge of the Army of Tennessee. Johnston was a competent and crafty general, seasoned by the war and not likely to make mistakes. Moreover, the terrain was hilly and cut up, favoring defense. The further Sherman advanced, the longer his supply line back to Chattanooga and the north, forcing him to leave troops for garrison duty along the rail line.

Johnston recognized the folly of attacking Sherman directly, so he tried a different strategy: he planned to keep Sherman away from Atlanta as long as possible, at least until the November elections. He had two reasons: he hoped many of Sherman's soldiers would leave when their enlistments were up before summer, and a war-weary North might replace President Lincoln with someone more willing to negotiate a peace that included Southern independence.

Johnston's plan was to take up defensive positions to forestall Sherman's movements, but Sherman was able to outflank Johnston in position after position until Sherman reached the outskirts of Atlanta. Tired of Johnston's retreats, President Davis relieved him of duty and gave his army to the younger and more aggressive John B. Hood.

Confederate Success at Richmond and New Market, Virginia

Like Sherman, Grant had the larger army and a steady flow of supplies, but he could not find a means of crushing or dispersing his opponent. Both Lee and Johnston were clever and accomplished generals, and the men they commanded were seasoned, passionate fighters.

After Spotsylvania, Lee moved quickly to stay between Grant and Richmond. The two armies sparred at the North Anna River and then again at Totopotomy Creek on May 30. Grant shifted left and south, settling in near a small town outside Richmond called Cold Harbor. A charge against Lee's trenches resulted in massive Union casualties.

Nor were Grant's plans going much better further afield. General Benjamin Butler's plan to attack Richmond from between the capital city and Petersburg stalled. Grant had ordered an army under Franz Sigel to march up the Shenandoah Valley, run Rebels out of that region, and occupy it for the Union. But Confederate general John Breckinridge defeated Sigel near New Market.

Meanwhile, Union general David Hunter had moved from West Virginia into Lynchburg, Virginia, a rail hub for supplies to Lee's army. Lee could not well afford for the North to control Lynchburg or to advance from there to help Grant at Richmond.

From Cold Harbor to Petersburg

Grant was tantalizingly close to Richmond, as close as McClellan had reached two years before, but he could not beat the Army of Virginia out of its miles of trenches. If Grant was going to capture the Confederate capital he would have to do it some other way. Then Grant pulled off one of the most stunning maneuvers of the war, and if his subordinates had acted well near the end of it—or if the Confederates had reacted less adeptly—Grant might have won the war in the summer of 1864.

In the six weeks from the Battle of the Wilderness on May 4 to the beginning of the siege of Petersburg, casualties to Grant's forces ran to 60,000 or 70,000 men. Although Grant made up the losses with replacements, the toll appalled the North and Grant was heavily criticized.

Rather than besieging Richmond, Grant stealthily withdrew his army and sent them toward the James River. He got much of his army across before Lee could react. The objective was Petersburg on the south side of the Appomattox River. All but one of the railroads coming from the south toward Richmond merged there. If Grant could capture Petersburg, Richmond would have to be abandoned.

The first Federal units to cross the James were meant to speed into Petersburg, which was only lightly defended, but the few Confederates there put up a stiff fight. As more Federals arrived, General Beauregard deftly organized the city's defense and held off the Federals until much of the Army of Northern Virginia could arrive. Three days after beginning to cross the James River, Grant had to admit that his hopes for capturing Petersburg swiftly had failed. He settled in for a siege.

CHAPTER 11

The Course of the War: 1864 Part II

Halfway through the critical election year of 1864, the North had little to show for its efforts. Grant had not broken the Army of Northern Virginia. He had lost tens of thousands of men and was stalled around the small city of Petersburg. Likewise, Sherman was pushing Johnston's Confederate army southward but had won no large prize. Guerilla bands plagued Tennessee. The North was discouraged, and even Lincoln thought he might not be re-elected. But the South was suffering, too, and it had few resources to fall back on.

General Early Heads for Washington, D.C.

Just after the Cold Harbor fight outside Richmond in early June, Robert E. Lee felt a threat to his rear. This was the small army of David Hunter, come east from the West Virginia mountains and down to Lynchburg east of the Shenandoah Valley. Hunter was a threat to Lee's supplies as well as a possible reinforcement for Grant, who was banging on the doors of Petersburg and Richmond. Lee detached General Jubal Early and his corps of 8,000 soldiers to push Hunter out of Lynchburg and relieve the pressure from this sector. If he could do that then he could return to Lee or march north in a raid toward Washington.

Early joined with the Confederate force that had recently defeated Sigel, and they pursued Hunter until the Union general had taken his army back into the West Virginia hinterland, leaving the entire Shenandoah Valley free of significant Union forces. Early and Lee were positioned to use the Shenandoah Valley as a kind of shotgun pointed toward Washington, D.C.

Even if the Confederates could not capture the capital they would likely frighten Lincoln into demanding a substantial force be recalled to man the Washington defenses. This would leave Grant weakened at a time when Northern sentiment was turning sour.

Early continued north, bypassing a strong Union garrison at Harpers Ferry, and crossed the Potomac near the old Antietam battlefield. Grant detached troops from his lines near Petersburg to reinforce Washington. Some of these men defended a line along the Monocacy River outside Frederick, Maryland. Early's Southerners defeated them and pressed on toward Washington, but the fight at the Monocacy River had delayed Early just enough to allow more of Grant's men to fill the Washington forts and trenches north of the city. When Early reached Washington on July 11 and 12, he determined he could not breach the defenses and so withdrew toward the Shenandoah Valley whence he came.

Sherman Wins Atlanta

Hood, now in command of the Army of Tennessee and tasked with saving Atlanta, led his men out of their trenches and attacked Sherman's army on

July 20 along Peachtree Creek, just ten miles outside of Atlanta. Hood's men were simply outnumbered. The Confederates suffered 4,800 casualties, and Hood was forced to retreat to Atlanta.

Sherman sent McPherson to attack Hood in retreat. On July 22, William Hardee's infantry division attacked Sherman's forces in what became known as the Battle of Atlanta. The Confederate forces, outmanned and outgunned, lost more than 8,500 men. Union losses were lighter, but McPherson was among the dead.

Major General William Tecumseh Sherman
Photo courtesy of the National Archives (111-B-1769)

Sherman replaced McPherson with Major General Oliver Howard and sent him around the western side of Atlanta with orders to sever Hood's communication lines. Hood successfully protected the railroad at Ezra Church on July 28, but he lost another 2,500 men in the process. At this point, the

Confederate army numbered fewer than 45,000 men. Facing overwhelming numbers, they fell back behind Atlanta's defensive lines and waited for Sherman to attack.

Rather than risking a frontal assault, which would have resulted in huge casualties, Sherman laid siege to Atlanta, bombarding the city with heavy artillery for more than a month and doing all he could to destroy its supply lines. But the South refused to give in that easily; Confederate cavalry commander Joseph Wheeler skillfully kept many supply lines in operation until the end of August.

"War is cruelty and you cannot refine it. . . . But when peace does come, you may call on me for anything. Then will I share with you the last cracker."—William Tecumseh Sherman, to the mayor of Atlanta after ordering the civilian population evacuated from the city

The standoff came to a head on August 28, when Sherman attacked the Montgomery & Atlanta Railroad south of the city. Hood, realizing the importance of keeping the line open, attacked the Union flank at Jonesborough but ultimately lost a valiant battle. With no remaining line of supply, Confederate forces evacuated Atlanta on September 2, and Sherman's troops marched in the following day.

The once proud city of Atlanta had been all but destroyed during the siege and final evacuation. What wasn't demolished by Union artillery was burned to the ground by fleeing Confederate troops, who also ransacked stores for all the supplies they could carry.

The Struggle for the Shenandoah Valley

Through the summer Grant could do little against Lee behind his defenses at Petersburg. The last two years had shown convincingly that sending infantry up against well-entrenched soldiers was no formula for military success. Grant did try to break the Confederate line by allowing Pennsylvania miners to dig a trench below the Confederate trenches and set off tons of explosives on July 30. The devastation blew a gap in the Southern works, but the Union attack bogged down in the hole from the explosion. The Battle of the Crater got the Union army nothing but bad press.

Grant turned his attention to the Shenandoah Valley. It supplied a good deal of the food that sustained the Army of Northern Virginia, and it had enough to support a Southern army in the valley if they were forced to find all their food by foraging. Grant wanted the supplies to Lee's army stopped. He also meant to preclude the possibility of some future Southern army—like Early's—operating in this troublesome area.

FACT

The grandfather of World War II general George S. Patton was George S. Patton I. A graduate of the Virginia Military Institute and commander of the Twenty-second Virginia Infantry Regiment, he was mortally wounded at the Battle of Winchester in September 1864.

Grant wanted an aggressive commander and chose Phil Sheridan for the job. He told Sheridan to make the valley barren so that no cattle, pigs, or crops could be used to sustain Southern forces. This, of course, meant the destruction of farmers' buildings and fields, but Grant felt it necessary, and the North sustained him.

Sheridan's Attacks on Early

With about three times as many men as Early's 15,000 Rebels, Sheridan set off toward the lower valley. His force defeated Early's men at Winchester on September 19, and Early retreated up the valley. Sheridan's army defeated Early again at Fisher's Hill three days later, and Early retreated again. Sheridan set out destroying barns, cribs, stables, and other structures that sustained the valley's rich agriculture.

Early sprang a surprise attack on Sheridan's left flank at Cedar Creek on October 19. Sheridan himself was miles away at Winchester. He set off at a gallop toward Cedar Creek, rallying his men and getting them to turn and face the advancing Southerners. This celebrated "Sheridan's Ride" helped turn the tide of battle. Early's men were crushed by Sheridan's counterattack. They would never be a force in the Shenandoah Valley again.

Hood Heads for Tennessee

When Hood and his Army of Tennessee abandoned Atlanta on September 2, they were diminished but not defeated. Hood was an aggressive commander, and he meant to continue the war.

Hood thought that if he marched northwest and attacked garrisons along the railroad line, Sherman would have to leave Atlanta to protect his supply line. Somewhere in those rugged hills, Hood might defeat him. Sherman did come out of Atlanta, but he left a substantial garrison behind. He also had enough men to spare to send General Thomas and a substantial part of the army to Nashville to help counter Forrest's cavalry.

All through September and into October Hood and Sherman sparred in the rough country northwest of Atlanta, but there was never an opening to make an all-out attack. Frustrated, Hood retreated into northern Alabama. Equally frustrated, Sherman settled back into Atlanta.

The generals devised opposite plans. Hood thought he could best serve the Confederacy by marching north into Tennessee, capturing Nashville, and showing that the Southern nation could still wield its sovereignty to the Kentucky border. Perhaps this would draw Sherman after him, restoring Atlanta and setting up Sherman for destruction. Sherman had another notion. He thought he could best cripple the South by marching through the heart of Georgia to the Atlantic Ocean and capturing Savannah. In mid-November, Hood set off north. Sherman, after sending General John Schofield and part of his army north to reinforce Thomas in Tennessee, set off southeast.

Hood nearly brought Schofield's army to grief in a planned ambush on November 29 at Spring Hill, Tennessee. Schofield's men escaped into the town of Franklin, south of Nashville. Furious that his men had missed an opportunity at Spring Hill, Hood ordered them into a massive charge at

Schofield's Franklin defenses. The attack was a disaster for Hood's army, and five Confederate generals were slain in the assault.

Schofield's small army was not large enough to turn and attack Hood, so Schofield continued his march north to join Thomas in Nashville. Hood pursued in hopes of throwing the Federals out of the Tennessee capital, but he did not have the strength. In the first days of December, he settled in for a siege.

Sherman Marches to the Sea

Sherman began his infamous March to the Sea on November 15. Atlanta was torched as he moved his men out, and smoke filled the skies as the city was reduced to rubble. Despite having sent both Thomas and Schofield back to Nashville with sizeable forces, Sherman still had 62,000 men at his command. They would not have a supply line back to Chattanooga and the north. They would have to live off of what they brought with them and what they could take from Confederate farmers and planters along the way.

Sherman's men burned many homes in their paths, generally leaving nothing standing except the masonry chimneys. These became known as Sherman Sentinels. Railroad ties that the soldiers heated and then wrapped around trees became known as Sherman Neckties.

Total War

Sherman split his army into two columns. Together, they presented a front that was twenty-five to sixty miles wide. Like army ants, they swarmed over the countryside, destroying railroads, bridges, telegraph lines, manufacturing plants, plantations, and anything else that Sherman deemed of value to the Southern war effort.

Although they were cut off from supplies coming by rail from the north, Sherman's men found plenty to eat. While Lee's army starved for lack of provisions, it was harvest time and Sherman's army had more food than it could possibly consume. Extra supplies were either abandoned or given to the growing contingent of runaway slaves who eagerly followed the army that had liberated them.

Sherman gave orders not to steal from private citizens, but these orders was not strictly enforced, and many Union soldiers took it upon themselves to punish the Southern citizenry. Families and entire towns fled the approaching army, rightfully fearful of retribution; they often returned to find everything they owned gone and their homes and farms destroyed.

By the late fall of 1864, low morale was beginning to show on the Southern ranks. According to Bruce Catton's *Never Call Retreat,* their sketchy records reveal that between 100,000 and 200,000 enlisted soldiers were not present for duty.

Sherman's army was so large that it faced little opposition from Confederate forces aside from a small number of state troopers, militiamen, and cavalry. There were occasional skirmishes, but Sherman's army quickly overran any opposing forces in its path. On December 10, Sherman reached the Atlantic coast after a march of 300 miles. He had inflicted an estimated $100 million worth of damage along the way.

The Move to Savannah

Savannah was Sherman's next objective, but as he prepared a major assault, Confederate general William S. Hardee withdrew his greatly outnumbered 10,000-man army rather than face certain annihilation. Sherman marched into Savannah on December 22 and wired Lincoln two days later to offer the city as a Christmas present. Lincoln was elated.

Meanwhile, Union general Thomas came out of Nashville's defenses and smashed Hood's worn-down army outside the city. The battle took place on

December 15 and 16. Hood's men, stretched to the limit even before the battle, gave way. The Army of Tennessee was never again a substantial fighting force.

Lincoln's Second Presidential Election

Despite doing his best to preserve the Union and bring the Southern states back into the fold, Lincoln almost wasn't re-elected in 1864. The public had grown weary of the war, especially the huge number of casualties and the tremendous amount of money required to keep the Union war machine rolling, and they placed blame for the whole mess squarely at Lincoln's feet. The Union had assumed the war would be over in a matter of months, and the longer it dragged on, the less support Lincoln had among the Northern states. So bleak did things look toward the end that Lincoln himself felt he would never win the Republican nomination for a second term. The front-runner, at least for a while, appeared to be Salmon P. Chase, who had long held presidential aspirations.

FACT

The first federal paper money, printed under the Legal Tender Act of 1862, carried the image of Secretary of the Treasury Salmon P. Chase, who aspired to be president and saw the greenbacks as a multitude of tiny campaign posters. Sadly for Chase, his dream of living in the White House never materialized.

Indeed, Chase did all he could to undermine Lincoln's chances while bolstering his own. As secretary of the treasury, he surrounded himself with a cadre of high-ranking Republicans who believed they were the true power brokers, and he did all he could to curry their favor. However, Chase's bid for the White House was cut short early in the game when a clandestine attempt to remove Lincoln from the ticket and replace him with Chase became publicly known. The coup made Chase look disloyal to Lincoln, and Chase offered his resignation, which Lincoln accepted a few months later.

Despite growing public dissatisfaction with the war, Lincoln did receive his party's nomination; however, Vice President Hannibal Hamlin was replaced by Andrew Johnson, the Democratic governor of Tennessee. Republican leaders felt the addition of Johnson increased regional balance and improved Lincoln's chances of winning a second term. The party also temporarily changed its name to the Union Party.

Lincoln's greatest opponent in the 1864 election was George B. McClellan, who won the Democratic nomination during the party's convention in Chicago. The race had all the makings of a true grudge match; Lincoln and McClellan had clashed often during the early years of the war during McClellan's command of the Army of the Potomac. Lincoln had eventually fired McClellan over McClellan's frustrating reluctance to pursue the enemy. McClellan regarded Lincoln with disdain and never missed an opportunity to say so.

McClellan ran on a platform of peace that included a vow to end hostilities with the Confederacy, though personally McClellan believed the war should be continued until the Union won. He felt Lincoln had not proved himself an effective leader during the war, and he also had problems with Lincoln's policy of emancipation. Lincoln countered by portraying the Democratic Party—and its candidate—as disloyal to the Union, and he reiterated the need to preserve the Union at all costs.

"Neither party expected for the war the magnitude or the duration which it has already attained. . . . Each looked to an easier triumph and a result less fundamental and astounding. Both read the same Bible and pray to the same God, and each invokes His aid against the other. . . . The prayers of both could not be answered; that of neither have been answered fully."—Abraham Lincoln, second inaugural address, March 4, 1865

One of the biggest thorns in Lincoln's side as the presidential race heated up was the lack of substantial Union victories. Increasingly, Lincoln's leadership and ability to control his fighting forces was called into question, and every Confederate victory was another nail in his political coffin. Newspaper editorials lambasted him at every turn, and his political foes rejoiced at every failure. But the race took a decided turn in Lincoln's favor when Sherman captured Atlanta and Farragut won the battle of Mobile Bay in late August. Suddenly, the Union was making decisive strikes against the Confederacy, and the end of the war seemed near.

Lincoln's star shone brighter than ever, and he soundly defeated McClellan. Lincoln received 55 percent of the popular vote, and his margin in the Electoral College was even more impressive—212 to 21. McClellan had won only his home state of New Jersey and the border states of Kentucky and Delaware.

CHAPTER 12

The End of the Civil War

As 1865 began, the Confederacy was teetering. Its army west of the Mississippi could do little to affect the outcome. The entire Mississippi River was under Union control. In Alabama, Tennessee, Georgia, and Mississippi, Confederate forces could do no more than harass Union outposts. Grant's army had Lee's Army of Northern Virginia locked in the trenches outside Petersburg, and Sherman was at Savannah, ready to go in just about any direction he chose. The Confederate soldiers still in the field were poorly clothed and poorly fed. The end was in sight.

Sherman's March Through the Carolinas

Sherman remained with his army in Savannah through January 1865. He had time to consider his options. No Confederate force could reasonably attack him. Sherman decided he could march north along the Atlantic much as he had marched southeast from Atlanta to Savannah. Once he got into northern North Carolina, he could coordinate his movements with Grant, whose army was then around Petersburg in southern Virginia. Along the way, Sherman could occupy major cities in South and North Carolina and continue his destruction of the Southern economy.

Ruins seen from the Circular Church, Charleston, South Carolina, 1865 *Photo courtesy of the National Archives (111-B-4667)*

Sherman and his army pulled out of Savannah on February 1. He was not likely to face any more opposition than 30,000 Confederates under Joseph Johnston. These were drawn from about 10,000 men who were the escaped Savannah garrison, portions of the Army of Tennessee that had been smashed in front of Nashville in December, and various militia and cavalry groups. Sherman would have as much problem with the lay of the land—many rivers and boggy country to cross—as with Johnston's men.

Sherman made a feint at Charleston, then sent most of his men to Columbia, South Carolina's capital, which they entered on February 17. So stalwart from the sea, the rebellious city could not hold out once its rail lines to the interior were cut; it was turned over to Union authorities on February 18.

The Union men, who had been relatively gentle in Savannah, took again to the kinds of destructive ways they had developed in Georgia. Most of them blamed South Carolina for having started the whole war to begin with. When they left Columbia, it was devastated by fire; whether the blaze was set on purpose or accidentally is still debated. Sherman continued northward. In middle and late March he battled Confederate forces in North Carolina, winning both contests. Soon he was ready to link up with Grant.

The Collapsing Confederacy

A number of diverse factors contributed to the Confederacy's ultimate demise. Foremost were the combined forces of Grant and Sherman, who put relentless pressure on the South's two principal armies. While Grant forced Lee's hand at Petersburg, Sherman effectively split the eastern portion of the South in half with his March to the Sea and up into the Carolinas. The combined attacks pushed the already battered and much smaller Southern armies to the brink. The Confederacy could no longer defend itself or its territories, ensuring a Union victory.

A Suffering Economy

The state of the Southern economy was also a contributing factor. The gravity of the situation became evident more than a year before the war officially ended, and it only grew worse as the conflict progressed. Its economy close to ruin, the fledgling nation had neither the credit nor the cash to buy foreign goods for its armies or its people. As a result, consumer goods became increasingly scarce and outrageously expensive, and the army was finally forced to literally beg the civilian populace—most of whom had long grown tired of the war—for food, clothing, and other essential items.

A Lack of Soldiers

Willing, able-bodied men also grew short in numbers as the war went on, forcing the military to take almost anyone willing to fight, including underage boys and old men. At the beginning, prisoner exchanges allowed both sides to maintain strong numbers, but the Union cessation of the program in 1863 hit the Confederacy hard; all of a sudden, tens of thousands of Southern soldiers were languishing in Union prisons. The manpower situation grew so dire toward the end that Confederate officials started conscripting slaves, a concept viewed with derision just a couple of years earlier. The huge number of casualties in many of the major battles also severely depleted Confederate forces. In many cases, the actual number of Union casualties was higher, but the overall percentage was smaller. In other words, the South lost fewer men on average but took a harder hit with the number it did lose. Not surprisingly, Confederate recruitment drives during the final year of the war provided fewer and fewer soldiers willing to lay down their lives for a cause many were starting to believe was hopeless.

At the northern portion of the Shenandoah Valley region of Virginia, the town of Winchester changed hands seventy-two times over the course of the war. Planned evacuations accounted for some of these transfers, but there was also fierce fighting in which contesting sides shot at one another through the streets.

Davis's Determination

Amazingly, President Davis had plans to continue the war no matter the fate of the Army of Northern Virginia or the capital at Richmond. An angry Confederate to the bitter end, Davis carried with him up to the moment of his capture the belief that the Confederacy would prevail if given enough time, but he was pretty much alone in that sentiment. By April 1865, the Confederacy had clearly lost its ability to fight, and no amount of rally cries could revive it. Most of Davis's closest advisors and associates knew the cause had been lost months before, but none could convince Davis to bargain for peace.

The Final Battles Around Petersburg

For Lee, calamity came in late March 1865. Realizing that Petersburg was a lost cause so long as Grant kept pressing with more men and resources to the southwest and the last rail line that supplied the city from the south, Lee developed a daring plan that called for him and his troops to flee the city, hook up with General Joseph Johnston to stop Sherman's assault, then return to take on Grant. It was a bold ploy that might actually have worked had Lee commanded a sufficient number of men, though even with his small army, he had no other choice.

Soldiers in the trenches before battle, Petersburg, Virginia, 1865 *Photo courtesy of the National Archives (111-B-157)*

Just before daylight on March 25, 1865, Confederate forces under General John Gordon attacked Union-held Fort Stedman, which lay directly east of Petersburg. The surprise assault was a success, and the Rebel forces pushed on to the Union secondary line. If they could break the line and hold it, Grant would have to pull troops back from the southwest and Lee's army could break out toward North Carolina and General Johnston. Unfortunately for Lee, the Union forces rallied with a mighty counterattack that destroyed the Confederate front. By midmorning, Lee's forces had been pushed back at a loss of nearly 5,000 men.

Fighting Southwest of the City

With that, Grant—assisted by Philip Sheridan's cavalry—made a major push against Lee's right flank in the hope of preventing Lee's escape to the south. On March 29, a full corps attacked Lee's right while Sheridan led a corps of cavalry and infantry in a wide sweep toward the small town of Five Forks on the Confederate right. Sheridan knew that if he could get behind Lee's army, he could stop it in its tracks and effectively end the war that day.

During the siege of Petersburg, the Confederate army was so desperate for able bodies to man its defenses that it resorted to using old men, young boys, and two unwilling members of Jefferson Davis's cabinet.

But Lee wasn't about to go down without a fight. He quickly realized what was happening and sent troops under George Pickett to oppose Sheridan's assault. Pickett managed to stop Sheridan at Dinwiddie Court House, just short of Five Forks, on March 31. But Sheridan wasn't defeated; he merely waited for reinforcements. Grant sent him a corps under General Gouverneur Warren.

The ensuing battle was hard fought, with Sheridan loudly rallying his troops, hell-bent on stopping Lee at all costs. Sheridan's goal was the Southside Railway, a Confederate central supply line. Sheridan's forces managed to all but annihilate Pickett's division and take the town of Five Forks. Grant cabled Lincoln that Five Forks was under Union control and Petersburg was next. Lincoln contacted the press, which carried the news under huge headlines. The end of the war was within the Union's grasp.

On April 2, Grant launched an all-out assault along the Confederate line defending Petersburg. Artillery battered the Rebel forces, softening the line and killing many. Then the guns stopped, and Union infantry attacked in a huge wave that eventually tore a hole in the middle of the Confederate line. The Rebels fought with all they had, but they were outnumbered and outgunned. Lee knew that Petersburg was lost and made plans to abandon the city. He wired Jefferson Davis that Richmond could no longer be protected and encouraged Davis and his cabinet to flee the capital as quickly as possible. Then Lee took his remaining army of hungry, ill-equipped men and headed west with the intention of joining Johnston's army.

Fleeing Richmond

News that the Confederate government was abandoning Richmond spread quickly, and soon the city's civilian population was fighting with government and military officials for all available vehicles. Those who were able joined Davis and his staff in flight. Those who couldn't leave took to their homes, locking doors and shuttering windows, unsure of what to expect as Union forces advanced upon them.

Fires were set and buildings destroyed in an attempt to keep anything useful out of Union hands. Before long, the city was engulfed in a blaze that could be seen for miles. The citizens of Richmond, having suffered for so long, began looting the city, looking for food and anything of value. Many got drunk on whiskey that had been left undestroyed. Chaos reigned as the once proud Confederate capital collapsed upon itself.

Grant's forces marched into Richmond on April 3, the day after the fall of Petersburg. The Crown of the Confederacy was finally under Union control.

The Surrender of Robert E. Lee

Lee's army got a one-day jump on Grant's Army of the Potomac, abandoning Petersburg for Danville, Virginia, where Jefferson Davis hoped to reinstate the Confederate government and keep the war going. Lee knew the continuation of hostilities was futile, but as a professional soldier, he couldn't bring himself to question his commander-in-chief.

Flight and Pursuit

On the night of April 3, 1865, Lee's army found itself in Amelia Court House, a little more than twenty miles from Petersburg. Lee had hoped to find rations for his starving men, but there wasn't a single morsel to be had. Desperate to move on, he had no choice but to remain an extra day while scouts foraged the countryside in search of food. This cost Lee his one-day head start and placed him and his men in great jeopardy. The area was swarming with Union troops. Following very close behind were three corps of Union infantry, marching a few miles south of Lee on a parallel course. On the night of April 4, some of Sheridan's cavalry made a tentative move into Amelia Court House. Lee knew he couldn't stay; to do so would have been folly.

The forage wagons upon which Lee had pinned his hopes returned nearly empty on April 5. This meant his men would have to march on empty stomachs, something they had been forced to do for far too long. After another brief delay so that additional Confederate forces under General George Thomas Anderson and General Richard Ewell could join him, Lee ordered his dwindling Army of Northern Virginia to move out—only to find his path blocked by Union infantry and cavalry.

FACT

Wilmer McLean's home was located near Manassas, Virginia, directly in the path of the First Battle of Manassas. The man was so shaken by the battle that he decided to move as far away from the war as possible, settling his family in Appomattox. But the war came back and ended in his parlor, where Lee formally surrendered to Grant.

Rather than directly face the larger Federal force, Lee shifted west toward Farmville, where he hoped to receive food and provisions for his men from nearby Lynchburg. The night march there took a heavy toll on Lee's hungry, exhausted men, many of whom stumbled out of the walking columns and were never seen again. And as always, Federal forces continued to harass the Confederates as they slowly made their way. Grant dogged Lee with unflagging determination, pressing closer and closer, unwilling to let his esteemed foe escape again. The end was close, and both men knew it.

Disaster at Sayler's Creek

On April 6, Union forces overwhelmed John Gordon's divisions, which were covering the Confederate wagon trains, at Sayler's Creek. During that battle, Union soldiers captured the majority of Lee's supply wagons and, even more heartbreaking, decimated the corps led by Anderson and Ewell. Lee's army lost more than 7,000 men. He was left with just 15,000 soldiers armed with only muskets and sabers. Opposing them were 80,000 Union infantry and cavalry.

QUESTION?

Could Robert E. Lee have continued the war despite being nearly surrounded at Appomattox?
Some of his officers suggested the army disperse to the hills and wage a guerilla war against the Union armies. Lee dismissed the idea, saying he was personally too old and guerilla warfare would cause as much harm to the South as to Union forces.

The following day, Lee's army stumbled into Farmville, where he and his men received food for the first time in many days. Once they had eaten their fill, Lee pressed on, crossing the Appomattox River and burning the bridges behind him. But even that failed to hold back Grant's forces, and Lee continued to feel the Union commander's presence just miles behind him. That evening, Lee received an invitation from Grant to surrender, an offer he quickly refused. A tiny ray of hope remained: if Lee could get his men to Appomattox Station on the rail line to Lynchburg, he could feed them from supply trains there, then swing south to Danville.

On April 8, Grant's army forced Lee into another rear-guard action to protect his remaining wagons. As Lee's men fought for their survival, Sheridan's cavalry and infantry under E. O. C. Ord quickly moved past Lee's southern flank and drove into Appomattox Station, where they captured Lee's supply railroad cars and placed themselves across his line of march. That evening, Lee's army entered Appomattox Court House a few miles from Appomattox Station and saw the extent of Sheridan's force. The Confederates were greatly outnumbered by heavily armed Union cavalry and infantry, far too many for them to engage. An assault would have been suicide, and all knew it. The end had finally come for Lee's Army of Northern Virginia.

Total Confederate and Union deaths attributed to the Civil War from both battle and disease is approximately 623,000. At least 471,400 more were wounded. The total casualty list for the war is about 1,094,400.

The following day, April 9—Palm Sunday—Lee put on his best dress uniform, including a red silk sash, a jeweled sword given to him by women in England, red-stitched spurred boots, and long gray gloves, known as gauntlets. He planned to meet with Grant to discuss surrender terms and wanted to look his best if Grant took him prisoner. It was an agonizing decision for Lee, who told Gordon he would rather "die a thousand deaths." But he had no choice. If he didn't surrender, thousands more would die needlessly.

Surrender at the McLean House

Grant and Lee were an exercise in contrast when they shook hands in Wilmer McLean's parlor in Appomattox Court House. Lee looked resplendent in his finest dress uniform, and Grant, who had been nursing a severe headache that morning and hadn't had time to clean up, appeared mud-spattered and disheveled. Grant arrived alone and found Lee standing with two aides. He removed his gloves and extended his hand to the man he had pursued for so long. The two officers then sat down as six of Grant's generals entered the room and stood behind their commander.

Grant did no gloating that day. He told Lee that his officers and men would have to surrender, then be paroled and disqualified from taking up arms again unless properly exchanged with Northern prisoners (which, of course, was never contemplated). All arms, ammunition, and supplies were to be delivered up as captured property. After a request from Lee, Grant promised to "let all the men who claim to own a horse or mule take the animals home with them to work their little farms." Grant also authorized all of the provisions Lee needed to feed his starving men. Lee was very appreciative of Grant's kind gesture, noting, "This will have the best possible effect on the men. It will be very gratifying and will do much toward conciliating our people."

After signing the declaration of surrender, Lee stood up and shook Grant's hand one more time. He bowed to the other men in the room and walked silently out the door. On the porch, Lee put his riding gloves on and gazed for a moment toward the hillside where his ragtag army awaited his return. He absently drove his right fist into his left hand three times, then mounted his beloved horse Traveller and rode away to deliver the difficult news to his men.

The first soldier buried at Arlington National Cemetery was a Confederate prisoner of war who died in a local hospital. In all, more than 200 other Southerners would be interred there. Most of the early plots were located in what had been Mary Lee's rose garden; Union brigadier general Montgomery Meigs wanted to make it impossible for the Lees to return to their prewar residence.

Three days later, on April 12, what was left of Lee's Army of Northern Virginia relinquished their weapons and received their paroles, which allowed them to return home. Though a handful of minor battles would be fought in the weeks ahead, the war was virtually over, and the Confederate States of America, so eager to prove its independence, no longer existed. On April 14, General Robert Anderson raised the American flag over Fort Sumter—the same flag he had been forced to lower exactly four years earlier. Later that evening, Lincoln was killed at Ford's Theatre by John Wilkes Booth. Others would die in skirmishes over the next few weeks, but in many ways, Lincoln was the final casualty in a war that took so many.

The Assassination of Abraham Lincoln

Few events in American history have become so ingrained in the public consciousness as the assassination of Abraham Lincoln. His murder by actor

John Wilkes Booth, coming literally at the end of the Civil War, plunged an already weary nation into deep sorrow. For many Americans, it was the ultimate tragedy following four years of overwhelming anguish and suffering. Tears at the loss of a great and noble leader flooded the land.

John Wilkes Booth *Photo courtesy of the National Archives (64-M-19)*

The assassination of Abraham Lincoln was not the act of a single disgruntled Confederate sympathizer. Booth and several associates spent months planning an attack on Lincoln, and his attendance at the theater finally gave them the perfect opportunity. Originally, they had planned to kidnap the president and exchange him for Confederate prisoners of war and possibly a peace treaty between the warring sides. However, as the Confederacy itself started to fall, Booth changed his plans and decided to kill Lincoln instead. Also on the conspirators' hit list were Vice President

Johnson, General Grant, and Secretary of State Seward, who was seriously wounded by a conspirator named Lewis Powell.

Lincoln and Booth at Ford's Theatre

A week after Lee's surrender at Appomattox Court House, an exhausted Lincoln decided to relax by attending a production of a light comedy, *Our American Cousin*, at Ford's Theatre in Washington, D.C. Nearly a dozen people were invited to join the Lincolns at the theater, but only two—Major Henry Rathbone and his fiancée, Clara Harris—did so. Among those who declined were General Grant and his wife—a decision that probably saved Grant's life.

At approximately 10 P.M., John Wilkes Booth walked into Ford's Theatre. He was well known to the theater staff, and the ticket taker let him in gratis as a professional courtesy. Though Lincoln's life had been threatened repeatedly over the course of the war, security surrounding the president was light. Only a White House footman stood guard outside Lincoln's box; the Metropolitan policeman assigned to protect the president had left his post for a few moments. Booth was admitted to the box upon showing his calling card. He quietly slipped in behind Lincoln and shot the president in the back of the head with a small single-shot derringer. Rathbone quickly stood up to grab Booth, but Booth stabbed him in the arm with a seven-inch dagger, then leaped from the box to the stage below. He landed awkwardly, breaking his leg. Booth shouted, "Sic semper tyrannis!" ("Thus always to tyrants!") before the stunned audience, then hobbled to the exit.

The first doctor to attend to Lincoln was a young army surgeon named Charles A. Leale, who had only recently graduated from medical school. Lincoln showed signs of life and was quickly transported to a home across the street from the theater, but there was little Leale or any of the dozens of physicians who flocked to Lincoln's bed could do. He was declared dead at 7:22 A.M.

Booth's Escape and Rumors of Conspiracy

After shooting Lincoln, Booth escaped to the countryside and sought aid for his broken leg. He stayed a week with a Southern sympathizer, then moved to a farm in Bowling Green, Virginia. There, he and an accomplice were surrounded by Union cavalry, who called for them to surrender. The accomplice did but Booth refused. The barn was set afire, and Booth was shot and wounded by Sergeant Boston Corbett. Pulled from the flames, Booth died three hours later.

Not surprisingly, rumors of a large Confederate conspiracy in the death of Lincoln and attacks on his cabinet swept through Washington. Some rumors suggested that Jefferson Davis and other prominent Confederate officials were in on the plot, but such was not the case; Booth and his cadre of Union haters had worked alone. In trials that reeked more of revenge than justice, all of the conspirators were found guilty, and four of them were executed by hanging. Three others, including Samuel Mudd, the doctor who set Booth's broken leg, were sentenced to life imprisonment, though Mudd served only four years before being pardoned and released.

Flight of the Confederate Government

After Lee had warned President Davis to leave Richmond, Davis put his evacuation plans into effect. Davis and others gathered what they could—including the Confederate treasury's remaining gold worth more than $500,000, Confederate bank notes, negotiable bonds, and a chest full of jewels—and boarded a train for Danville, Virginia. A day later, Union troops entered Richmond and Petersburg.

Davis had hoped to establish a new Confederate capital in Danville and continue the war for Southern independence. Following Lee's surrender to Grant on April 9, Davis and his cabinet scattered to escape arrest. Davis continued south into Georgia, where he was reunited with his family and planned to travel to either Texas or Mexico, where he and many other members of the Confederacy hoped to find sanctuary. However, the Federal army wasn't about to let Davis escape.

Davis was finally captured near Irwinville, Georgia, on May 10 by a detachment of the Fourth Michigan Cavalry. He and his family were taken to Macon, Georgia, and forced to endure the constant taunts of Union soldiers singing, "We'll hang Jeff Davis from a sour apple tree." On May 22, Davis was imprisoned in Fort Monroe, Virginia, and kept in shackles. Still proud and defiant, he resisted being chained and finally had to be subdued by his jailers. Davis sat in Fort Monroe for almost two years without benefit of trial, under constant watch by soldiers who had orders never to speak to him.

FACT

When the Confederate government arrived in Danville, Virginia, by train, the treasury in their possession was estimated at $327,022— about $120,000 less than its calculated sum when the government fled Richmond. Attempts to account for the discrepancy proved fruitless, and rumors that President Davis had stolen the funds dogged him for years. However, most historians agree that Davis did not take the money.

Davis suffered tremendously during his incarceration. Captivity exacerbated his already weak physical condition. He might have died but for Dr. John Craven, who tended to Davis's health and provided him with whatever comforts he could arrange.

At the start of his incarceration, Davis's family was moved to Savannah. Varina Davis, worried about the safety of the children, who were being threatened on the streets by soldiers and Unionists, moved them to Canada under the care of her mother. Mrs. Davis then devoted herself to lobbying for her husband's release.

Very Last Battles

Lee's surrender at Appomattox Court House on April 9, 1865, effectively brought the Civil War to an end; however, Lee's surrender was not the conclusion of hostilities. Three other Confederate commanders continued to do battle with the Union for another two and a half months.

General Joseph E. Johnston followed Sherman's march through North Carolina even after receiving news of the fall of Richmond and Lee's surrender. He finally agreed to discuss surrender terms with Sherman on April 17, 1865. Sherman offered his foe a very generous surrender agreement, so generous that it was rejected by the Federal government. A second agreement was accepted by both parties on April 26, and Johnston's troops formally surrendered on May 3.

In Mobile, Alabama, Confederate general Richard Taylor, the son of former President Zachary Taylor, also continued to fight with a force of 15,000 troops after hearing of Lee's surrender and the dissolution of the Confederate government. Taylor finally surrendered to E. R. S. Canby on May 4.

"With an unceasing admiration of your constancy and devotion to your Country, and grateful remembrance of your kind and generous consideration of myself, I bid you all an affectionate farewell."—Robert E. Lee, last order to the Army of Northern Virginia

On May 12 and 13, General E. Kirby Smith, unaware of Lee's surrender, waged the last land battle of the war in west Texas. Smith's force of 300 Rebels won a surprising victory at Palmito Ranch over more than 800 Union soldiers under Theodore Barrett. Smith's men disbanded after hearing that Richmond had been taken, but Smith refused to give up the fight and went to Houston to rally more troops. His plan never panned out, however, because General Simon Buckner, acting in Smith's name, surrendered the Trans-Mississippi Department in New Orleans on May 25.

Finally, there was Stand Watie, leader of the Cherokee Nation and commander of the largest Native American force in the Confederate army. Watie continued to wage war against the North until he was finally convinced to surrender to Lieutenant Colonel Asa C. Matthews on June 23, 1865.

CHAPTER 13

War off the Battlefield

The battles of the Civil War may be the most memorable images of the struggle, but there was more to the war than massed lines of hundreds of thousands of infantry. Important naval battles along the Confederacy's rivers and coastal waters were hugely important in the outcome of the Civil War. And because the Confederacy was so vast, guerrilla actions by Southerners—uniformed and not—harassed Northern forces. Confederates also worked to carry out sabotage in Northern cities.

Naval Warfare Begins

The navies of the two opposing sides were not ready for an intense or protracted war, but they adapted fast. Previous naval wars were waged among sailing ships. Both sides quickly realized that the most effective ships would be steam powered and that for protection from shot and shell they would need thick hulls of iron, now in more abundance than in previous ages. Ironclad gunboats suitable for warfare on rivers rather than on oceans soon appeared. Yet along the coasts and against the Confederate ports, Union sailing ships composed most of the fighting fleets, and Southerners relied on swift sailing ships to rush supplies in through the blockade.

The Union Blockade

The first naval involvement of the war was a blockade of Southern ports, which was ordered by President Lincoln within days of the attack on Fort Sumter. Lincoln believed a blockade would strangle the new republic's ability to do business with foreign powers and thus force it toward a quick peace. But while Lincoln's intentions may have been good, the U.S. Navy's ability to carry out the plan was not.

USS *St Louis*, an ironclad gunboat *Photo courtesy of the National Archives (165-C-630)*

At the onset of the war, the U.S. Navy's fleet was in shambles. It had only ninety ships, and most of them were obsolete. In fact, when Lincoln first called for a blockade, only three ships were available for immediate duty to cover more than 3,500 miles of Southern coastline. In addition, the majority of Union navy personnel were spread across the world and unavailable for immediate service; of those that were available, nearly 10 percent resigned their commission to join the Confederacy. As a result, Confederate blockade runners, which were typically painted gray to avoid detection, came and went with impunity for the first couple of years of the war.

The Union blockade became more effective as the war progressed. In 1861, at the beginning of the war, only one in ten blockade runners was captured. By 1864, that number had risen to one in three.

Some Southern ports were close-blockaded and attacked by a combination of army and navy forces. Out at sea, a cruising blockade was often established in international waters, along well-traveled sea lanes, and in neutral ports. Not surprisingly, the Confederate government balked at these blockades, calling them a violation of international law. But the Union found them effective.

As the war progressed the U.S. Navy also patrolled inland waterways such as rivers and bays, often assisting army forces in penetrating Confederate defenses, especially along the Mississippi River. More than once, naval forces played an important role in deciding the outcome of a land battle. Prime examples are the battles for Forts Henry and Donelson and the battle for Vicksburg. Even at Shiloh, Federal gunboats shelled Confederate infantry charges on the evening of the first day, helping to stave off a near Southern victory.

The role of the U.S. Navy in the Civil War cannot be underestimated. Many people tend to forget that the navy was even involved in the conflict, but history shows that it played a decisive role. Abraham Lincoln noted during a tribute to Union servicemen late in the war, "It is hard to say that anything has been more bravely, and well done, than at Antietam, Murfreesboro,

Gettysburg, and on many a field of lesser note. Nor must Uncle Sam's web-feet be forgotten. At all the watery margins they have been present. Not only on the deep sea, the broad bay, and the rapid river, but also up the narrow muddy bayou, and wherever the ground was a little damp. Thanks to all. For the great republic—for the principles it lives by, and keeps alive—for man's vast future—thanks to all."

Beginnings of the Confederate Navy

The Union navy may have been less than adequate at the onset of the war, but even with its many faults, it was still superior to the Confederate navy. Stephen Mallory, Confederate secretary of the navy, described the Confederate navy in 1861 as consisting only of an unfurnished room in Montgomery, Alabama, in which naval policy was formed. However, under Mallory, the Confederate navy quickly made up for its deficiencies and soon proved a viable threat to the Union war effort. It's estimated that one-sixth of Confederate naval officers came from the North at the beginning of the war, among them navigator Matthew Fontaine Maury and Franklin Buchanan, former commandant of the Washington Navy Yard.

FACT

Despite a less-developed maritime tradition and a smaller iron industry, the Confederacy developed a workable submarine. The *H. L. Hunley* was the first submarine to sink an enemy warship, a feat it carried out in February 1864, at Charleston, South Carolina. The *Hunley* sank in the attack and Confederate submarine warfare was over.

The Confederate naval forces consisted primarily of two types: commerce destroyers (modeled after the piratelike privateers that preyed on British merchant ships during the Revolutionary War and the War of 1812) and ironclad ships that were used almost exclusively to protect rivers and ports. Although they lacked an industrial base or the same sort of naval traditions of New England, Southerners did astonishingly well with making warships and putting up a naval response to the Union blockade and naval assaults.

The Monitor Versus the Merrimac

One of the best known naval battles during the Civil War is the duel between the Union ironclad *Monitor* and the Confederate ironclad *Virginia*, formerly the USS *Merrimac*, on March 9, 1862.

The Confederacy dredged up the *Merrimac*, which had been torched and scuttled by Union forces when the Confederacy took control of the Norfolk shipyards, and turned it into the first ironclad vessel built on American soil. News of the venture quickly reached Union officials, who immediately approved the development of ironclads for the Union navy. The first to be constructed (in a remarkable 101 days) was the *Monitor*. Like the *Virginia*, the *Monitor* was protected by four-inch steel plates. However, it had two guns on a revolving turret, which provided more accurate firepower. It also was smaller, faster, and more maneuverable than the *Virginia*.

According to *Civil War Day by Day*, the U.S. Navy had ninety ships at the beginning of the war. During the war it built 208 and bought 418 more. The Confederates had no ships but managed to buy, convert, or build about 500 vessels of all sorts for use during the war.

The *Virginia* sailed into Chesapeake Bay on March 5 and headed for Hampton Roads, a major Union blockading base. Around 1 P.M. on March 8, the ship confronted five wooden Union ships, which didn't know what to make of the bizarre vessel facing them. They fired all they had at the partially submerged craft but quickly found that their shells had little impact. The *Virginia* immediately set about its task, ramming and sinking the *Cumberland*, one of the Union's most impressive frigates; grounding and burning the fifty-gun *Congress*; and knocking the flagship *Minnesota* out of commission. The only damage to the ironclad was a broken ram and injuries to its captain, Franklin Buchanan.

The USS *Monitor* steamed to the rescue, though it almost didn't make it. The ship nearly sank as it sailed ponderously to Hampton Roads, arriving around 1 A.M. on March 9. Officials in Washington feared the Union ironclad would be no match for the *Virginia*, but the *Monitor* soon proved otherwise. The two ships faced off, just 100 yards apart, at 9 A.M. on March 9 and began pounding each other with all they had. Shells bounced off their iron skins, and the two ships collided several times, sometimes by accident and sometimes not. The furious duel lasted four hours, with neither ship gaining an advantage. The *Monitor* finally drew back when its captain, John L. Worden, was temporarily blinded by a shell blast, and the *Virginia*, which was slowly taking on water and experiencing engine difficulties, took that as its cue to withdraw. The battle ended in a draw, though it could be said that the Union was the real victor because its blockade of Hampton Roads survived.

Once McClellan began marching his Union troops up the peninsula between the York and James rivers to start the Peninsular Campaign, the *Virginia* was doomed. It could not go far up the James River to help defend Richmond because the water was too shallow, and it could not steam out to the ocean because it was too unseaworthy for the open ocean. The Confederates blew the *Virginia* up on May 11 to keep it from falling into Union hands.

Island No. 10

After Grant's army and Foote's navy had captured Forts Henry and Donelson on the Tennessee and Columbia rivers for the Union in February 1862, the Confederates abandoned their stronghold of Columbus, Kentucky, on the Mississippi because it was too far north to be supplied. They moved Columbus's guns south to near the Tennessee state line and mounted most of them on a two-mile long spit in the river called Island No. 10 to halt any Union advance along the waterway.

The barrier was prodigious. Island No. 10 was at the bottom of a huge bend in the river. The Mississippi flows west at Island No. 10, then north for several miles, then west again at the settlement of New Madrid, then south again. The Confederates placed most of their guns on Island No. 10 with a bunch at New Madrid for good measure. When Foote saw the strength of the position, he stopped up short and wouldn't let any of his gunboats forward.

Sending Reinforcements

But the Federals were determined to continue their drive downriver. They sent a small army under John Pope to work in tandem with Foote. Pope captured New Madrid, but from there he could do nothing. He had to cross the mile-wide river to cut the supply line to Island No. 10, and he could not cross because he had neither the transports nor the gunboats to protect transports.

Although the naval war is often overlooked, there was a naval action at sea almost every day of the war. Blockade runners sought to evade Union blockading ships, and chases and captures kept the Union navy busy. *Civil War Day by Day* places the number of attempted violations of the blockade at 8,200.

The transport problem was solved by clever engineers and the grueling labor of 600 soldiers. Upriver of Island No. 10 they cut a canal through swampy and flooded forest to the top of the river loop near New Madrid. The Federals floated transports along the new canal to New Madrid, but the gunboats needed deeper water; at least one would have to run past the guns of Island No. 10.

Commander Henry Walke, captain of the gunboat *Carondelet*, won permission to try to make a run. In preparation, he strapped bales of hay to the *Carondelet*'s port side and muffled the exhaust lines of his engines. In the darkness of April 4, he made his attempt and made it safely to the Union sanctuary at New Madrid, the bales of hay shot up but otherwise in good shape.

Pope could then move enough of his men in relative safety to the eastern shore of the river. Again the Confederates were forced to give up a river fortress, this on the day after Grant's success at Shiloh. And again, a large segment of the Mississippi River fell to the control of the Federals; most of the way to Memphis now lay open.

The Battle of New Orleans

In the spring of 1862, the Union looked toward New Orleans, the largest city in the Confederacy. Military actions in other regions had left the city lightly defended. Its greatest protection from Union invasion came from Fort Jackson and Fort St. Philip, which guarded the water approach seventy-five miles downriver. Both forts were heavily fortified and armed with large cannons; a barricade of sunken ships in the river itself forced approaching craft to stop directly in front of their line of fire. Such a defense seemed insurmountable, and Confederate leaders were confident the two forts could hold off any naval assault the Union might attempt.

But Union military leaders thought otherwise. Naval commander David Porter believed a strong mortar attack from boats on the river could disable the forts' firepower and allow a fleet to pass all the way to New Orleans, and such an attack was readied in early 1862.

To facilitate the invasion, Union general Benjamin Butler captured Ship Island, near the mouth of the Mississippi. The Union's ships were renovated to make them lighter so that they could pass over the river's many sandbars, and the fleet began its long trip up the Mississippi in April, supported by Butler's 15,000 troops for a possible land invasion.

Attacking the Forts

On April 18, Porter began a six-day mortar attack. His nineteen mortar ships lobbed more than 3,000 shells at the forts each day, but they did little damage to the forts' defenses. The bombardment did act as a distraction, and on the night of April 20, two Union gunboats approached the river barricade and cleared a small path for the rest of the fleet.

Squadron captain David Farragut ordered his fleet to proceed, hopeful that enough ships would survive to invade the city of New Orleans. The fleet began the treacherous run under cover of darkness early on the morning of April 24 and was quickly met with cannon fire, which they returned. Confederate officers tried to halt the invasion by sending out a small fleet of wooden ships to ram the approaching Union vessels. Several rafts that had been set on fire were deployed in an attempt to slow the advance.

Farragut's flagship was damaged during the attack, but its crew quickly brought it back into the fray as the Union fleet sank or disabled most of the Confederate ships. All but four of Farragut's fleet made it safely past the supposedly impassable Confederate forts.

Farragut sailed into New Orleans on April 25 and captured the city with little resistance, though the mayor of the city refused to officially surrender. The soldiers manning Forts Jackson and St. Philip laid down their guns on April 28, and Butler and his troops arrived the next day.

FACT

The residents of New Orleans weren't particularly happy about the Union occupation of their city. To show her disapproval, one woman dumped the contents of a chamber pot on the head of David Farragut.

Farragut's bold attack on New Orleans placed the city and its port under Union command, a striking defeat for the Confederacy. By taking New Orleans, located 100 miles above the mouth of the Mississippi River, the Union effectively controlled the very gateway to the Deep South.

The Battle of Memphis

After the bloodless victory at Corinth, Mississippi, in late May, the Union army turned its attention to Memphis, Tennessee, the Confederacy's fifth largest city and a key port along the Mississippi River. But before Henry Halleck had a chance to invade, the city fell during one of the war's most impressive naval engagements.

Steaming past Island No. 10, the Union army and navy confronted Fort Pillow fifty miles above Memphis. It was armed with forty guns, and Confederates had hedged their bets with a fleet of eight steamboats converted into armed rams, a throwback to the days of the Roman galley. These rams surprised the Union fleet with a hit-and-run attack at Plum Run Bend, located just above Fort Pillow, and disabled two Union ironclads by punching holes in them just below the waterline.

The Union navy vowed never to be caught unprepared again and fitted several steamboats of its own with sturdy rams. The brains behind the operation was Charles Ellet, a fifty-seven-year-old civil engineer from Pennsylvania who, having failed to convince the Union navy of the value of ram power, found a believer in Secretary of War Stanton. Ellet supervised the construction of nine steamboats, developing his own calculations for maximum strength. Ellet commanded the fleet's flagship and placed eight relatives aboard the others.

Ellet was eager to take on the Confederate fleet at Fort Pillow, but his plans changed when Confederate general Beauregard ordered the fort's evacuation; Beauregard had determined the location was too far north with Corinth in the hands of the Federals. Instead, the Confederates decided to make a stand at Memphis, and early on June 6, the Southern ram fleet sailed out to take on five Union ironclads and four of Ellet's self-designed ram ships. Thousands of Memphis residents lined the bluffs above the river to cheer the Rebels.

"We propose a powerful movement down the Mississippi to the ocean, with a cordon of posts . . . the object being to clear out . . . this great line of communication in connection with the strict blockade of the seaboard, so as to envelop the insurgent States and bring them to terms with less bloodshed than by any other plan."—Winfield Scott, in a letter describing the Anaconda Plan to General George B. McClellan

There turned out to be little for them to cheer about. It took the Union ships less than two hours to reduce the Confederate vessels to driftwood. Only one Confederate boat escaped the battle. It was a devastating defeat for the Confederate river force, and it opened the door for the Union to capture Memphis. The residents who had so loudly cheered during the early minutes of the river battle stood silent as a four-man detachment led by Ellet's son, Charles Ellet Jr., raised the American flag over the Memphis post office. Charles Ellet Sr. was wounded in the fighting and died two weeks later. Charles Ellet Jr. was promoted to colonel—at nineteen, he was the youngest person to hold that rank—and took command of his father's ram fleet. He was killed in combat a year later.

The Battle of Mobile Bay

Alabama's Mobile Bay became increasingly important to the Confederacy as the war progressed. The Union blockade had effectively closed other ports, but Mobile Bay was still relatively free, making it the only open Gulf port east of Texas and the primary site for the smuggling of arms and provisions from Europe. David Farragut, promoted in July 1862 to rear admiral, wanted to launch an assault on the port immediately following his success at New Orleans in April 1862, but circumstances forced him to wait until January 1864 to begin preparations, though the attack itself wouldn't come for another seven months.

When the time came, however, Farragut had an impressive fleet behind him: fourteen wooden boats and four ironclads. He began the assault early on the morning of August 5, easing the fleet into the bay, which was heavily mined with explosives, known as torpedoes. The fleet was met by heavy Confederate gunfire from Fort Morgan, the bay's main defense, as well as a Confederate fleet of three wooden gunboats and the South's largest ironclad, the CSS *Tennessee*, led by Confederate admiral Franklin Buchanan.

FACT

Admiral Franklin Buchanan, commanding the Confederate naval forces at Mobile Bay from his flagship the CSS *Tennessee*, had been the first superintendent of the Naval Academy in Annapolis. He felt naval tradition dictated that he keep the fight going as long as his ship could fight. He ordered it out against overwhelming odds and fought until it could neither fire nor steer.

As the battle commenced, Farragut tied himself high in the rigging of his flagship, the *Hartford*, so that he could better direct his ships. From his perch, he watched his lead ironclad, the *Tecumseh*, strike a mine and sink with almost all hands in a matter of minutes. The rest of Farragut's ships stopped where they were, confused and fearful of other mines, as the cannons at Fort Morgan continued to roar. It was then that Farragut shouted the rallying words for which he is still remembered today: "Damn the torpedoes! Full speed ahead!" Moving the *Hartford* out in front, Farragut successfully led the rest of his fleet through the minefield and past the fort into Mobile Bay.

The *Tennessee*, commanded by Buchanan himself, tried to ram the Union ships, then engaged in a gun battle with them before slinking off to safe harbor at Fort Morgan. The Union crews took that quiet moment to have a quick breakfast, only to have their meal interrupted by the *Tennessee*, which returned for another attack. The Confederate ironclad was a formidable ship, but Buchanan soon found himself surrounded by Union vessels, which rammed and fired upon his ship until it was a helpless hulk. Buchanan was injured during the battle and his ship surrendered. In just four hours, Mobile Bay had come under Union control. Fort Morgan, however, was not captured until August 23, and the city of Mobile would remain in Confederate hands until the end of the following April.

Sabotage and Far-Fetched Plots

With the war turning badly for the Confederates in the autumn of 1864, some of them turned to desperate measures, including sabotage in Northern cities.

St. Albans Raid

Twenty raiders from Canada descended on the town of St. Albans, Vermont, fifteen miles south of the border on Lake Champlain. Escaped or exchanged prisoners, these men had organized in Canada and slipped into St. Albans by twos and threes, checking into various boarding houses. In the afternoon of October 19, 1864, they assembled in the town square, removed their topcoats to reveal Confederate uniforms, and announced they were seizing the town. They took $200,000 from the town's three banks before the townspeople began shooting at them. One townsman was killed and three Confederates wounded before the Southerners fled north again into

Canada with their loot. The money never reached Richmond to shore up the war effort; instead, it was used to plot further mischief against the Yankee north.

Saboteurs in New York City

Another group of Confederates operating out of Canada converged on New York City in November. Their plan was also economic of a sort: burn the city down or at least damage it enough to hurt the Northern economy. The conspirators checked into twenty hotels and set their rooms on fire on November 25. Some also set fire to a celebrated New York landmark, Barnum's Museum. The hotel fires did not work well, and local firefighters put them out with little trouble. The fire at Barnum's was more spectacular but was also brought under control. All but one of the saboteurs escaped.

General John Mosby raided Fairfax, Virginia, in March 1863 and caught Union general Edwin Stoughton in his headquarters sleeping. He spanked the Vermonter awake and asked "General, have you ever heard of Mosby?" "Yes," said Stoughton groggily. "Have you caught him?" "No," Mosby said. "He has caught you."

The Plot to Capture the USS Michigan

Another plot involved capturing vessels on Lake Erie, including the U.S. Navy's only warship there. The USS *Michigan* was guarding Southern prisoners on Johnson Island in Sandusky Bay of Lake Erie. Confederate officers organized a team that was to overpower small vessels, then overwhelm the *Michigan* and free thousands of prisoners. The Confederates were then to sail to Cleveland and Buffalo, exacting tribute before escaping to Canada. The band did indeed capture smaller vessels on the lake in late September but could not make an organized attempt on the *Michigan*, which in any event had been forewarned.

Guerilla Warfare

Not surprisingly in an area of land as large as the Confederacy, Union armies left their supply lines vulnerable to rebel sympathizers the further they moved into enemy territory. Guerilla soldiers of the Confederate armies and informal partisan bands of men posed a threat to the Union's supply lines. The more formal bands attacked Union supply depots, garrisons, and the like, hoping to improve Southern military prospects. Some were quite effective. Nathan Bedford Forrest often worked behind Union army lines in guerilla-like raids through Tennessee, Mississippi, and Kentucky.

In Virginia, a notable guerilla leader was John Mosby. Early in the war, Mosby was a cavalry leader attached to larger units, but he later operated behind Union lines in northern Virginia as the Forty-third Virginia Battalion. Northern Virginia was ripe for guerilla warfare because tremendous supplies passed through it to the Army of the Potomac to any Union armies near or in the Shenandoah Valley. Mosby became known as the "Grey Ghost" for his hit-and-run tactics. He was never captured.

CHAPTER 14

The War in the West and Other Places

Much of the national memory of the Civil War centers on the battles between the Army of the Potomac and the Army of Northern Virginia. In part, this has to do with noted writers Bruce Catton and Douglas S. Freeman, who concentrated on the war in Virginia. In his trilogy *The Civil War: A Narrative*, Shelby Foote redirected attention to the struggle outside Virginia, especially Tennessee, Mississippi, and Georgia. But the war was fought in thousands of locations, including New Mexico Territory and even the Arctic Ocean.

14

The War in Kansas, Missouri, and Arkansas

Missouri was vital to the Union cause. If it went to the Confederacy and became an active Confederate area, Union forces would not have been able to move down the Mississippi. In order to hold Missouri for the Union, Kansas had to be protected. Once Missouri was more or less secure, the Union had to press large Southern forces out of Arkansas. The Union managed to do all of these things, but it took a great deal of time and effort, and Kansas, Missouri, and Arkansas were never entirely free of Southern influence and forces.

Kansas

Kansas was the scene of fighting even before the Civil War broke out in 1861. Having been a territory that would be admitted to the Union based on popular sovereignty, that is, how many of its enfranchised population voted to have the state admitted as a slave or free state, both Northerners and Southerners raced to the region in the 1850s to bolster support for their respective views. Fighting broke out between groups of the opposing ideologies, and the territory became known as "Bleeding Kansas." Roving fighters were not averse to mayhem and murder.

Charles Francis Adams, the U.S. minister to England, with the help of the able Secretary of State William H. Seward, did much to prevent England and other European powers from recognizing and aiding the Confederacy.

The most notorious partisan raid was carried out by a band led by William Quantrill against the town of Lawrence. Quantrill led his guerillas into Lawrence to avenge the deaths of Missourians imprisoned by Federal authorities; a jail roof had collapsed, killing a number of women. Before Quantrill's men left, much of the town was destroyed and more than 150 men and boys lay dead.

A month and a half later, Quantrill's Raiders fought elements of a Union force near Baxter Springs near the southeast corner of the state. The partisan group of 400 defeated the Union men, then rode on south to spend the winter in Texas.

The only battle in Kansas between regular Confederate and Union forces took place at Mine Creek in October 1864. This was during the Sterling Price raid up through Missouri and continued while Price was attempting to return to Arkansas. Union cavalry under Alfred Pleasonton defeated Price, who continued his retreat southward.

Missouri

Missouri suffered the same sort of partisan warfare as Kansas, though it did not see as much violence before the war began. Missouri was a slave state, but there was considerable sentiment to stay in the Union. The governor at the time Fort Sumter was attacked was pro-Confederacy, but the legislature was not inclined to secede. A stalemate ensued between pro-Northern and pro-Southern troops in and around St. Louis.

FACT

Jesse James and his brother Frank began their lives of violence as Confederate guerillas during the Civil War. Under the command of partisan leader William Quantrill, they roamed Missouri, wreaking havoc on Union forces and Northern sympathizers. Quantrill was killed late in the war, and the James brothers set out with the Younger brothers for a life of crime after the war ended.

Washington sent a feisty soldier named Nathaniel S. Lyon to command the Union troops. In May, Lyon broke up the pro-Southern militia but then got into a fight marching back into St. Louis; twenty-eight civilians were killed, but Missouri stayed in the Union despite its status as a slave state.

Lyon then marched his men into southwest Missouri, the stronghold of Southern sentiment. At Wilson's Creek on August 10, 1861, Lyon fought a Confederate force under Sterling Price and Benjamin McCulloch. Lyon was killed in the hard-fought battle and the Federals were repulsed. But the Rebels could not make much of their victory, and the state was not threatened with a Southern advance. General John Fremont, in command of the

Federals in the region, secured the Union gains, along with the vital town of Cairo, where the Ohio and Mississippi rivers join. From this time, Missouri fell into guerilla and partisan warfare. The fighting was often vicious, and neighbors found themselves on opposing sides. In late 1863, Confederate cavalry leader Joseph O. "Jo" Shelby led a raid of 600 men out of Arkansas as far north as the Missouri River and back again.

In 1864, long after Vicksburg had fallen to the Federals, Sterling Price headed north into Missouri with 12,000 Confederate horsemen. At first, not many Union forces were arrayed against Price's small army, and it battled garrisons on its way to St. Louis, hoping to seize war materiel there. But Federals along the Mississippi who were meant to be transferred to Sherman in Georgia were instead ordered to St. Louis, and Price had to bypass the city. He then headed west, and two Federal columns set out to crush the little Southern army. The result was the Battle of Westport on October 23 near Kansas City. This was the largest battle in the Missouri; about 30,000 men engaged. Price avoided destruction, then took his army south again. The two forces fought again two days later near Mine Creek, Kansas, and a few days after that at Newtonia, Missouri, before Price took his men back into southern Arkansas.

Arkansas

Like Virginia, Arkansas seceded from the Union only after Fort Sumter demonstrated that the North was not going to let the South go without a fight. In early 1862, Confederate general Earl Van Dorn, using McCulloch and Price's troops, attempted to defeat the Union army that had advanced into Arkansas from Springfield, Missouri, to the north. The result was the Battle of Pea Ridge or Elk Horn Tavern, the largest battle west of the Mississippi. Van Dorn's men included many Cherokee and Creek Indians, and the fierce battle raged for two days before the Union men defeated the Southerners. The battle ensured Missouri would be safe from large Southern armies and helped open the way for the Union advances on Memphis and Vicksburg. Van Dorn's men were sent east to help with campaigns in Mississippi and Tennessee and, as in Missouri, the war in Arkansas fell to irregulars. Northern troops occupied the capital of Little Rock a few months after Grant took Vicksburg in 1863.

The War in Texas

Texas joined the Confederacy in March 1861 and was its largest state. Texas was an important asset; it had cotton plantations and controlled the Gulf Coast ports through which cotton was exported. The Confederacy also counted on Texas for its fighting men, and the state responded by sending thousands of able-bodied males to Confederate armies further east. Besides dozens of regiments, Texas also sent General Albert Sydney Johnston, who eventually commanded the western theater of the war and was killed at Shiloh in 1862, and John B. Hood, whose Texas Brigade became famous in eastern battles. Hood became one of Robert E. Lee's hardest hitting division commanders. He and his men fought with distinction at Antietam and Gettysburg, among other battles. Hood was eventually given command of the Army of Tennessee and tried to defeat Sherman's army around Atlanta in 1864. Hood went on to lead the army at the battles of Franklin and Nashville.

"Who are you, my boys?" General Robert E. Lee asked of troops coming up to plug a critical gap in the line during the 1864 Battle of the Wilderness. "Texas boys!" they shouted. "Hurray for Texas," Lee shouted back. "Texans always move them. Hurray for Texas!"

The most important Gulf Coast ports in Texas were Galveston and Sabine Pass. The Union navy attacked and occupied Galveston in October 1862. Confederate general John Bankhead Magruder led a combined land and naval attack against the occupying forces on January 1, 1863. He fashioned what he called cotton-clads, steamboats protected with bales of cotton to absorb the shock of cannon balls. These descended on the Yankee ships while Magruder's infantry rushed the Federals on land.

The Federals again attempted an invasion of Texas in September 1863 and instigated an astonishing battle, one Jefferson Davis likened to Thermopylae. The Federals mounted an invasion force of 5,000 from New Orleans and aimed at Sabine Pass, defended by Lt. Dick Dowling and forty-seven men. The idea was to push aside the small force at Sabine Pass, march on

Beaumont and Houston, and then swing down and pick up Galveston. But Dowling used his men and armaments to good effect. His cannons disabled the first two Federal ships that entered Sabine Pass. The other ships retreated while the Confederates captured the crews of the first two—more than 300 men—and all their armaments.

Later in the war, Northern troops under General Banks out of New Orleans occupied Brownsville and surrounding areas. The point was less to injure Confederate Texas than to demonstrate to the French in Mexico that they should not attempt to aid the Confederacy.

Texan residents generally supported the Confederate government during the war, but planters were upset when they were asked to withhold their cotton for exporting. By 1863 and 1864, many Texans were angry at the martial law imposed by the Confederate government, the harsh conscription laws, and perceived infringements of local rights.

War in Florida

At the outbreak of war, Florida had only been part of the Union for fourteen years. Moreover, it was a largely unsettled frontier state. Its population was only about 140,000, half of whom were African-American slaves working on agricultural plantations. Much of the political and economic power rested in the hands of large planters, who agreed politically with the planter class throughout the South. Florida became the third state to secede after the election of Abraham Lincoln. Federal soldiers held onto Fort Pickens in Pensacola Bay, though Southern forces surrounded it and demanded its surrender. The Civil War could have begun here rather than at Fort Sumter, but by agreement the North did not reinforce the garrison there and the Confederates did not attack it. Months later, so many Florida troops were sent north to help with the Confederate armies that Fort Pickens remained in Union hands. The transfer of native Florida troops to Confederate forces further north weakened the ability of Florida to defend its immense coastline, and Union forces seized towns and cities along the northeast coast, Jacksonville among them.

Florida was important to the Confederacy for its cattle, fish, fruit, and salt, the latter to preserve food for the armies' long marches and encampments. Florida's principal ports—Jacksonville, Pensacola, and Key West—were blockaded by the Union navy, but blockade runners slipped through to beaches and inlets on Florida's long coast line to deliver supplies for the Southern states.

Approximately 14,000 Floridians fought for the Confederacy, and about 2,000 fought for the Union. About 5,000 Floridian soldiers died during the war. The Battle of Olustee in northern Florida was one of the bloodiest Civil War battles in terms of the percentage of casualties; 3,000 of the 10,000 were dead, wounded, or missing by the battle's end.

In June 1862, the Union attempted to capture Tampa. Gunboats sailed into the bay, but a force of Confederates refused to surrender or retreat. The gunboats held off for a while so civilians could flee, then opened fire. But the Southerners still would not yield, and the Union forces abandoned their attempt to capture the town.

Eager to disrupt the supply lines of food moving north and bring Florida back into closer relation with the Union, an expedition of 5,000 Federal troops were sent from Jacksonville west into the interior toward Lake City in 1864. The advancing Union army had a large contingent of African Americans, and they were looking for others in the interior of the state to swell their ranks. Confederate general Joseph Finegan blocked the way to Lake City near Olustee with 5,100 militia. The ensuing battle was won by the Southerners, and the Union men retreated toward Jacksonville again. After the Battle of Olustee, Florida was relatively quiet for the remainder of the war.

War in the Far West

From the beginning, the Confederacy had wanted to expand west. In his prewar days, Jefferson Davis had helped engineer the Gadsen Purchase of southern Arizona and New Mexico. In California lay gold, a rich treasure for any country, and its ports promised trade with Asia. With these in their hands, the Confederacy might gain control of northern Mexico. Between California and the Confederate state of Texas lay the New Mexico Territory. To link the Confederate states to the Pacific meant securing this territory, and a Confederate named Henry Sibley tried to do just this.

A good deal of Federal supplies and some of its forts along the Rio Grande had fallen into Confederate hands after Fort Sumter, so the Southerners had a good jump on their expedition into the New Mexico Territory. They started off from El Paso and marched up the Rio Grande. They fought a battle at Valverde near Fort Craig on February 21, 1862, against a Federal garrison under Edward Canby. The struggle did not slow the Southerners appreciably, and they continued north to Albuquerque and then Santa Fe. But by early March they found these cities barren of the supplies they had counted on seizing; Canby had sent orders ahead to burn anything the Confederates could use.

FACT

Both the North and the South relied on Native Americans. The Confederacy wanted to enlist Native Americans both to help man its armies and to help defend Texas from invasion from Kansas. Many Indians remained neutral; others hoped to take advantage of the Union's distraction back east to reclaim land in the west, and some enlisted with Confederate forces.

The Federal stronghold near Santa Fe was Fort Union. Sibley believed that soon its garrison would come out to fight them, and it did in late March. First it lured a portion of Sibley's men into an ambush. Then the Federals defeated Sibley's little army in the Battle of Glorieta Pass on March 28. Sibley was out of supplies and didn't feel welcome by the civilians. His only good option was to retreat back down the Rio Grande to Texas. This he did, and Confederate hopes of reaching through New Mexico to California were never revived.

War on the Atlantic and Pacific

The Civil War actually reached as far as the Bering Sea and Arctic Ocean, and warships pursued and confronted each other through both the North and South Atlantic. Southerners conspired to have British shipbuilding yards construct fast ships, ostensibly for sale to European owners, only to refit them as warships for the Confederacy. Northern diplomats complained vociferously, sometimes with effect, sometimes not. In any event, several Confederate commerce raiders escaped into the world's oceans. They were generally commanded by Southern officers but manned by men from many countries in search of adventure and reward.

The devastation caused by the Confederate commerce raiders was so great that it was a source of contention between the United States and Great Britain after the war. The United States sued Britain for billions of dollars lost, contesting Britain's actions prolonged the war, increased insurance rates, and caused other damages. The two countries settled in 1871 after an international tribunal awarded the United States more than $15 million in damages.

The Alabama

Built in British shipbuilding yards and launched under the fictitious name of *Enrica*, the CSS *Alabama* received its Confederate navy commission in August 1862. It was a 1,050-ton steam-powered sloop that set out under the command of wax-tipped mustached Captain Raphael Semmes. The *Alabama* attacked merchantmen plying the Atlantic between Europe and America. By the end of the year it had captured more than a score of Union merchant ships, burning most after taking what treasure it could.

In all, the *Alabama* took more than sixty ships.

When the *Alabama* returned to Europe for repairs in June 1864, a Union warship, *Kearsarge*, fitted with iron chain beneath an overlay of wood, sank the *Alabama* in a shootout that lasted only ninety minutes.

The Florida

Originally named the *Oreto,* the CSS *Florida* was ordered by Confederate agent James Bulloch, the maternal uncle of future U.S. president Theodore Roosevelt. The *Florida* was able to make it out of England after Bulloch provided forged papers showing that the ship was owned by a merchant of Palermo. The ship was put to sea unarmed in March 1862 (its heavy guns following on another vessel), then set out on a two-year career that saw the capture of more than fifty ships, mainly in the North and South Atlantic. Together, the *Florida* and the *Alabama* made the Union's northern Atlantic commerce quite perilous.

FACT

The *Shenandoah* was launched toward the end of the war in October 1864. It weighed 1,160 tons and could sail at an average speed of thirteen knots. It took nearly 1,000 prisoners during its around-the-world raid without a single battle death, though two men died of disease.

During the fall of 1864, the USS *Wachusett* heard that the *Florida* was en route to Brazil and set out in pursuit. It found the Confederate raider in the Brazilian harbor of Bahia, a neutral port. No action was supposed to be taken against a warship in a neutral port, but the *Wachusett* captain Napoleon Collins steamed his warship into the port and rammed the Confederate vessel when its captain and half of its crew were enjoying a night ashore in a hotel. The *Wachusett* then towed the *Florida* out of the harbor under gunfire from the Brazilians. The *Wachusett* took the *Florida* to Norfolk where the commerce raider sunk under mysterious circumstances. Collins was court-martialed, but the Secretary of the Navy set aside the sentence and Collins eventually went on to become an admiral.

The Shenandoah

Like its two famous predecessors, the *Alabama* and the *Florida*, the *Shenandoah* was built in Britain under a surreptitious name. Instead, it sailed to the Madeira Islands, where it was fitted with guns and rechristened the CSS *Shenandoah*. Under the command of Captain James Waddell, it struck out on a career of attempting to ruin Northern finances by disrupting its merchant fleet. In particular, the *Shenandoah* was meant to disrupt the New England whaling fleet, a key support to the Northern economy. It had a hull of iron and was steam powered, though its propeller could be lifted out of the water if coal was low or its sails could send it more swiftly through the waves.

The *Shenandoah* set out for the Indian Ocean, taking prizes in the South Atlantic as it went. It reached Australia in January 1865, then cruised north in search of New England whalers. The *Shenandoah* found a good many of them in the Bering Sea and Arctic Ocean, once seizing and sinking eleven ships in less than half a day.

The crew of the *Shenandoah* discovered that the Confederacy had collapsed when it was off the west coast of America and decided to make a run for England rather than surrender to a Northern warship. It made the voyage without mishap and surrendered to British authorities in November 1865.

The "War" in Europe

When the Southern states left the Union, their leaders hoped the Confederacy would quickly be recognized as an independent republic by the major foreign powers—England, France, and Russia. Such recognition would add strength to its legal claim of independence, as well as provide much needed financial and weapons support for the war with the North. However, the issue was not an easy one to settle. England and France had defeated Russia in the Crimean War, and both would have been ecstatic at the fall of the United States government. Russia, on the other hand, needed the United States as an ally to help control its European enemies.

"There is no doubt the South has made an army. They are making, it appears, a navy. And they have made . . . a nation."—British Chancellor of the Exchequeur William Gladstone, October 1862; his remarks caused an uproar in the Union, which was afraid Britain would officially recognize the Confederacy

Shortly after the fall of Fort Sumter, England's Queen Victoria declared her nation neutral in the conflict but acknowledged the Confederacy as a belligerent nation, which meant it could buy arms from neutral nations and capture merchant and military vessels. Confederate leaders had hoped for more concrete recognition but accepted the status in the hope that full recognition would come later. The Lincoln administration, on the other hand, viewed England's neutrality as a hostile act and expressed its displeasure.

The Union had expected that England would disavow the Confederacy, specifically over the issue of slavery, which most Britons considered a loathsome institution. But while the British government acknowledged its disgust over the Confederacy's continued use of slaves, it ultimately decided on a position of neutrality primarily for financial reasons—British textile manufacturers were dependent on Southern cotton.

Particularly adept at garnering Southern sympathy among the British was Henry Hotze, a Swiss-born Alabamian and talented propagandist who worked ceaselessly to sway British opinion regarding the Confederacy. Hotze sweet-talked his way into the British social elite and wrote pro-Confederate editorials for a number of British newspapers. Hotze told liberals that the South was fighting for its right to self-determination, and he told conservatives that the South's ruling class was defending its liberties against a greedy Union government. British businessmen were courted with the promise that the Confederacy would open its ports to free trade without protective tariffs.

Building Blockade Runners

Much to the Union's anger, England's neutral position meant that it could still aid the Confederacy in a number of ways. One of the most damaging to the Union war effort was British production of Confederate blockade runners and warships, particularly in Liverpool, where Southern sympathies ran high. Technically speaking, the construction of these ships violated Britain's Foreign Enlistment Act, which forbade the construction and arming of warships in British territory for a belligerent power, but the South and its British sympathizers found a number of helpful loopholes.

The Trent Affair

On the night of October 11, 1861, a Confederate blockade runner slipped out of Charleston Harbor. Its mission was to transport James Mason, the Confederacy's envoy, to England, and John Slidell, Mason's associate, to London and Paris to discuss the issue of Confederate recognition.

Arriving in Havana, Cuba, the two men transferred to the *Trent,* a British mail steamer bound for England. The next day the *Trent* was intercepted by the Union ship *San Jacinto.* Two shots were fired across the bow of the *Trent,* and the ship was boarded in clear violation of international law. Charles Wilkes, the captain of the *San Jacinto,* demanded Mason and Slidell's surrender. The *Trent* sailed to Boston, where Mason and Slidell were arrested and jailed. The *Trent* then continued on to England.

Union officials had no qualms over Captain Wilkes's behavior and commended him on his "patriotic conduct" in capturing the Confederate diplomats. The British, however, were outraged. With rhetoric reaching a fever pitch on both sides, British prime minister Lord Palmerston issued an ultimatum that the Union couldn't ignore: release Mason and Slidell or face war. England still sent an imposing 8,000 soldiers to Canada as a show of force. Worse for the Union, the incident only increased sympathy for the Confederacy.

Lincoln, realizing that the Union needed England more than England needed the Union, quickly backed down on the issue. By late December, he acknowledged that Mason and Slidell had been arrested illegally and agreed to release them. On January 1, 1862, the two men were turned over to British officials and allowed to continue to England.

CHAPTER 15

Weapons of War

Although it's common to think of Civil War soldiers ramrodding their shoulder arms in the same way soldiers of the American Revolution did, there was a very dramatic improvement in weaponry—a major reason why the war had so many casualties. Smooth-bore muskets gave way to rifled muskets that were more accurate and deadly over long distances. Soldiers also began to use breechloading and repeater rifles, vastly increasing their firepower. And artillery could cause more human and material damage than ever before.

Weapons Innovations

The Civil War marked a dramatic turning point in the evolution of warfare. The years immediately preceding the war and the period of the conflict itself saw important advances in small arms, such as the rifle musket, the revolver, and the magazine rifle (also known as the repeater), as well as a huge array of innovations, including the use of balloons for reconnaissance, the first land mines and machine guns, and even the first military use of a primitive submarine. The telegraph, which had been invented by Samuel Morse just seventeen years before the war began, also played an important role in the formation and implementation of combat strategy. The telegraph allowed officers in the field to remain in close touch with their counterparts in other regions, and it also allowed combat officers to relay important information to their superiors in Washington and Richmond.

The impact of advances in small arms can't be overestimated. The rifle musket, which replaced the smoothbore musket as the most commonly used infantry weapon in the 1850s, marked the first improvement in shoulder arms in nearly 150 years. Because of their limitations, smoothbore muskets were most effective only in massed units, but the rifle musket offered a number of improvements that resulted in greater accuracy, distance, and ease of use.

Two entirely new types of firearms appeared during the Civil War: the breechloader and the magazine rifle. Breechloaders became safer and more effective during the Civil War, although they still saw limited use during the war because many ordnance officers thought the weapons were wasteful. The magazine rifle loaded from a "magazine," which stored bullets on the rifle itself. One type, called the Henry Repeating Rifle, could fire twenty-eight shots a minute and was much favored by Union soldiers, who would buy them with their own pay.

Small Arms

Small arms are any weapons carried by a soldier. During the Civil War, the most common small arms included the following:

- Muskets—smoothbore, long-barreled shoulder arms
- Rifles—shoulder arms with spiral grooves cut into the inner surface of the barrel
- Carbines—short-barreled rifles, commonly used by the cavalry
- Handguns—pistols and revolvers

Small arms were commonly designated by their caliber, method of loading (breech or muzzle), and manufacturer. The most frequently used small arms in both the Union and Confederate armies were the .58 caliber Springfield musket and the .69 caliber Harpers Ferry rifle. Both were muzzleloaded weapons that fired the Minie ball, a revolutionary hollow-based bullet that greatly accelerated the loading and firing process.

The increased use of these weapons resulted in a remarkable change in infantry tactics. Smoothbore muskets were notoriously inaccurate and had a relatively short range; firing lines as close as 100 yards inflicted little damage. For maximum effectiveness, soldiers usually had to run toward the enemy firing en masse and hoping they hit something, then use their bayonets for close-quarter fighting.

The rifled musket introduced just before the Civil War was a completely different weapon, however. It offered accuracy at a considerable distance; skilled snipers could hit their target as far as a half mile away. This accuracy made a frontal assault especially hazardous. Unfortunately, many commanding officers failed to take these new weapons into consideration when formulating battle tactics, resulting in a huge number of casualties.

Muskets and Rifles

During the first weeks of the Civil War, as both sides scrambled to put together a fighting force, Union ordnance officials weren't too concerned about the state of the nation's arsenals. Secretary of War Simon Cameron and Chief of Ordnance James Ripley both believed that the number of guns readily available for service, though small, would be sufficient for a war everyone thought would last three months. After all, the number of troops necessary to bring the Southern rebellion under control was estimated at 250,000, and the Federal weapons stores housed more than 400,000 rifles and muskets, which would also be supplemented with weapons brought by state militias.

FACT

At the Battle of Chickamauga, the 535 members of the Twenty-first Ohio Infantry Regiment used their Colt revolving rifles to help prevent a Union rout. During five hours of fighting, the Twenty-First Ohio fired off more than 43,500 rounds, proving the superiority of repeating rifles. Commented one captured Confederate soldier: "My God, we thought you had a division there!"

The picture of the war changed dramatically after the first few battles, which demonstrated that the South was not going down without a long and costly fight. By July 1861, few weapons remained in the national arsenal except a number of very obsolete .69-caliber altered smoothbore muskets— long, awkward weapons that had their original flintlock ignition systems converted to percussion. Not surprisingly, the Union's entire supply of modern rifled weapons, which included 40,000 Model 1855 Harpers Ferry rifles, rifle muskets, and other weapons, were disbursed during the first six weeks of the war. Many of them went to influential politicians who gave them to favored regiments, rather than to the militia and three-year volunteers to whom they had originally been slated.

New Rifled Muskets

It wasn't until mid-1861 that the Federal armory in Springfield, Massachusetts, started producing what would become the favored weapon during the war—the Model 1861 Springfield rifle musket. Before that, the average Union soldier had to make do with the traditional smoothbore musket, a weapon with a high risk factor because of its inaccuracy and time-consuming loading procedure. Demand for the Model 1861 was tremendous. The Springfield Armory produced more than 250,000 of the weapons over two years, and the government still had to contract with twenty private manufacturers to make an additional 450,000. Each cost the U.S. Treasury between $15 and $20.

Some of the most impressive weapons in the federal arsenal were the .58-caliber rifled arms, most of them altered Mississippis and U.S. Model 1855s. Manufactured to conform to the new standards for arms established by Jefferson Davis, who was secretary of war in 1855, the guns were designed to fire the .58-caliber Minie ball, which was easier to load and offered greater accuracy. The elimination of all calibers but the .58 from its muzzleloading regulation arms helped the government simplify weapons production.

Repeaters and Carbines

Repeating rifles were magazine fed and fired metallic cartridges. The most popular brands of repeating rifles were the Spencer and Henry, and though limited in number, they had a demoralizing effect on the Confederate soldiers who faced them. Because they were multishot weapons, repeating rifles could make a handful of well-trained soldiers seem like a regiment. Unfortunately, the Federal Ordnance Department bought only 15,000 Spencer and Henry rifles for the entire Union army, making the weapons extremely coveted among the fighting forces.

FACT

In 1848, French army Captain Claude F. Minie created a hollow-based bullet that could be easily rammed into a rifle's bore. When fired, the lead bullet expanded, catching the rifling and spinning out of the barrel. This improved range (up to a half mile) and accuracy (a skilled marksman could hit a target with precision up to 250 yards away).

For members of the cavalry, the weapon of choice was the carbine, a short-barreled rifle that was lightweight and easy to use, especially on horseback. As with many weapons, there was a shortage of these popular rifles at the onset of the war, but manufacturers soon corrected that, flooding the Union ordnance offices with a number of unique carbine designs. Realizing the value of the carbine to the soldier in the field, the government adopted nearly seventeen different makes and models. The most advanced version was the magazine-fed metallic-cartridge breechloader, which could be mass-produced in volume. Other innovations included barrels that tipped up or hinged downward, cylinders that revolved, and breechblocks that slid vertically or swung to the side.

Confederacy Challenges

The Union suffered from a weapons shortage at the beginning of the war, but the Confederacy had it even worse. The new republic's arsenals contained just 296,000 shoulder arms, most of them outdated flintlock muskets and altered percussion smoothbores. When hostilities first broke out, the Confederate army had just 24,000 modern rifles to distribute among its troops.

The vast majority of Confederate infantrymen marched into battle armed with .69-caliber smoothbore muskets, which were quite effective at close range but wildly inaccurate at distances of more than 100 yards. The Union soldiers opposing them knew about this limitation and enjoyed taunting the rebels by dancing just out of range. Things changed dramatically in late 1862, when Confederate ordnance officials finally managed to bring the military arsenal up to date. Smoothbore muskets were replaced with much more accurate rifle muskets that extended the firing range up to 600 yards. Within just a few months, Northern soldiers stopped dancing and started ducking.

The individual Confederate states did their part by opening up state arsenals and requesting donations from private citizens. The call was met with enthusiasm, and a great number of privately owned rifles, shotguns, and other firearms were donated to the Confederate cause. The Southern states also contracted with small-gun manufacturers and repair shops to alter muskets and rifles so that they would meet military specifications. Thomas Riggins, who owned a gun repair shop in Knoxville, Tennessee, employed sixty assistants working night and day to convert donated rifles and flintlocks into percussion carbines for a volunteer cavalry regiment known as the East Tennessee Squirrel Shooters. Riggins was a skilled craftsman, and the soldiers who came into possession of his weapons knew their guns would get the job done.

Additional weapons used by the Confederacy came from the North, primarily from federal arsenals that fell under Confederate control when the Southern states seceded. In 1859, a standing order was issued by the secretary of war to periodically supply Southern arsenals with weapons from Northern armories. As a result of that order, more than 18,000 percussion muskets, 11,000 altered muskets, and 2,000 rifles were shipped to the Baton Rouge Arsenal in 1860 and 1861—just in time to arm Confederate soldiers. And just a week into the war, the Confederacy captured the U.S. armory at Harpers Ferry, Virginia. In addition to firearms, the raid also gave the South a tremendous amount of arms-producing machinery.

FACT

Union ordnance men turned down the Spencer repeating breechloading rifle in 1860 with the explanation that soldiers would fire too quickly and waste ammunition. Smarter minds prevailed, and the Spencer eventually made its way to the battlefield, but not until near the end of the war.

Weapons were also obtained from foreign manufacturers. In April 1861, for example, Captain Caleb Huse was sent to Europe by Confederate officials to purchase as many small arms as he possibly could. The result was a wide array of weapons that varied greatly in quality. British Enfield rifle muskets were greatly coveted by Confederate infantry, but others, such as the Austrian Lorenz rifle musket, proved to be shoddily made and fairly ineffectual in the battlefield.

Rebel Cavalry

Like their Northern counterparts, members of the Confederate cavalry preferred breechloading carbines above all other weapons because they were reliable, lightweight, and easy to use. However, only a few thousand Southern cavalry actually got to use breechloading carbines because they were in such short supply. Southern gun manufacturers couldn't meet the demand because of a lack of supplies, machinery, and technical know-how, and the breechloading carbines they did produce were of poor quality. As a result, many cavalry soldiers were forced to use long, unwieldy, muzzle-loading shoulder arms, which were next to impossible to load and shoot on a charging horse.

Also popular among Southern cavalry were sawed-off shotguns, which were found to be extremely effective in close quarters. In fact, a regiment armed with 12-gauge shotguns was a force to be reckoned with.

Handguns

Of the many weapons used during the Civil War, handguns proved to be the least desired. Rifles provided much greater accuracy and distance, and sabers and bayonets were much more effective during a charge or in close-quarters fighting. Noted Major Leonidas Scranton of the Second Michigan Cavalry: "Pistols are useless. I have known regiments that have been in the field over two years that have never used their pistols in action."

For the average Union soldier, the issue was moot anyway. The government cheerfully handed out shoulder arms to all who needed them, but only cavalrymen and mounted light artillery were issued sidearms; everyone else had to provide their own.

Weapons fire was often wildly inaccurate due to the limitations of the weapons and the panic of the men. Some soldiers estimated it took a man's weight in lead to kill a single enemy. According to a Union munitions expert, it required 140 pounds of powder and 900 pounds of lead to kill each Confederate who was shot on the battlefield.

The Union purchased 370,000 handguns over the course of the Civil War. The most preferred were the Colt .44 caliber and .36 caliber six-shooters. They were well-made, reliable, and accurate weapons that packed a punch. The U.S. government bought about 12,000 Lefaucheux .41-caliber revolvers. By the end of the war, a great many sidearms had been given away, sold, sent home, or merely tossed aside by Union soldiers, who found them unnecessarily heavy and just plain unhelpful.

Southern cavalrymen preferred sidearms because they were lightweight and extremely accurate at short range. Limited supplies prompted Secretary of War Benjamin to order that handguns be taken away from the infantry and given to the cavalry, which needed them more.

The handguns that were used to arm Confederate soldiers came from a multitude of sources, including Southern manufacturers, seized arsenals, fallen soldiers in the battlefield, foreign manufacturers, and private donations from Confederate citizens. The preferred Adams & Deane and the Kerr revolvers were manufactured by the London Armoury Company, the largest single producer of handguns imported into the South.

Swords and Sabers

Swords and sabers are traditional weapons of war and were an important part of every officer's dress uniform on both sides of the Civil War. Among the enlisted men in the Union army, however, only sergeants, cavalrymen, select artillerymen, and musicians were issued swords, and rather plain ones at that, since they were designed more for fighting than dress. The swords issued to officers tended to be much more ornate and served as a symbol of rank rather than a fighting weapon. Only the sabers carried by cavalry and light artillery officers were actual weapons, though they weren't used as often as rifles and sidearms.

Federal army battle deaths during the war numbered 67,088, plus another 43,012 who died of wounds. Those who died of disease probably numbered 224,000, and the number of Federal wounded is put at 275,175. The Confederates lost approximately 95,000 from battle deaths or from mortal wounds. About 164,000 died from disease. The approximate number of wounded is 194,000.

The vast majority of regulation swords issued to Union soldiers were patterned on weapons of the French army, and most were made by private firms or purchased from foreign manufacturers. European sword makers provided nearly all officers' blades, which were based on an 1850 pattern. It was also common for citizens and military subordinates to give specially made presentation swords to officers as tokens of appreciation for exceptional service or bravery or as a symbol of esteem. Most of these ornate swords, which were quite expensive, were for formal occasions rather than actual fighting.

Swords held much greater appeal among Confederate soldiers because they harkened back to an era of chivalry and romance, an era that was still in effect in the midcentury South. As in the North, swords were both a symbol of rank and a fighting weapon, though they were rarely used. Instead, cavalry and artillery forces relied on sidearms for self-defense because they were reliable and effective. Confederate infantry officers commonly wore swords but used them in combat only when absolutely necessary.

Most Confederate swords were variations of models used by the U.S. Army and were manufactured by Southern companies. A large number of Confederate officers, however, wore imported swords, cherished family heirlooms, or U.S. swords acquired during service in the prewar army.

In addition to their sidearms, many Confederate soldiers carried large bowie knives, named after James Bowie, one of the heroes of the Alamo, who was said to have originated the knife's design. The knives were large—blades ranged from six to eighteen inches in length—and served a number of functions, including skinning wild animals, scaling fish, whittling branches, and self-defense. During man-to-man fighting, a well-honed bowie knife could take off a man's arm with a single swipe.

Artillery

All firearms larger than small arms are known collectively as artillery or cannon. Several dozen different types of artillery were used over the course of the Civil War, but they all fell into one of two distinct categories: smoothbore or rifled cannon. Artillery was further identified by the weight of the projectile, the caliber of the bore diameter, the method of loading (muzzle or breech), and sometimes the name of the inventor or manufacturer. Further distinction was made by the path of a weapon's trajectory (guns had a flat trajectory; mortars a high, arching shot; and howitzers a trajectory that fell between the two) and its tactical deployment, such as seacoast, field, and siege artillery.

Guns and Ammunition

The most commonly used artillery on both sides was the Napoleon, a smoothbore, muzzleloaded howitzer whose projectile weighed twelve pounds. It was developed in France during the reign of Louis Napoleon and was first introduced in the United States in 1856. The Napoleon was a reliable, sturdy piece of machinery that worked as an offensive and defensive weapon. Napoleons were first made of bronze, but Southern manufacturers were forced to make later versions out of iron when bronze fell into short supply. The maximum range of the Napoleon was 1,000 yards, but the weapon proved most effective at shorter ranges—250 yards or less. It used both grape shot and canister ammunition and is believed to have killed more men on both sides than all other artillery weapons combined.

A 200-pound Parrott rifle in Fort Gregg on Morris Island, South Carolina, 1865
Photo courtesy of the National Archives (165-S-128)

Second to the Napoleon were the three-inch ordnance and Parrott guns, rifled cannon that had greater accuracy and range than smoothbore artillery. On a good day, a three-incher could lob a shell up to 2,500 yards, but such long-range artillery proved ineffective during most battles because the gunner had to see what he was shooting at. Rifled cannon did have their valuable uses, however. They were very good at destroying fortifications and played an integral role in the battles of Vicksburg and Atlanta. Most of the artillery used during the Civil War was muzzleloaded. Breechloading cannon were available, but most gunners found them unreliable and difficult to use.

Size played an important role in the use of artillery; the heavier guns were more difficult to transport, especially over hilly or muddy terrain. The most portable artillery and thus some of the most widely used were the six- and twelve-pound mountain howitzers, which proved very effective during battles fought in mountainous areas. Naval and siege cannons were some of the heaviest and provided the greatest power. The eight- and ten-inch siege howitzers had ranges of more than 2,000 yards and could fire forty-five and ninety-pound shells, which inflicted tremendous damage on their targets.

The big guns fired an array of ammunition, including solid shot, grape, canister, shell, and chain shot, most of which came in any of the nine common artillery calibers. Solid shot and shell were used to destroy distant, fixed targets such as fortifications, while chain shot, which consisted of two balls connected by a short chain, was employed primarily against the masts and rigging of ships. Grape shot and canister were used most commonly in the field. Both were scattershot projectiles consisting of several iron balls in an iron casement. When fired, the casement would disintegrate, releasing the shot in a deadly spray very much like a giant sawed-off shotgun. At close range (250 yards or less), these weapons could inflict serious damage.

The Union Advantage

The Union had artillery in greater quantities and better quality than the Confederacy, and its officers used the weapons to tremendous advantage. Typically, Confederate infantry would move forward against Union infantry, often through fields and woodlands, until they were within a specific range. At that point, the Union artillery would be moved into place, and iron death would rain down upon the hapless Confederate troops, breaking their charge and forcing them back. This tactic repeated itself throughout the war and enabled Union victories in such battles as Shiloh and Gettysburg.

One of the biggest reasons the Union was able to maintain superiority in the area of artillery was its manufacturing might. The North contained far more manufacturing plants and skilled technicians than the South, as well as far greater access to the raw materials needed to build reliable weaponry. The South did its best to keep up, but in the long run it was simply out-manufactured. Quite a bit of artillery was acquired from foreign manufacturers, but the Northern blockade of Southern ports played an important role in keeping the Confederate army undersupplied. General Henry Hunt, chief of artillery for the Army of the Potomac, noted, "While the South had at the beginning of the war the better raw material for infantry and cavalry, the North had the best for artillery. A battery requires many mechanics, with their tools and stores, and also what are called handy men. No country furnishes better men for the artillery proper than our Northern, and particularly our New England, states."

FACT

Firing artillery required the efforts of several men working in a sort of ballet. Experienced gunners could load and fire a fieldpiece every thirty seconds, even in the face of enemy fire. Not surprisingly, gunnery teams were a close-knit bunch who treated their weapons as members of the family, often giving them special names.

Once the war began in earnest and it became apparent that hostilities would not be quickly concluded, foundries in the North worked almost around the clock to produce cannons and ammunition for the Union army. The greatest output was of twelve-pounder smoothbore Napoleons and three-inch ordnance rifles, which quickly became the muscle of the Union artillery because of their reliability, durability, and accuracy. A huge number of Parrott guns were also produced, primarily at the West Point Foundry. The Parrott came in various sizes, from ten- and twelve-pounder field versions to huge cast-iron cannons that fired 100- and 200-pound shells. However, the larger cannons were greatly disliked by the Union soldiers because they had a nasty habit of exploding if they were fired repeatedly.

Union Work on the Battlefield

The U.S. regular army artillery was a small but extremely well-trained corps of specialists that provided expert guidance in the art of field gunnery and tactics. These soldiers made sure their weapons hit their targets with deadly accuracy. During the Battle of Antietam, Brigadier General John Gibbon placed six Napoleons of Battery B, Fourth U.S. Artillery, on a knoll overlooking a cornfield to protect his right flank but realized too late that his gunners had aimed the cannons' muzzles too high and were shooting over the heads of advancing enemy troops. Before too long, forty of his battery's 100 men had fallen. As Confederate troops charged the Union battery, Gibbon leaped off his horse, ran to one of the guns, and quickly adjusted the elevating screw. On his orders, the crew fired several more volleys into the cornfield, blasting away a fence as well as a high number of Confederate troops. Gibbon's daring saved Battery B from almost certain annihilation.

Horse artillery consisted of small but powerful cannons disassembled, packed onto horses, and carried over rough terrain. It was commonly used by the cavalry, and both Jeb Stuart and Nathan Forrest made excellent use of it during the Civil War.

Artillery played an equally important role in the Battle of Malvern Hill, the last of the Seven Days Battles. Almost the entire artillery arm of George McClellan's retreating army, approximately 250 cannon, was positioned on a bluff flanking the James River as Robert E. Lee's pursuing forces attacked. The big guns did extraordinary damage to the Confederate forces, cutting wide swaths within their ranks.

The Confederate greatest use of field artillery was on the third day of Gettysburg, when Southern artillerists assembled almost hub-to-hub more than 130 guns they had hauled all the way from Virginia. For more than an hour they fired; it was the largest bombardment on troops in North America. However, the Confederates' aim was slightly too high and they did not significantly impact the Federals. Pickett's Charge, which followed the artillery bombardment, failed to break the Union line.

CHAPTER 16

Life in the Service

The Civil War was decided by battles, but day by day, battles were the exceptions. For the soldiers, life was mainly in camp or marching to a place to set up new camps. During the worst winter months, camp life was about all there was. Life in camps held innumerable struggles: for proper diet, for adequate clothing, for dry bedding, and more. And, to be sure, there were also amusements, from gambling to music making.

Camp Life

Camp life during the Civil War harbored a host of problems, but it was better than marching or combat. For many soldiers, camp was home for up to three years, and they coped as best they could.

Living Quarters

Army regulations required camps to be laid out in a grid pattern, with officers' quarters at the front end of each street and enlisted men's quarters aligned to the rear. The camp was set up approximately along the same lines as the line of battle, and each company proudly displayed its colors on the outside of its tents.

Winter quarters: soldiers in front of their wooden hut, "Pine Cottage" *Photo courtesy of the National Archives (111-B-256)*

During the summer months, most soldiers slept in canvas tents. At the onset of the war, both sides used what was known as the Sibley tent, named after its inventor, Henry H. Sibley, a brigadier general in the Confederate army. The Sibley tent was a large canvas cone about eighteen feet in diameter, twelve feet tall, and supported by a center pole. It had a circular opening at the top for ventilation and was heated by a cone-shaped stove. The Sibley tent was designed to house twelve men comfortably, but a shortage of supplies often increased occupancy to up to twenty men per tent. As might be expected, the conditions within these tents often bordered on the intolerable; bathing was a rare luxury for soldiers in the field.

Bands were common on both sides, and it wasn't unusual for musicians from both sides to jam together in the evening following a day of combat. A U.S. Sanitation Commission inspection of Union military camps in October 1861 found that nearly 75 percent of all regiments had one. Most bands were disbanded by July 1862; they were simply too expensive.

Overcrowding was alleviated somewhat when the Sibley tent was replaced by smaller tents that were easier to carry. The Union army primarily used the wedge tent, a six-foot length of canvas draped over a horizontal pole and staked to the ground at the sides, with flaps that closed over each end. The wedge tent also saw use in the South, but when canvas became scarce, many soldiers were forced to make open-air beds by piling leaves or straw between two logs and covering it with a blanket or poncho. During the winter, crude huts were made out of wood—when wood was available.

Daily Routine

Soldiers in the Civil War did not see battle every day, or even every week. Most were inactive about 75 percent of the time, thanks to the hurry-up-and-wait nature of warfare. During these down periods, the typical day started at 5 A.M. during the spring and summer months and 6 A.M. during the fall and winter. Soldiers were awakened by reveille, roll call was taken by the first sergeant, and then everyone sat down to breakfast, which usually consisted of biscuits, some kind of cured meat, and coffee. Eggs and fruit were added to the menu when they were available.

During the rest of the day, soldiers engaged in as many as five two-hour drill sessions on weaponry or maneuvers. Most soldiers found these drills extremely boring and tedious; they wanted to fight, not practice, though they realized the drills could mean the difference between life and death when fighting did occur.

FACT

Sutlers were associated with armies on both sides of the war. These were vendors who supplied goods—newspapers, tobacco, tinned meats, shoelaces—not usually provided by the government. Most sutlers charged exorbitant prices for their often shoddy goods, but soldiers desperate for news from home, a cigar, or a piece of candy paid them without hesitation.

Soldiers also cleaned and readied the camp, built roads, dug latrines, gathered wood for cooking and heating, and sometimes foraged for food to supplement their meals. One of the biggest problems facing soldiers in the field was proper sanitation. Access to clean water for drinking and bathing was often limited, and illness from contaminated water or poor hygiene was rampant. Because army camps were tight-knit groups, a contagious disease such as measles or chickenpox could decimate a camp within days. Indeed, most soldiers had more to fear from illness than enemy bullets.

Food

Food shortages became a serious problem for the Confederacy, and even some Union forces during the later years of the war. Early on, soldiers on both sides were relatively well fed. By mandate, daily rations for Union soldiers in 1861 included a minimum of 20 ounces of fresh or salted beef, or 12 ounces of salt pork; more than a pound of flour; and a vegetable, usually beans. Soldiers also received regular allotments of coffee, salt, vinegar, and sugar.

In the field during long campaigns, however, mandated allotments often fell short. Quality meat and vegetables were in short supply, and soldiers were forced to subsist primarily on salt pork, dried beans, corn bread, and hardtack, a biscuit made of flour and water that more often than not was contaminated with weevils and other critters. The lack of fresh vegetables and fruit often led to outbreaks of scurvy, a disease caused by a vitamin C deficiency.

Log hut company kitchen, 1864 *Photo courtesy of the National Archives (111-B-252)*

As the war progressed and supply trains found themselves unable to reach forces in the field, soldiers on both sides often had to live off the land. Hunting helped provide meat, but sometimes armies were forced to take what they needed from nearby homes and businesses. Confederate soldiers, who usually found themselves fighting on the home field, preferred to request provisions from sympathetic citizens. Sometimes they stole supplies or took them by force, though pillaging was something most soldiers did only under the most dire of circumstances.

Coping

Boredom was a chronic problem in most army camps. Drilling helped take up some of the day, but the soldiers had to devise other forms of recreation to help them while away the rest of the hours. Those who were able wrote long letters home or read books, magazines, and newspapers when they could get them. Others played cards or engaged in various sports, such as baseball, boxing, and cockfighting. Some camps, desperate for activity, even staged cockroach and lice races. Drinking and gambling were discouraged by military officials, but both activities were nearly impossible to control, especially after payday. Contact with prostitutes also was strongly discouraged but, again, nearly impossible to stop. Soldiers on leave frequently visited brothels, and prostitutes were known to visit military camps in specially equipped wagons.

Asked by gleeful Southerners how he was going to feed his army after Confederate forces captured his food supply at Holly Springs, Mississippi, in 1862, General Ulysses S. Grant later recalled, "I told them that I was not disturbed; that I had already sent troops and wagons to collect all the food and forage they could find for fifteen miles on each side of the road."

Alcohol was a huge problem on both sides. Soldiers on duty were prohibited by army regulations from buying liquor, but soldiers found a number of ingenious ways to smuggle alcohol into camp and keep it hidden from their commanding officers. The members of one clever Mississippi company managed to sneak a half-gallon of whiskey past guards by pouring it into a watermelon; they then kept the watermelon hidden by burying it beneath the floor of their tent and drinking from it through long straws.

Of all the hardships soldiers faced in camp, homesickness was probably the most rampant and difficult to cure. Furloughs were rarely given—both sides needed as many able bodies on the battlefield as they could muster—and often impractical, since most units were so distant that it would have taken soldiers days or even weeks to reach home. Many soldiers became so homesick that they deserted, sometimes for a short while, sometimes forever. During the war, 141 Union soldiers were executed for desertion, though Lincoln signed numerous pardons for the common offense. "I prefer to take the risk on the side of mercy," he explained.

Uniforms

The Civil War is commonly known as the War of the Blue and the Gray, describing the colors of the uniforms worn by Union and Confederate soldiers. In truth, there was very little conformity of dress on either side, at least during the first months of the war. The regular army had an established uniform, but the majority of participants were volunteers from state militias who often demonstrated their independence and esprit de corps by dressing in flamboyant (albeit impractical) uniforms of their own design. When these units got together, it looked more like a circus show than a fighting force.

The various units fighting for the Confederacy were even more independent in their attire, showing their disdain for the concept of a centralized government by dressing as colorfully and uniquely as they could. Only later in the conflict would both sides establish a standard for military dress, though many units tenaciously continued to flaunt their independence by adding flourishes and various accouterments.

Growing Pains

One of the biggest problems during the first months of the war was finding enough uniforms to dress the participants on both sides. In the North, a great many clothing manufacturers received lucrative government contracts to make military uniforms, but in the rush to meet quotas, factory-made uniforms were often of poor quality and design. The system also fostered corruption. Eventually, the government cracked down on manufacturers who pocketed huge profits and churned out inferior clothing, and the quality of uniforms improved dramatically.

The U.S. Quartermaster Department was responsible for dressing the Union's fighting forces, having supervised the design and manufacture of clothing for enlisted men at the Schuylkill Arsenal since the War of 1812. However, the army was hard pressed to adequately dress the huge influx of new soldiers at the beginning of the war, so the War Department asked the various states to dress their own regiments—preferably in the traditional dark blue uniform—and apply to the government for reimbursement. But the states were unable to supply adequate numbers of uniforms on such short notice, so many early volunteer regiments wore uniforms paid for by their local communities, with perhaps a little help from the state.

Several regiments left for Washington without any uniforms at all. The First and Second Ohio, for example, were sent to the nation's capital so soon after they were organized that their leaders decided to pick up uniforms during the trip rather than wait. None were available, so they bought materials and made them as they traveled.

The average Civil War soldier was paid very little for laying his life on the line. Top pay for a Union infantry private was just $16 a month. His Confederate counterpart received $18 a month, but it was worth considerably less due to skyrocketing inflation.

Following the Union defeat at the First Battle of Manassas, Congress immediately authorized a call for 500,000 volunteers to serve for three years, and the states started working overtime to clothe the new recruits. New York, for example, decided to issue all of its new regiments a standard outfit that included a dark blue woolen jacket that closed in front with eight state-seal buttons, light blue pants and overcoat, and a dark blue fatigue cap. Unfortunately, many were made of cheap material, and the soldiers who received them complained bitterly of the poor workmanship.

Federal Improvements

The uniform situation improved dramatically by the fall of 1861. The government purchased a large number of uniforms from foreign manufacturers, and the high quality of the garments forced American manufacturers to improve the quality of their own product, as well as increase production quotas. On September 13, 1861, the U.S. War Department, in a much needed attempt to stop Union soldiers from accidentally being killed by their own men, asked the officials of Northern states to stop furnishing gray uniforms to their soldiers. By mid-1862, gray uniforms had all but disappeared from Union regiments as Quartermaster General Montgomery Meigs assumed the job of contracting and distributing uniforms to Union troops.

The Schuylkill Arsenal in Philadelphia could not keep up with the huge demand for uniforms, so additional manufacturing and purchasing depots were established in New York, Boston, Cincinnati, and elsewhere. Federal inspectors checked every piece of clothing that was produced or purchased, and uniforms were stamped with labels that identified the inspectors and the maker. This greatly increased the quality of the clothing that eventually reached the Union soldiers.

Confederate Efforts

The Confederacy faced similar problems. The newly formed government struggled to find sufficient manufacturers to meet the demand for uniforms, and the civilian population often sewed uniforms for local soldiers. Still, some Confederate soldiers had nothing to wear but their own clothes, and the situation only worsened. In some cases, entire units were forced to march from battle to battle lacking shoes and other garments.

Few Southern states had dress regulations for their militia, which formed the backbone of the Confederate fighting force at the beginning of the war. The troops' uniforms were inspired by everything from Scottish Highlanders and frontiersmen to French chasseurs and Zouaves, and many continued to wear their exotic dress even after they were made a part of the Confederate regular army.

By October 1862, an effective depot system had been established, and the Confederate government assumed the responsibility of supplying all clothing to its troops. The new issue system set annual allotments for articles of clothing. Of course, soldiers who participated in lengthy campaigns went through their allotted clothes in no time. Rather than spend their hard-earned money for replacements, many asked their friends and family to help by buying or making clothes for them.

What the Average Soldier Wore

Standard uniforms included all major forms of clothing, from shoes to underwear. Both Union and Confederate forces found ways to show rank and affiliation in their uniforms. Neither side was preoccupied with comfort.

What the Average Union Soldier Wore

The typical Union infantryman wore a dark blue, loose flannel sackcoat that hung at midthigh, blue trousers made of wool or jersey, a light blouse, heavy leather shoes that were derisively known as "gunboats," and a blue forage cap (also known as a slouch cap). Additional clothing and protective gear included an overcoat with a blue cape, a thick wool blanket (which weighed approximately five pounds), a gum blanket that served as a tent floor or a poncho, a thick flannel pullover shirt, and a pair of wool socks.

D. W. C. Arnold, private in the Union army *Photo courtesy of the National Archives (111-B-5435)*

Affiliation with a specific branch of the service was indicated by stripes down the outer seam of the uniform—yellow for cavalry, red for artillery, light blue for infantry, emerald green for mounted rifleman, and crimson for ordnance and hospital personnel. Distinctions in rank were denoted by the type of frock coat worn—majors, lieutenant colonels, colonels, and all general officers wore double-breasted coats; lower ranking officers wore single-breasted coats. Additional rank distinctions included the number and placement of buttons and shoulder boards or sleeve chevrons.

What the Average Southern Soldier Wore

The uniforms worn by Confederate troops were quite similar to their Union counterparts, except the color was gray or yellow-brown. The standard infantryman wore a gray or yellow-brown wool shell jacket; gray, yellow-brown, or blue pants; low-heeled leather shoes; and a gray or yellow-brown forage cap. Frock coats similar to those worn by Union infantry were also part of the uniform, but supplies were limited and not all soldiers received them. Additional garments traditionally included a homemade coverlet, a cotton shirt, a wool vest, and wool socks. All officers and enlisted men on both sides also received ankle-high boots.

Private Edmund Ruffin, Confederate soldier who fired the first shot against Fort Sumter *Photo courtesy of the National Archives (111-BA-1226)*

In the Confederate army, affiliation with a particular branch of service was indicated by the colored facing on a man's coat—yellow for cavalry, red for artillery, light blue for infantry, and black for medical personnel.

Variations in rank within each branch was designated by colored stripes on outer trouser seams—regimental officers had a ¼-inch stripe; generals wore a 2 ⅝-inch stripe; adjutant, quartermaster, commissary, and engineer officers wore one gold ¼-inch stripe.

Rank was also indicated by buttons and insignias. Soldiers on both sides were expected to carry all of their provisions, including clothing, equipment, personal effects, and weapons, on their backs, and a fully equipped infantryman might carry a load of fifty pounds or more.

The Issue of Comfort

While the quality of the uniforms received by Union and Confederate soldiers gradually improved as the war progressed, their comfort did not. When the clothing arrived at training camps, it was placed in piles, and the soldiers lined up and took what was on top. The issue of fit was not a big concern, and it wasn't uncommon for soldiers to receive clothing that was much too big or small for them. The lucky ones were able to trade with someone else.

Even if a soldier received a uniform that was a perfect fit, he still experienced great discomfort. Northern mills, following orders from the War Department, used wool to make almost everything—including underwear. The material was stiff, scratchy, and often unbearable against the skin, but unless a soldier had brought underclothes from home, he was stuck with what he got.

FACT

During the First Battle of Manassas, soldiers on both sides dressed in a wide variety of colorful uniforms that sometimes made it difficult to differentiate friend from foe. Some Southern units wore blue, and some Northern soldiers were decked out in gray. More than one soldier was accidentally killed by friendly fire.

During the thick of the war, when soldiers were marching, skirmishing, and fighting for their lives, the majority of fighting men tried to lighten their load to the bare necessities. When spring came, many soldiers discarded their heavy winter coats and other clothing. When soldiers were engaged in a major campaign, very often the only clothes they carried were those they were wearing. Speed on the battlefield meant much more than a wardrobe.

Flags of the North and South

The national flags of the Union and the Confederacy were more than colorful pieces of cloth; they quickly came to symbolize everything each side stood for, rallying troops and private citizens into an unprecedented patriotic fervor. In New York City, for example, an angry mob took over the offices of the *New York Herald*, which professed a strong pro-Southern sentiment, and threatened to burn everything in sight if the publisher didn't display the Stars and Stripes. He quickly complied.

Before the war, the army's flags were made at the Schuylkill Arsenal, but with increased demand, the Quartermaster Department created additional depots in New York and Cincinnati. The contractors to the three depots accounted for nearly 2,400 national flags and 2,300 regimental flags over the course of the war.

It became quite fashionable to display the flag at one's home and office, and to wear the flag on one's person as a show of support for the Union cause. The same was true for the Confederate Stars and Bars. Communities nationwide presented specially made flags—either traditional designs or variations thereof—to local militia units gearing up to go to war, hopeful that the colorful banners would inspire the troops to victory.

In 1861, U.S. Army regulations required infantry units to carry two silk flags, a national flag and a regimental flag, each nearly six feet square. The regimental designation was to be embroidered on the center stripe of the national flag. The embroidery was to be in silver on infantry flags and gold on artillery flags, but a shortage of qualified embroiderers often forced quartermasters to have the designations painted on instead.

Until 1862, the individual states were given responsibility for recruiting and outfitting the militias that came out of them, and they were usually responsible for their flags as well. The result was a plethora of colorful and creative patterns that helped distinguish one unit from another.

FACT

Beginning in the winter of 1861–62, Union troops started marking their national and regimental flags with the names of battles in which they had participated, a practice that dated back to the 1830s in the regular army.

In the thick of battle, the regimental flag was often the only visible sign of a unit amid the smoke and chaos, and thus it typically received a huge amount of enemy fire. As a result, casualties were usually the highest closest to the colors. To compensate for expected losses, the color guard of a Union regiment, whose sole job was to keep the colors flying, was fairly large, consisting of between six and nine men. If one man fell, another would quickly grab the flag and keep it aloft. To be a member of a regimental color guard was an esteemed honor. The color guard of a cavalry regiment was much smaller, usually just a standard-bearer followed by a single corporal.

The Flags of the Confederacy

The Confederate congress successively adopted three designs for the new republic's national flag. The first, adopted on March 4, 1861, looked very much like the Stars and Stripes—so much so that it was nicknamed the Stars and Bars. It consisted of a field of three equal horizontal bars of red, white, red. Its blue canton extended two-thirds the height of the flag and featured a circle of stars equal to the number of states in the Confederacy.

Two years later, the new flag debuted. Nicknamed the Stainless Banner because it had a plain white field, it featured a red canton crisscrossed by a white-edged, dark blue St. Andrew's Cross emblazoned with thirteen white stars. Unfortunately, its white field made it look like a flag of truce. In March 1865, the Confederate congress changed the flag's proportions and added a wide red vertical bar to its fly edge. This decision was made mere weeks before the war ended, and very few flags were made.

Because the Stars and Stripes and the Stars and Bars looked so much alike at the beginning of the war, General Pierre G. T. Beauregard proposed a separate battle flag to prevent the possibility of mistaken identity on the field. The Battle Flag of the Confederacy is the design most people envision when they think of the Confederate flag.

CHAPTER 17

Horrors of War

Few men who marched away to war in 1861 could imagine the deprivations, dangers, and dreadfulness that awaited them. The battles were chaotic, cacophonous, and terrifying. Wounds were often massive and horrible. Medical care, when it was available at all, was excruciating and barely effective. Prisoners suffered through disease and disgusting conditions. There were some lights in this darkness—Red Cross founder Clara Barton prominent among them—but the general suffering was immense.

Battlefield Conditions

Many of the volunteers who joined the armies of the North and South did so more as a means of escape than because of patriotic pride. A great many had spent their lives on family farms and in small towns, and they saw the war as an opportunity to experience some excitement and see the rest of the country. In their fantasies, the war was a clean, bloodless affair that would be over in a matter of months with nary a bullet fired. The reality, unfortunately, was much different.

Many soldiers were sent into battle with weapons they barely knew how to use, a situation made worse by the terror of battle. On the field at Gettysburg, Union ordnance officers collected thousands of muskets loaded with up to ten charges. In the fever of the fight, many of the soldiers had apparently loaded and reloaded without actually firing.

While camp life was filled with interminable boredom, the battlefield was filled with gut-wrenching terror. Once a battle commenced, the scene was usually one of chaos. The noise was deafening as cannons roared and hundreds and sometimes thousands of soldiers fired on each other. Officers would try desperately to rally and guide their troops in the throes of battle, but the smoke and the noise made the task difficult, if not impossible. In addition, as many as half of the soldiers typically had little knowledge of the terrain, and it wasn't unusual for entire units to get lost.

The Instinct for Panic

Many soldiers, especially those experiencing their first battle, panicked at the first sounds of gunfire and fled to the rear. One common tactic was to help a wounded comrade to the medical tent and then not return to the fighting. Commanding officers quickly became wise to the ruse and ordered cavalry officers in the rear to challenge fleeing soldiers with the cry, "Show blood!" Those who could not were ordered to take up arms and return to the front.

Most of the soldiers on both sides were raw recruits, inexperienced teen-agers, or young men barely out of their teens who had never been involved in a gunfight in their lives. In most cases, their only experience with fire-arms was hunting with friends. Now they were being ordered to face an often-unseen enemy and attack, knowing full well that there was a chance they might not survive.

Feats and Acts Beyond the Everyday

Every battle was different. The terrain changed, as did the weather and even the number of men available to fight. Officers did the best they could under these ever-changing circumstances, and many of the most skilled officers managed to pull off some spectacular feats in the face of overwhelming odds.

Different too were the leadership styles of commanding officers. Some were skilled tacticians and strategists, others were exceptionally skilled at leading their men, and a few could do both. Generals tended to stay toward the rear lines during a battle, guiding the action with the aid of subordinates who would carry orders down to unit leaders. But a few reckless generals liked to lead by example and were out in the front of the charge. Both sides lost a great number of talented leaders as a result.

FACT

Battlefield deaths weren't always the direct result of enemy bullets. Many wounded soldiers perished in raging brushfires that were ignited during heavy fighting in dry fields and forests. A number of battles were tempo-rarily halted while both sides struggled to save their wounded from brush-fires that threatened to engulf them.

During major battles, it wasn't uncommon for soldiers to fight non-stop for hours, fueled by pure adrenaline and completely unaware of the passage of time. Only when the sun went down and the battle ceased did their rhythms return to normal, as did their need for food, drink, and sleep. This was the battlefield experience for hundreds of thousands of Civil War soldiers, sometimes for days on end, battle after battle. Those lucky enough to return home never forgot the sights, sounds, and smells of combat.

Amazingly, once the shooting stopped, opposing forces often put their differences aside in order to barter for various goods. There are innumerable examples of Union and Confederate soldiers meeting in a truce zone to tell jokes and swap food, coffee, tobacco, newspapers, and other goods. Occasionally, even the officers joined in. In one notable incident, a Union officer was invited by his Confederate counterparts to attend a country dance at a farmhouse near the area where both armies were camped. The officer accepted the invitation, enjoyed the dance, and was safely returned to his lines by his hosts before daybreak.

Casualties

Causes of death during the Civil War were many. Bullets and artillery took their share of lives on both sides, but more than twice as many men died from illness than from enemy fire.

Soaring Casualties

The casualty statistics are staggering. According to an analysis of government records, slightly more than 350,000 Union soldiers died from various causes during the Civil War. The majority of deaths were from disease. Nearly 25,000 men died from causes such as suicide, execution, sunstroke, and accidents. The Union navy lost nearly 5,000 men to illness, accidents, and battle injuries.

Records of Confederate deaths aren't nearly as comprehensive as those of Union casualties; military and government files were destroyed during and after the war. However, a generally accepted estimate is 150,000 dead of disease and 95,000 killed or mortally wounded in combat. No statistics survive regarding deaths among Confederate naval personnel.

To put these figures in perspective, consider that more Americans died of disease and battlefield wounds during the Civil War than all other American wars combined, from the Revolutionary War to Vietnam, including both

World Wars. In fact, the Battle of Antietam resulted in four times the casualties as the landings on the Normandy beaches on D-Day, June 6, 1944.

Casualty by Disease

The high number of battlefield deaths during the Civil War is easy to understand. Civil War-era weapons caused massive physical damage when they hit their targets, and outdated battle tactics often put large numbers of soldiers in harm's way. But the number of deaths related to disease requires a little explanation.

"I have a mortal dread of the battle field, for I have never yet been nearer to one than to hear the cannon roar & and have never seen a person die. I am afraid that the groans of the wounded & dying will make me shake, nevertheless I hope & trust that strength will be given me to stand up & do my duty."—Private Edward Edes

The Civil War took place shortly before a number of important advances in human medicine. There were no vaccines for the most common of illnesses, and hygiene was poor, especially in mobile military camps. Young men who had lived their entire lives in relative seclusion in small towns and hamlets simply didn't have immunity to many types of illnesses, and they fell sick from the most innocuous of diseases.

One of the leading contributors to wartime illness was the latrine, usually a simple hole or trench used by all members of the camp. When the stench of the latrine became unbearable, it was covered over and a new one dug. As might be expected, camp latrines were veritable breeding grounds for every imaginable form of illness. They also attracted a lot of insects, particularly flies, which would deposit germs and bacteria on the food the men ate and the water they drank. Numerous outbreaks of diarrhea and epidemics of cholera and other contagious diseases resulted. Whooping cough, measles, scarlet fever, smallpox, and dysentery also took a huge toll, as did environmental ailments such as sunstroke, frostbite, and tetanus. Many soldiers suffered from gastrointestinal ailments and other complaints for almost the entire length of their enlistment.

Civilian Casualties

Soldiers weren't the only ones to die during the Civil War. The conflict also took a huge toll on the civilian population, particularly in the South. While the number of Northern citizens who died as a direct result of the war is relatively small, some historians estimate that up to 50,000 Confederate citizens may have perished from various causes, including stray bullets and poor sanitation following the devastation of entire towns and cities.

Prisoners of War

For the most part, soldiers who were taken prisoner by both sides were relatively well treated. This was the Victorian era, after all, and chivalry still had its place during wartime. More importantly, however, the soldiers of the North and South weren't fighting some unknown, foreign enemy; they were fighting people who spoke their language and had been their own countrymen. To abuse another American—even a rebellious one—wasn't in the nature of most men, though there were exceptions. In addition, every soldier knew there was a strong possibility he could be taken prisoner, so it behooved all to act with kindness toward captured enemy forces—today it was them; tomorrow it could be you.

Paroles and Exchanges

At the beginning of the war, captured soldiers were expected to "give parole," or promise not to escape. Paroled soldiers could expect to be sent back to their own lines under a flag of truce, at which time they would be sent home until an exchange was effected. Union and Confederate military officials reached an agreement in 1862 that stipulated that all prisoners were to be exchanged within ten days of capture. The fact that promises were made and kept demonstrates the gentlemanly nature of the Civil War during its first years—a man's word was his honor. However, if a soldier broke his promise by returning to the field unexchanged, he ran the risk of being shot or hanged.

The value of a prisoner depended on his rank. A general was worth up to sixty privates; a major general was worth up to forty privates. At the bottom end, a noncommissioned officer was worth two privates, and privates were traded one for one. Approximately 200,000 soldiers from both sides were freed through prisoner exchanges.

FACT

The Union and the Confederacy both employed sharpshooters to pick off the enemy at a great distance. Southern snipers were particularly effective as a result of their incredibly accurate rifles. At the battle of Spotsylvania, one sniper shot Union General John Sedgwick dead at 800 yards.

In 1864, the Union ceased prisoner exchanges altogether in an attempt to bring the Confederacy down by attrition. Union officials finally realized that every Confederate soldier in a POW camp was one less rifle aimed at Union soldiers. The policy had a devastating effect on the South, where manpower shortages were rampant. Unfortunately, many POWs also suffered greatly as a result of the no-exchange policy.

The conditions at POW camps varied greatly. At the beginning of the war, when prisoner exchanges helped keep prisons relatively empty, conditions were fairly good on both sides. Prisoners were usually well treated, well fed, and adequately clothed. This remained true for most prisons in the North throughout the war, but the conditions of POW camps in the South deteriorated greatly as the Confederacy gradually found itself unable to feed and clothe even its own citizens and soldiers. Most prison officials did their best to maintain humane conditions, but they had less and less to work with during the final year of the war.

Northern POW Camp Conditions

The North had its share of less-than-ideal facilities. Point Lookout in Maryland, for example, was designed to house 10,000 men in tents, but it often contained 20,000 or more. Fort Jefferson in the Dry Tortugas, off the

Florida Keys, was another prison known for its brutal conditions. An old fort converted into a military prison in 1861, Fort Jefferson housed Union army criminals. The tropical climate at Fort Jefferson was stifling, and the work conditions unmerciful. Worse, unsanitary conditions promoted the spread of disease among the prison population, killing many.

FACT

Fort Jefferson's most famous prisoner was Dr. Samuel Mudd, who set John Wilkes Booth's broken leg following the assassination of Abraham Lincoln. Mudd claimed he hadn't recognized Booth when he set his leg, but he was sentenced to life in prison. He was pardoned and released by President Andrew Johnson in 1869 but was never able to escape the stigma of his association to Lincoln's assassination.

Probably the worst Union POW camp was located in the town of Elmira, New York. More than 2,960 Confederate soldiers died there—almost a quarter of the prison population. According to government records, the death rate at Elmira was only slightly less than that of Andersonville, and it was more than double that of other Union prisons. The most common cause of death was disease exacerbated by starvation and filthy living conditions. Many prisoners, denied warm clothing and even blankets, froze to death during the harsh winter months. Those who survived the camp referred to it as "Hellmira." It remains an indelible black mark on the conduct of the Union army.

Andersonville

No prisoner of war camp was more reviled than the Confederate prison constructed near the village of Andersonville in Sumter County, Georgia. Its name has become synonymous with barbarism and ill treatment.

Andersonville, officially known as Camp Sumter, was opened in February 1864 after the high number of Northern prisoners started taking a heavy toll on the food supplies in Richmond, where prisoners had previously been housed. When the first prisoners arrived at the new camp, they were greeted by sixteen acres of open land surrounded by a fifteen-foot-tall stockade. Originally designed to house 10,000 men, the facility soon contained more than three times that number and was expanded to twenty-six acres. Nearly 400 new prisoners arrived each day, straining the prison's meager resources to the breaking point.

Almost from the start, rations were scarce and of poor quality, and few prisoners had adequate shelter from the summer sun and the winter cold. The only fresh water came from Stockade Creek, a small stream that flowed through the prison yard. Waste was often dumped into the water, and downstream it was used as a latrine for all prisoners. The entire region was soon contaminated, but prisoners continued to drink from it. Health care was nonexistent.

At Vicksburg in 1863, General Grant paroled 31,000 Confederate soldiers rather than go through the chore of sending them all to prison camps in the North. He captured many of them again at Chattanooga. After taking command of all the Union armies, Grant ordered an end to prisoner exchanges until Confederate officials agreed to honor a one-for-one exchange.

The first commander of Andersonville was John Henry Winder, who oversaw all Confederate prisons. Winder died from exhaustion in February 1865 and was succeeded by Henry Wirz, a Swiss-born Confederate officer known for his hatred of the Union. According to reports, Wirz did little to alleviate the suffering of his inmates, and the prison's increasingly poor conditions took a heavy toll—approximately 13,000 prisoners died there, a mortality rate of about 29 percent.

At the end of the war, Henry Wirz became the only Confederate officer to be tried and convicted for war crimes. Numerous prisoners who suffered under his sadistic command testified against him, as did Clara Barton, who was outraged when she visited the prison site at the war's end to identify the dead and missing and see that they received a proper burial. Wirz was held accountable for the conditions at Andersonville, found guilty, and summarily executed. Wirz claimed he simply didn't have food, clothing, or medical supplies to give the prisoners and that his own staff suffered equally as the Confederacy began to crumble.

Acts of Kindness and Respect

In contrast to the brutality and horrifying conditions of some POW camps in the North and South are numerous reports of gallantry and kindness at others. For the most part, officers were especially well treated on both sides. They occasionally dined with the commanding officers of the camp and were often given new uniforms (minus their military buttons) when exchanged. In one example of unexpected chivalry, Union general Benjamin Butler, who was not particularly well known for his generosity, went to astounding lengths to find a special horse belonging to Confederate cavalry brigadier William H. F. Lee, the son of Robert E. Lee. The horse had been stolen during the younger Lee's capture in 1863.

Battlefield Medicine

Medicine was still crude during the Civil War, and the wounded and ill paid a horrible price for this lack of knowledge. Ironically, a number of important medical advances were made in the years immediately following the war, but they proved of little use to the poor wretches who found themselves under a battlefield doctor's care. In the eyes of many, those who died in battle were luckier than the wounded.

At its height, the Confederate POW camp near Andersonville, Georgia, contained more than 33,000 Union prisoners, making it the fifth largest city in the Confederacy. As Union armies neared Atlanta, 100 miles away, Confederates worried that a cavalry raid might free the prisoners and form an army in the Confederate rear.

The treatment of choice for broken or lacerated limbs was immediate amputation. The majority of patients were anesthetized with chloroform, ether, nitrous oxide, or, at the very least, a glass of whiskey. When anesthesia was unavailable, a cloth or bullet was placed in the patient's mouth for him to bite on, and he was held down by several strong orderlies while the doctor attended to the damaged limb with a knife and saw. Many field doctors could amputate a leg in less than two minutes. Following large battles with heavy casualties, doctors often worked nonstop for hours, tending

Amputation being performed in a hospital tent, Gettysburg, July 1863 *Photo courtesy of the National Archives (79-T-2265)*

to a seemingly endless stream of injured soldiers. Field hospital observers reported the grisly scene of severed limbs stacked like cordwood beside the operating table, waiting to be disposed of.

Amputation was only the beginning of a wounded soldier's troubles. Though his wounds had been treated, chances were better than good that he would soon fall victim to infection or, worse, gangrene.

The type of amputation played a role in patient survival; the smaller the limb, the less likely the chance of death. For example, of more than 8,000 finger amputations performed over the course of the war, fewer than 200 patients died. The deadliest type of amputation was that of the thigh; more than half of the patients receiving this procedure died within days, usually from massive blood loss and overwhelming infection.

War Doctors

One of the biggest medical problems during the Civil War was the inadequate training most doctors received. Just before the war, the majority of physicians served as apprentices rather than attending medical school, which meant that many were woefully unprepared for what they encountered on the battlefield.

As horrible as Civil War surgery was, it was often amazingly successful in saving a wounded soldier's life. According to U.S. Army records, of nearly 29,000 amputations performed during the war, only 7,000 or so patients died as a result. The most successful were those surgeries performed within forty-eight hours of injury; wounds tended later than that had a much poorer prognosis.

In Europe, four-year medical schools were fairly common, and students received a great deal of laboratory training. As a result, European physicians had a far better understanding of the causes and treatments of disease and infection. Students in American medical schools trained for less than two years and received almost no clinical experience and very little laboratory instruction. Amazingly, Harvard University didn't own a single stethoscope or microscope until after the war.

At the onset of the war, the Federal army had fewer than 100 medical officers, and the Confederacy had only twenty-four. By 1865, however, more than 13,000 Union doctors had served in the field and in hospitals. In the Confederacy, approximately 4,000 medical officers and a great many volunteers tended to the wounded.

Despite their lack of training and the horrible conditions under which they often worked, Civil War doctors did an astounding job of caring for the sick and wounded. Millions of cases of injury and disease were treated in just forty-eight months, and for the most part, doctors were compassionate and caring individuals who tried to put the concerns of their patients first.

Nurses and Clara Barton

Clara Barton is well known as the founder of the American Red Cross, but it was her remarkable humanitarian efforts during the Civil War that established her reputation as the "Angel of the Battlefield." She was also an ardent feminist, the first female diplomat, and an important advocate of health and education reform and civil rights.

Clara Barton *Photo courtesy of the National Archives (111-B-1857)*

Barton worked as a clerk in the U.S. Patent Office in Washington, D.C., where she saw the first casualties of the Civil War. She observed the inadequate medical care and noted that the wounded frequently went without sufficient food or clothing. Working independently of other relief agencies, Barton started lobbying to change the horrific conditions of battlefield medicine.

In July 1862, Barton received permission from the U.S. surgeon general to take medical supplies directly to the front lines and field hospitals. She risked her life to help the soldiers on the front at important battles such as Cedar Creek, Second Manassas, Antietam, and Fredericksburg. She also provided medical aid during the Carolinas campaign and in Virginia during Grant's 1864 offensives, where she was granted an official position with the Army of the James under the command of General Benjamin Butler.

As the war began to wind down, Barton was given a nearly overwhelming task by President Lincoln. He asked her to oversee the search for missing and captured Union soldiers, compile lists of the sick and wounded, and identify the Union dead buried in mass graves at Andersonville prison and elsewhere. The endeavor took Barton four long years to complete, but her efforts went a long way toward ensuring that Union soldiers who died on the battlefield and in prison were given decent burials and, more importantly, were remembered for their sacrifice.

Clara Barton was not the only woman who made tremendous sacrifices for the men who served in uniform. Women were by and large denied the opportunity of attending medical school, but thousands volunteered for medical service during the war. Union records show that approximately 4,000 women served as nurses in Union hospitals. Three thousand of these were recruited by Dorothea Dix, who volunteered for the Union in 1861 at the age of fifty-nine. She had worked before the war improving conditions for prisoners and the mentally ill. She was placed in charge of all female nurses for the Union and served in that capacity throughout the war at no salary. The number of Southern women who acted as nurses in Confederate hospitals is unknown but believed to be as high as that for the Union.

CHAPTER 18

Away from the Mainstream

The Civil War was far more textured an experience than it appears on the surface. About a quarter of the soldiers were foreign born. Another 200,000 were African Americans, some of whom fought for the South. For the first time in history, newspapers made detailed account of a war in progress, complete with illustrations. The new art of photography brought the horrors of war to communities that had sent their sons but had experienced no fighting themselves. And the role of women in the war must not be forgotten. Notable spies—even celebrated soldiers—were female.

African-American Participation in the Civil War

A large number of black men saw battle during the Civil War, fighting for both the North and the South. Bringing blacks into the military was an extraordinarily difficult task, but when they finally received their uniforms and guns, most proved to be exceptionally brave and skilled soldiers.

Early Prejudice

Many Northerners were reluctant to advocate the enlistment of blacks because it was commonly believed that black people had been held in servitude for so long that they were too cowardly to make good soldiers. Even Abraham Lincoln, a strong advocate of abolition, felt the concept had merit. Lincoln also feared that recruiting black soldiers would turn those border states with strong Confederate sympathies against the Union, something he was loath to do.

Despite the prejudice, several officers tried to enlist black men in defiance of the government. General David Hunter organized a regiment of black soldiers on the South Carolina Sea Islands in 1862, but the War Department refused to sanction it. In Kansas, General James Lane raised two regiments of fugitive slaves from Missouri and free blacks from the North. Lane's soldiers were not officially recognized by the War Department until early 1863, although they participated in several battles against Confederate sympathizers in Kansas and Missouri. In New Orleans, General Benjamin Butler initially turned down a regiment of black soldiers following the Union conquest of the city. He changed his mind and recruited three regiments of black soldiers when he was threatened by a sizable Confederate attack in August 1862.

Progress

Sentiments regarding the recruitment of black soldiers slowly changed in the summer of 1862 as the North experienced a number of defeats and morale began to plunge. People were growing weary of the war, and there was a noticeable decline in the number of able-bodied white men who enlisted for military service. This forced the government to seriously consider the idea of black recruitment, and in July 1862, Congress passed two acts that opened the door. The first was the Confiscation Act, which gave the president power to "employ as many persons of African descent as he may deem necessary and proper for the suppression of this rebellion." The second was an act that repealed the provisions of a 1792 law barring black men from joining a militia.

The Twenty-sixth U.S. Colored Volunteer Infantry on parade, Camp William Penn, Pennsylvania, 1865 *Photo courtesy of the National Archives (165-C-692)*

The passage of the two acts did little to quell Northern opposition to the recruitment of African-American soldiers, but on August 25, 1862, General Rufus Saxton, military governor of the South Carolina Sea Islands, was authorized by the War Department to raise five regiments of black soldiers to be commanded by white officers. Aiding the recruitment effort were prominent Northern black leaders, who did all they could to rally their brethren and encourage them to sign up in support of their rights as free citizens.

It took tremendous courage for black men to join the Union army. Despite promises from the government, most knew that taking up arms against the Confederacy—where many had previously been held in bondage—placed them in tremendous jeopardy. Southern soldiers were more likely to kill black soldiers than take them prisoner, and those who were captured risked execution or being resold into slavery. The risks were high for the white commanders of black regiments as well. In May 1863, the Confederate congress authorized President Jefferson Davis to have captured officers of black regiments put to death or otherwise severely punished, though history has shown that few white leaders of African-American regiments suffered at the hands of Confederate captors.

An estimated 200,000 blacks served in the Union army over the course of the Civil War, and more than 37,000 perished in battle. In some instances they were murdered after they had surrendered.

Despite these concerns, black regiments for the most part fought well and with exceptional bravery, often in the face of overwhelming odds. During the Battle of Port Hudson, a heavily fortified Confederate stronghold on the lower Mississippi, two regiments of black soldiers fought valiantly in the face of blistering rifle and cannon fire. The attack failed, but the troops demonstrated incredible heroism as they fought across open ground, and they earned effusive praise from their general.

From a Trickle to a Torrent

Equally brave was the Fifty-fourth Massachusetts, a black regiment commanded by Colonel Robert Gould Shaw and made famous in the motion picture *Glory*. It was composed of 650 African Americans from a number of Northern states; Shaw hailed from a vocal abolitionist Massachusetts family.

The regiment was sent to the South Carolina coast in May 1863. Major General Quincy Gillmore had devised a very risky plan to take back Fort Sumter and capture Charleston. The biggest obstacle was Battery Wagner on a tip of Morris Island, which stood a little more than a mile from Fort Sumter. The battery was small and fairly isolated, but it was well defended with 1,200 troops and much heavy artillery.

Union forces bombarded Battery Wagner for almost a week before Gillmore ordered an assault by 6,000 infantry—with the Fifty-fourth Massachusetts leading the way. The regiment fought a bloody hand-to-hand battle atop a palmetto parapet before being pushed back. Colonel Shaw was killed by a bullet through the heart, and nearly 40 percent of his regiment was slaughtered. The bodies of the dead, including Shaw, were buried on the beach in a mass grave.

"It is not too much to say that if this Massachusetts Fifty-fourth had faltered . . . two hundred thousand troops for whom it was a pioneer would never have put into the field . . . But it did not falter. It made Fort Wagner such a name for the colored race as Bunker Hill has been for ninety years to the white Yankees."—the *New York Tribune*

Despite the failure of the assault on Battery Wagner, the noble efforts of the Fifty-fourth Massachusetts contributed greatly to bolstering the image of black soldiers. Sergeant William Carney became the first African American to win the Congressional Medal of Honor as a result of his bravery in that ill-fated charge, though he didn't receive the honor until 1901. In fact, twenty-three black soldiers received the Congressional Medal of Honor for their bravery and service in the Civil War.

Black soldiers played an increasingly important role during the final year of the Civil War. Recruitment proved very successful, and by October 1864, there were 140 black regiments in the Union army containing a total of 101,950 men. Fifteen African-American regiments served in the Army of the James and twenty-three in the Army of the Potomac during the Union invasion of Virginia in the summer of 1864. In fact, black troops participated in every major military campaign in 1864–65 except William Sherman's invasion of Georgia and the Carolinas.

African Americans in Southern Armies

Blacks also served in the Confederate army, especially during the latter part of the war, when fighting men were in desperately short supply. Some hoped that by volunteering they would receive better treatment; others felt it was better to volunteer than to be forced into military service. More than a few hoped that by fighting side by side with white soldiers they could finally put to rest the common belief that blacks were inferior.

Most free blacks and slaves pressed into Confederate military service were used as laborers, harvesting food and cotton and constructing fortifications and entrenchments. Some laborers found themselves suddenly "recruited" as soldiers in the thick of battle, when the Southern army needed more armed bodies. Large numbers of these soldiers quickly deserted to Union lines. In August 1861, the U.S. Congress passed a confiscation act that allowed the seizure of all property used to aid the Southern rebellion—including slaves who had worked on Confederate fortifications or other military efforts. The act laid the foundation for an eventual declaration of emancipation.

Very late in the war, the Confederate Congress did pass a bill permitting slaves to be formally enrolled as soldiers. It was a desperate measure and many Southerners were against it; however, no African-American fighting units reached the battlefield.

Ethnic Makeup of the Civil War

Soldiers from a wide variety of ethnic backgrounds participated in the Civil War. Of approximately 2 million Union soldiers, nearly a quarter were foreign born. An estimated 175,000 were German, 150,000 were Irish, and 50,000 were English or Canadian. Native Americans also fought on both sides, as did a number of Hispanics and Scandinavians. Immigration continued almost unabated in the North throughout the war, and many newcomers showed their gratitude by joining the Union army within months of their arrival.

Irish Americans in particular played an integral role in the war. Many had immigrated in the thirty years before the war; New York and Boston both contained large Irish enclaves. According to the 1860 census, more than 1.5 million Americans claimed to be from Ireland. The number of soldiers of Irish descent in the Union army is well verified, but statistics regarding the Confederacy are almost unknown. Still, Southern songs of the era suggest a strong regional Irish influence.

Northern Europeans

The Irish at this time in American were singled out for distrust and harassment. Many factories and businesses refused to hire people with Irish names. After the war, many Irish veterans returned home to face the same bigotry and biases that had hounded them prior to military service.

A large number of Germans also immigrated to the United States in the decades preceding the war. Most German, Austrian, and Dutch immigrants made their homes in areas that reminded them of their homeland, places such as Pennsylvania, Delaware, and Virginia. When the war broke out, they enlisted without hesitation, and many German Americans rose to positions of great importance within the Union army.

Scandinavian Americans served primarily in the Union army because the vast majority of them had settled in the Northern states. In addition, most Swedes, Norwegians, and Danes were opposed to slavery. A large percentage of the Scandinavian Americans who fought for the Union joined the navy. One of the most prominent was John Ericsson, a Swede who invented the propeller and designed the first Union ironclad ship, the *Monitor*.

Native Americans

The war years were difficult for the Native American peoples, most of whom were struggling for their own independence and autonomy. Some tribes, such as the Cherokee, participated directly in the war; others, especially those in the east, decided whether to get involved on an individual basis. Many tribes realized that the war offered an opportunity for them to reclaim lands that had been taken from them, because it meant fewer federal soldiers overseeing their territories.

According to government records, approximately 3,600 Native Americans served in the Union army. One of the best known was Colonel Ely Parker, a Seneca who served as an aide to Ulysses S. Grant and transcribed the terms of Lee's surrender at Appomattox.

Statistics regarding Native American participation on the Confederate side are unavailable, but many did serve the Southern cause. Probably the best known is Brigadier General Chief Stand Watie, who was three-quarters Cherokee and organized a regiment known as the First Cherokee Mounted Rifles. Watie and his men fought bravely in a number of battles, and Watie has the distinction of being the last Confederate officer to lay down arms—more than two months after Lee's surrender.

Chronicling the Civil War

The Civil War was one of the first wars to be extensively covered in the press on both sides. Newspaper and magazine journalists from the North, the South, and overseas were given amazing freedom to follow armies, observe battles, and talk with commanders. The resulting stories have helped historians understand what happened during the war and why.

FACT

William T. Sherman, who found himself the frequent subject of journalistic ridicule, was not a fan of the press. He once noted: "Reporters print their limited and tainted observations as the history of events they neither see nor comprehend." Others, however, avidly followed the war in their favorite newspapers. Generals sometimes learned more from enemy newspapers than from spy reports.

Abraham Lincoln and Jefferson Davis were often pilloried in the press for their actions and policies, and their military leaders also found themselves subject to ridicule and attack, especially when they didn't win. Indeed, military success always seemed to play a role in whether the government was perceived positively or negatively. Reporters covering field action risked their lives to get the story. Daily newspapers and weekly news magazines such as *Harper's Weekly* and *Leslie's Weekly* sent reporters, photographers, and artists out by the dozens to cover the action, and many lost their lives. Photography was still in its infancy, so most newspapers and magazines relied on sketch artists to capture the essence of a particular event or scene. It wasn't uncommon for artists to sit on hills overlooking violent battles, sketching as fast as they could, with the intent of fleshing out their illustrations afterward.

Photography

Though it was a relatively new art form, photography helped put a human face on warfare. People on the home front were confronted with hundreds of images of war's inevitable death and destruction. Famous photographers include George Barnard, Alexander and James Gardner, George Cook, Timothy O'Sullivan, and, of course, Mathew Brady.

Studio photographers in cities and towns across the nation captured the many emotions of families who found themselves thrown into conflict. Understandably, photographs of family and friends were cherished mementos among soldiers in the field. Mathew Brady has been called the father of contemporary photojournalism, and with good reason. The photographs taken by Brady and his staff chronicled a war in progress for the first time.

Brady's photographic outfit in the field near Petersburg, Virginia, 1864 *Photo courtesy of the National Archives (111-B-5077)*

Before discovering photography, Brady worked as a painter and a craftsman of jewelry boxes. His life changed when he started experimenting with the daguerreotype photographic process. He opened a portrait studio in New York in 1844, found great success photographing celebrities, and opened a second studio in Washington, D.C., in 1858. By the time the Civil War started, Brady was using a new wet-plate photographic process. Its mobility, he realized, would allow photographers to document the conflict at the scene, and he turned his back on studio portraits to follow Union troops. Brady's photography wagon, which went with him to the battlefield, was a marvel. He started calling it his "What-is-it-wagon" because that's what people would ask wherever he went. Soon Brady and his staff became well known, and soldiers realized that at least one photographer would probably be present at every major battle.

The photographic process was slow and exposures were typically long, which explains why there are very few actual battle scenes. As the war went on, Brady's eyesight began to fail, so he hired a staff of photographers to continue his work. Few, however, received the credit due them, and Brady's name appeared on many photographs that he did not shoot. Several of the photographers under Brady's employ eventually went off on their own, seeking fame and fortune by covering the war for newspapers, magazines, and historical archives.

"It took unceasing care to keep every bit of the apparatus, as well as each and every chemical, free from contamination which might affect the picture. Often a breath of wind, no matter how gentle, spoiled the whole affair."—J. Pitcher Spencer, Civil War photographer

Brady and his staff managed to produce more than 3,500 photographs covering nearly every aspect of the war, including camp life, military portraits, and the aftermath of battle. Brady realized the importance of composition in a photograph and encouraged his staff to pose live soldiers as if they were going off to battle and to rearrange corpses for better visual effect.

Espionage During the Civil War

Spying during the Civil War was in one sense easy: nothing could distinguish a person's loyalty, except perhaps accent. The work, of course, was extremely dangerous. If caught, a spy risked death by hanging. Yet there was a constant stream of willing participants, not the least of which were women. Rose O'Neal Greenhow, for example, was a member of Washington society, a friend of numerous Northern politicians, and a Confederate spy. She sent information on Union plans to Confederate military leaders via coded messages transported by women on horseback.

Yet another femme fatale was actress Pauline Cushman, a Unionist who gained the confidence of Southern officials by toasting the Confederacy from the stage following a performance in Kentucky. Caught, she was condemned to death, but the end of the war saved her.

Belle Boyd

According to lore, Belle Boyd decided to become a spy for the Confederacy at age seventeen, after Union soldiers ransacked her family's Virginia home. Boyd operated from a Front Royal hotel owned by her father and was especially helpful during Stonewall Jackson's Shenandoah Valley Campaign of 1862. She provided important information regarding the movement of Union troops, as well as other secrets she managed to extract from Union officers by using her feminine wiles. Boyd delivered her reports via bold nighttime rides through enemy territory. She proved so helpful to the Confederate cause that Jackson named her an honorary aide-de-camp, and she became known throughout the South as "La Belle Rebelle."

FACT

Prostitution was a flourishing enterprise during the Civil War. Just one year after the war began, Washington, D.C., was home to more than 450 bordellos and an estimated 7,500 full-time prostitutes. The Confederate capital of Richmond boasted an equal number.

In June 1862, Boyd was placed in a Washington jail after being betrayed by one of her lovers, but she continued to aid the Confederacy by tossing rubber balls containing detailed notes from her jail cell window to an operative on the street below. Boyd was released in a prisoner exchange after four weeks but found herself behind bars again the following year, this time for five months. Boyd was released in December 1863 after contracting typhoid fever; she immediately went to Europe. She told people she was traveling abroad to recuperate, but in fact she was delivering letters from Jefferson Davis to the British government.

Boyd tried to return to the South aboard a Confederate blockade runner in May 1864, but the ship was stopped by a Union ship. The vessel's captain, Samuel Hardinge, fell in love with Boyd and helped her escape to Canada. They later married in England, but Hardinge died shortly after. When the war ended, Boyd published her autobiography and spent several decades entertaining lecture audiences in both the North and the South with tales of her adventures as a war spy. She died on tour in 1900.

Elizabeth Van Lew

Boyd's Union counterpart was Elizabeth Van Lew, a prominent Richmond citizen who loathed slavery and often lectured her neighbors on its evils. Given the nickname "Crazy Bet," she used her reputation as an eccentric to hide the many plans and schemes she concocted to aid the Union war effort from within Richmond, and she succeeded grandly.

Van Lew's first spy mission brought her to Libby Prison, a facility in downtown Richmond used to house Union POWs. She managed to get past the guards by bringing food, medicine, and books to the prisoners, and she came away with a wealth of information regarding Confederate troop movements and numbers. Van Lew helped a number of prisoners escape, and she enticed valuable information out of the camp's commandant. She even infiltrated Jefferson Davis's home, placing one of her former servants on his staff.

Van Lew also sent former servants into Northern territories carrying baskets of farm produce with coded messages in hollowed egg shells. Van Lew's courier system was fast and efficient; in fact, General Grant often received fresh flowers from Van Lew's garden via courier. Following the war, President Grant showed his appreciation for Van Lew's services by making her postmistress of Richmond.

Women and Children on the Battlefield

Contrary to popular belief, the Civil War was not fought only by adult males. Women and children also participated in the conflict in a variety of capacities, often giving their lives for a cause they deeply believed in.

Women in Camp

Many women did their part by traveling with soldiers as members of the so-called soapsuds brigade, whose sole job was to clean the clothes of military units. In most cases, members of the soapsuds brigade were the only women given official status in camp. Others, including officers' wives, were simply labeled camp followers. In the Union army, each company was permitted four laundresses. Many washerwomen were married to soldiers and lived with their husbands in the area of camp commonly known as suds row. If they were not married to a soldier, washerwomen were expected to be at least somehow related to a member of the unit. A washerwoman named Hannah O'Neil, for example, followed her son, who was a member of Company H of the First Minnesota Volunteer Infantry.

Far more rare were women who followed their loved ones into battle as more than washerwomen. A few military units adopted women as mascots or aides, and these women faced the same dangers as the male soldiers. One example is Kady Brownell, who was married to a member of the First Rhode Island (later the Fifth Rhode Island). Brownell was made the official "daughter" of the regiment and followed her husband to the front. According to some accounts, Brownell showed tremendous heroism during a battle in New Bern, North Carolina, on March 14, 1862, when she saved the Fifth Rhode Island from a friendly fire attack by rushing into the thick of battle and waving the flag. Brownell's husband was seriously wounded during that battle, and she spent the rest of her life caring for him.

Women Soldiers

Rarer still were women who disguised their gender in order to enlist and fight at the front. Pulling off such a feat was not easy, but many women did so successfully, slipping through the enlistment process and fooling their fellow soldiers. Those who were exposed because of injury or illness were either honorably discharged or merely dismissed, depending on their commanding officer. Many of those who were lauded for their military service drew veterans' pensions following the war.

Jennie Hodgers left Ireland as a stowaway, disguised herself as Albert D. J. Cashier, and served in the Illinois Volunteer Infantry from 1862 to 1865. Hodgers successfully kept her secret until the age of sixty-six, when she was struck by a car. A doctor at the veterans' hospital where she was treated discovered her true gender, but he kept it secret at Hodgers's request so she could continue to receive her veteran's pension.

Probably the most amazing tale of hidden identity was that of Loreta Janeta Velazquez, the Cuban-born widow of a Confederate soldier who raised and equipped at her own expense an infantry unit known as the Arkansas Grays. After her husband's death early in the war, Velazquez left her home and passed herself off as Harry Buford.

Velazquez was twice wounded and cited for gallantry. She was eventually stationed in Richmond, where her secret was discovered. Arrested as a spy, she convinced Confederate officials of her allegiance to the South and began work as a secret agent. In her autobiography, she wrote—truthfully—that she was as good a soldier as any man.

Children Rally

Children—that is, boys under the age of eighteen—also saw quite a bit of military service. Many lied about their age when enlisting; others were adopted as mascots by various military units. The exact number of underage soldiers is unknown, but some historians estimate the figure could be as high as 400,000. Many children were able to slip into the armed forces because recruiters were eager to fill quotas and usually didn't question boys who looked eighteen years old. However, even boys who were obviously underage succeeding in getting in, and many were assigned as regimental musicians.

Probably the most famous child to participate in the war is Johnny Clem, who became a legend in the Northern press. Clem ran away from home in 1861 at age nine to join a Union army regiment that had traveled through his hometown in Ohio. He was turned away but later joined another unit and served as its drummer boy; he also performed other camp chores.

According to U.S. military records, 127 Union soldiers were just thirteen years old when they enlisted, 320 were fourteen years old, nearly 800 were fifteen years old, 2,758 were sixteen, and approximately 6,500 were seventeen. Statistics regarding the number of underage soldiers in the Confederate army are unknown, but most historians believe the numbers to be even higher.

Clem was first immortalized in the press following the Battle of Shiloh, during which his drum was apparently destroyed. Officially enrolled in the army, complete with a miniature, hand-carved musket, Clem received additional press coverage as "the Drummer Boy of Chickamauga." During that battle, Clem allegedly shot and captured a Confederate soldier who tried to take him prisoner.

Despite his young age, Clem was captured once, wounded twice, and rose to the rank of lance sergeant before his fourteenth birthday. A few years later, Clem tried to enroll in West Point but was denied admission because he lacked a formal education. As a result of a direct appeal from President Grant, he was given a commission as second lieutenant and placed in command of a unit of black soldiers. He made the military his career, retiring as a major general shortly before the start of World War I. He died in 1937.

CHAPTER 19

Family Life During the Civil War

The Civil War was an all-encompassing event that touched the lives of almost every American. Whether you lived in the backwoods of Kentucky or a thriving eastern metropolis, the effects of the war were pervasive and inescapable. An astounding number of families on both sides of the conflict watched fathers, sons, and neighbors march off to battle, and many grieved when their loved ones and friends did not return.

America on the Eve of Destruction

The United States saw remarkable growth and prosperity during the three decades prior to the onset of the Civil War. Occasional economic corrections like the Panic of 1857 did not permanently disrupt the larger pattern of American well-being. The nation's population, encouraged by seemingly endless expansion, multiplied by leaps and bounds. By 1860, the nation was home to nearly 32 million people, including 4 million slaves. Since 1810, the American population had grown four times faster than Europe's, a growth rate that was almost six times the world average.

Rapid Economic Change

Most Americans continued to live in rural areas—that is, towns with fewer than 2,500 people—but the urban population was growing by leaps and bounds as people headed to burgeoning cities to seek their fortunes. The rate of urbanization during this period was the highest in American history; the urban population grew three times faster than the rural population in the five decades between 1810 and 1860.

FACT

Civil War memorabilia has become incredibly collectible today, especially handwritten letters from soldiers in the field. A family letter with interesting war-related content can sell for hundreds, even thousands, of dollars at auction.

Americans witnessed a huge evolution in lifestyle in the decades prior to the Civil War. The telegraph made communication almost instantaneous, and a network of canals, highways, and railroads made transportation faster and easier, dramatically reducing the cost of shipping goods.

Of equal importance was the rise of the middle class, which took advantage of dramatic advances in manufacturing. In the past, specialized craftsmen had been responsible for producing most common goods. Everything from shoes to guns to farm equipment was made by hand, but the American Industrial Revolution, with its emphasis on interchangeable parts and factory assembly, quickly changed the way Americans shopped. Increasing numbers of Americans bought factory-made or premade goods simply because they were so affordable.

Better, More Affordable Housing

At the beginning of the nineteenth century there were three basic types of housing: rough-hewn log cabins; homes made from brick or stone; and homes made from fastened, heavy timbers cut to shape by carpenters. Log homes were the least expensive and easiest homes to make, but most middle- and upper-income families wanted something nicer. However, the craftsmen needed to build stone or timber homes were in short supply, so the wait could be long.

The education of slaves was considered a very low priority by the majority of slave owners. As a result, only one-tenth of slaves could read and write with any fluency. Education for southern whites lagged behind northern standards. In 1860, roughly one southern white man in five was illiterate, but the illiteracy rate for southern white women was higher.

The answer came in the form of balloon-frame houses. The construction of a balloon-frame home didn't take as long or cost as much as one made from stone or hand-hewn timber, and the resulting structure was both attractive and sturdy. The first balloon-frame homes were built in Chicago and Rochester, New York, in the 1830s and quickly revolutionized the housing industry.

Improved Education Opportunities

In addition to the rapid expansion of industrialization, the growing use of mass production, and the rise of the middle class, the decades preceding the Civil War saw yet another positive social mark—the education of the American public. In years past, children often skipped a formal education in lieu of some sort of apprenticeship, but by the mid-1800s, a formal education was almost mandatory as increasingly affluent parents sought a better life for their children. More than 95 percent of adults in the New England states could read and write, and three-fourths of the children between the ages of five and nineteen were enrolled in school.

Education in the South was not quite as commonplace as it was in the North. But at midcentury, approximately 80 percent of the white population could read, write, and perform basic math, and one-third of white children attended school for an average of three months per year. These rates were higher than those for Britain and northern Europe at the time.

At the onset of the Civil War, the vast majority of Americans—North or South—were enjoying a fairly comfortable lifestyle. There was still much poverty in the nation, but work was readily available, the majority of families enjoyed financial prosperity, and an increasingly wide variety of consumer goods was available at affordable prices. It would be difficult to find a nation with more potential than the United States at midcentury, and its citizens were reaping the rewards.

Family Life

The Civil War was especially difficult on the family unit, which tended to be close knit and often extended. In most families, the husband and the eldest sons were the primary breadwinners, and it was a great loss when they had to go off to war. This was especially true among middle-class families, in which wives and mothers often had little experience providing for their families. A farmer's wife knew how to hold down the family stake in her husband's absence, but city women were in a much more difficult position.

Women of the era had an indomitable spirit, however, and they drew from deep reserves of strength and ingenuity when it came to supporting their families. Those who had been sheltered their entire lives, which was common, often found the transition traumatic, but they persevered as never before. In many ways, Civil War wives were the forbearers of World War II's Rosie the Riveter and the trendsetting feminists of the 1960s and 1970s. Many women found themselves running farms, plantations and businesses while their husbands were away. Thousands of women on both sides worked as nurses or aided the troops through such organizations as the United States Sanitary Commission.

Coping with Loss and Trauma

While they may have disagreed on ideology, families on both sides of the war shared one common trait: the pain of personal loss. Husbands and fathers died by the hundreds of thousands in both the North and the South, and thousands more returned home wounded and maimed. Many men were so shattered by their wartime experiences that they were little more than emotional and physical invalids, a situation that placed a huge burden on their already struggling families.

When the Civil War erupted, it often divided families. Lieutenant David H. Todd, commandant of the Confederate Libby Prison in Richmond, Virginia, was the half brother of Mary Todd Lincoln. John J. Crittenden, the former governor and U.S. senator from Kentucky, had tried to prevent the war in 1860 with a compromise; his sons fought on both sides of the war.

In addition to the financial hardship, the families of wounded veterans often had to face tremendous psychological pain. Many soldiers returned home suffering from what today would be diagnosed as posttraumatic stress disorder, and there were few resources available to help them or their families. Many women, initially ecstatic when their husbands returned home, watched their lives slowly crumble as they realized the rest of their years would be spent tending to their husbands' permanent wounds. Some women found they couldn't tolerate their postwar family existence and fled for a better life elsewhere.

Maintaining Bonds

Soldiers in the field maintained a strong sense of family by bonding with their comrades through common experience and background. Many senior officers went even further by appointing actual family members to their staff. During the winter months, when the war all but came to a halt because of the weather, entire families often joined their husbands and fathers in camp, happy to have the time together despite the conditions. In the summer, wives and children occasionally made short camp visits when their husbands and fathers were close enough.

Soldier's Aid

On the home front, many women participated in military assistance and relief efforts, such as sewing bees, food drives, and medical collections. Not only did these activities help provide soldiers with desperately appreciated items they probably wouldn't have been able to find elsewhere, but they gave the women a sense of unity and purpose. Weeks and months alone without their husbands plunged many women into severe depression; military relief efforts gave them something to do with their time and placed them in contact with others who understood their emotions. Families and soldiers also kept bonds strong by writing long letters back and forth. Nothing made a soldier's day like a letter from his loving wife, and vice versa.

Women performed front line work of the aid societies—nursing, sewing, and packaging—but they also did a good deal of the organizing and management. Elizabeth Blackwell, the nation's first officially degreed woman doctor, helped organize the Women's Central Relief Association, making it an effective and efficient organization that coordinated local efforts across the northern states. Abigail May ran the New England auxiliary of the U.S. Sanitary Commission, coordinating local chapters so that the most aid possible reached soldiers' camps.

Southern Suffering

Northern families lost a great many loved ones over the course of the war and experienced their share of problems and grief, but Southern families suffered far more. In the South, the threat of warfare was almost a daily occurrence. Numerous Southern towns and cities were destroyed over the course of the war, and the impact on the Confederate civilian population was enormous in virtually all areas. In many regions, it took all the coping skills families could muster to survive each day.

As the war progressed, the Northern blockade of Southern ports took a heavy toll on the general population. Items that Northerners took for granted became increasingly difficult to find in the South, and prices for basic necessities such as sugar and salt skyrocketed. Confederate money became almost worthless, and inflation reached staggering levels. For women who were the sole support of their families, it became a daily struggle to put together the most meager of meals.

A refugee family leaving a war area *Photo courtesy of the National Archives (200-CC-306)*

Worse still for Confederate families were the indignities they were forced to endure when Union forces invaded their towns. Many watched in helpless horror as their livestock and produce was taken from them or simply destroyed on the spot by vengeful Federal soldiers. Many families simply fled, wandering from area to area in search of food and shelter. This way of life was extremely hazardous, and the children suffered the most. An entire generation grew up hating the North, often justifiably.

For a great many soldiers, the horrors they had witnessed on the battlefield only increased their compassion for civilians caught in the middle. Most soldiers had families back home, and they understood well the emotional trauma the war caused. A good deed on their part might result in a good deed by others later on.

City Life

The vast majority of the nation's largest cities were located in the Northern states; the South lagged far behind. One of the reasons for this was the huge influx of foreign immigrants—primarily from Ireland and Germany—who poured into the nation in the decades before the war. While many new arrivals spread out to settle in regions that reminded them of home, the majority stayed in the cities—New York, Chicago, Boston, and other metropolitan areas—in the hope of finding well-paying jobs in the factories and businesses. This influx of immigrants would continue as the war raged, making many American cities some of the most populous in the world.

The population of many Northern cities exploded in the years prior to the war. The population of New York, for example, rose from 515,000 to more than 800,000 in the 1850s alone, and the population of Chicago, which was just over 4,000 when the city was incorporated in 1837, rose to 112,000 by 1860.

In many respects, life in the cities during the Civil War wasn't that much different from city life today. There were the very rich, the very poor, and the many in between. The poor tended to live in tenements; the rich lived in fine homes that often resembled palaces.

Bustle in the North

The streets of midcentury American cities were as busy and bustling as they are today. There was lots of coming and going, which meant lots of traffic—horse-drawn, of course.

Entertainment was rich and diverse in both the North and the South. Stage plays drew huge audiences. Operas, musical concerts, and lectures were also quite popular, as were ethnic stage shows that catered to a region's particular immigrant populations. If you had the money, there was seldom a lack of something to do. One of the most popular amusements in New York during the Civil War era was P. T. Barnum's curiosity museum in lower Manhattan. The veteran showman sold a huge number of tickets as New Yorkers flocked to see amazing animals and exhibits from around the world.

Southern Worries and Deprivations

Things were a bit more relaxed in the largest cities of the South, which included New Orleans, Richmond, Savannah, and Atlanta. The pace of the Southern states in general was much slower, a phenomenon that often baffled visiting Northerners before the war. One reason, of course, was that much of the region's hard labor was performed by slaves, giving its wealthier citizens plenty of free time in which to relax and indulge their personal passions.

Immigration brought a strong, cheap labor force to the United States during the mid-1800s. However, many immigrant women were unable to find decent paying work and were forced into a life of prostitution. An estimated one in twenty women who had come to the United States from abroad was forced by circumstance to sell her body in order to survive.

Southern cities were bustling but not overly crowded. Just prior to the beginning of the Civil War, Charleston, Richmond, and Savannah each had fewer than 40,000 citizens. Only New Orleans was comparable to the largest Northern cities, with a population of around 150,000. People traveled by carriage, cart, or horseback and very often lived on the outskirts of the city itself.

The Civil War had a far greater impact on Southern cities than those in the North. As the war encroached farther and farther into the Confederacy, many Southern cities found themselves under assault and eventually under Union control. But even if Northern troops never actually invaded a particular city or town, the good life eventually stopped as supplies, both luxury and essential, became increasingly difficult to get and prices skyrocketed. Southern city dwellers did all they could to keep their spirits high, but every Confederate defeat made it more difficult.

Citizens of the Confederacy were also asked to give what they could to the military, which eventually ran desperately short on essential supplies. The situation was particularly dire during the winter months of 1863. In October of that year, Captain W. M. Gillaspie, who was responsible for outfitting the army in Alabama, made an eloquent plea for supplies via the newspaper:

I want all the blankets and carpets that can possibly be spared. I want them, ladies of Alabama, to shield your noble defenders against an enemy more to be dreaded than the Northern foe with musket in hand—the snows of coming winter. Do you know that thousands of our heroic soldiers of the West sleep on the cold, damp ground without tents? Perhaps not. You enjoy warm houses and comfortable beds. . . . If the immortal matrons and maidens of heathen Rome could shear off and twist into bowstrings the hair of their heads to arm their husbands in repelling the invader, will not the Christian women of the Confederacy give the carpets off their floors to protect against the chilly blasts of winter those who are fighting with more than Roman heroism, for their lives, liberty, and more, their honor? Sufficient blankets cannot be had in time. Food and clothing failing the army, you and your children will belong to Lincoln.

By contrast, most Northern cities were overflowing with material goods and people with the money to buy them. The *New York Herald* reported in October 1863:

All our theaters are open . . . and they are all crowded nightly. The kind of entertainment given seems to be of little account. Provided the prices are high and the place fashionable, nothing more is required. All the hotels are as crowded as the theaters; and it is noticeable that the most costly accommodations, in both hotels and theaters, are the first and most eagerly taken. Our merchants report the same phenomenon in their stores: the richest silks, laces, and jewelry are the soonest sold. At least five hundred new turnouts may be seen any fine afternoon in the park; and neither Rotten Row, London, nor the Bois de Boulogne, Paris, can show a more splendid sight. Before the golden days of Indian summer are over these five hundred new equipages will be increased to a thousand. Not to keep a carriage, not to wear diamonds, not to be attired in a robe which cost a small fortune, is now equivalent of being a nobody.

Farm Life

The life of farmers in both the North and the South was considerably different from that of their city-dwelling brothers. Farmers tended to live far from the city, often spending their entire lives in the small town of their birth, growing sufficient crops to feed their families and make a small profit.

Farm life in the middle of the nineteenth century was hard work, even with the many labor-saving devices that had become available as a result of the Industrial Revolution. Once the animals had been fed at dawn, the farmer would spend the rest of his day tending to his crops, which varied greatly from one region to another.

Support Through Hardships

Farming communities in both the North and the South tended to be fairly close knit, with farmers coming to the aid of others when necessary. Most farmers used hired help to tend the land, though smaller farms were typically family affairs, especially if the family included several strong boys. Despite the common notion regarding slavery in the South, most small to midsize Southern farms did not use slaves because of the high cost of purchase and maintenance; slaves were more a luxury for wealthy plantation owners.

Women and Immigrants in Charge

As the war depleted the nation's male population, farmers' wives in both the North and the South suddenly found themselves the heads of their households. Unlike their overly protected city sisters, however, farm wives tended to be robust in nature and unafraid of hard labor. When their husbands went off to war, they picked up the hoe and plow and went to work. It was seldom a question of yes or no; for most farmers' wives, it was a simple issue of survival.

Many farmers, especially those in the North, were European immigrants striving for a better life in the Land of Plenty. They brought their customs and traditions with them, including a strong worth ethic and a sense of family and religion. Church usually played a vital role in the life of the average farmer, and Sunday was commonly a day of rest, reflection, and prayer, except during harvesting season, when crops waited for no one. But even then, most farmers tried to attend church whenever possible.

Day-to-Day Struggles

Farmers often suffered greatly during the Civil War, especially in the South. They usually lived far from town, which made them easy targets for marauders and invading forces, especially those in desperate need of food. Hungry Confederate soldiers begged for whatever a farmer could spare, but Union soldiers were seldom as considerate. Pillaging was discouraged by most officers, but the rule was difficult to enforce, and Union soldiers often took whatever they wanted and destroyed crops and livestock simply to keep them from falling into Confederate hands. Sadly, many farmers were unjustly punished by this reasoning, and it wasn't uncommon for a fleeing farmer to return to his homestead only to find it burned to the ground. This was especially true during Sherman's March to the Sea and his campaign through the Carolinas.

Plantation Life

Contrary to popular belief, which has been fueled by movies such as *Gone with the Wind*, the South was not one huge collection of large plantations. There were far more small and midsize farms—most of which were tended without slaves. However, the easy lifestyle of the landed gentry has become firmly embedded in the public consciousness.

The Deep South was home to the majority of plantations—large, almost palatial homes overseeing hundreds and often thousands of acres of prime farmland tended by slaves. Louisiana and Virginia both contained a large number of plantations, most of which grew cotton, tobacco, indigo, and rice, but plantations could be found in almost all of the Confederate states. Indeed, the plantation embodied the Southern sensibility and lifestyle in the eyes of most Northerners, even if they had never seen one.

QUESTION?

What is a plantation?

A functioning plantation usually consisted of a large family home, slave quarters, smokehouses, gardens, a stockyard, and the farmland itself, which could be quite expansive. Many large plantations contained everything necessary for daily maintenance and were virtually self-sufficient. The slaves worked the fields, occasionally assisted by paid white laborers, and in a good year each field slave produced a profit of $250.

Plantation owners were, for the most part, wealthy individuals with a taste for the finer things in life. They typically left the daily maintenance of their estates and farms to their staff, which allowed them time to indulge their particular hobbies. Hunting was a favorite pastime among wealthy plantation owners, and most Southern men—rich and poor—learned to ride and shoot at a very young age. Horse racing was another popular activity, and one that usually resulted in sizable bets between local plantation owners; many brought surplus slaves to the races to back large wagers.

Wealthy Southern planters, like the Northern rich, also enjoyed entertaining. Large, lavish house parties, balls, and banquets were held quite frequently. Attire was often formal, and the women reveled in showing off their best dresses, including the hoop skirts that have come to typify the classic Southern belle. Anyone who has viewed the scene in *Gone with the Wind* in which Scarlett O'Hara is stuffed into a corset and then a hoop skirt will understand the pains to which Southern women went in order to be fashionable.

Slaves on the Plantation

Most planters were doted on by a house staff that included butlers, maids, and cooks, as well as nannies for the planter's children. Like the farmhands and plantation overseers, the majority of plantation house staff were slaves. The nannies, commonly referred to as mammies, played an especially important role in the daily running of the household, and the children of a plantation often grew up with a closer bond to their nannies than to their own mothers. It was the responsibility of the nanny to care for the children—to see that they were fed, went to school, and behaved themselves. When they misbehaved, it was usually the nanny who punished them as well; it was one of the few instances in which a slave was allowed to lay a hand on a white person.

"Arlington House . . . has one of the most beautiful situations imaginable. . . . It was evidently in its day a grand affair; and its arrangement, furniture, pictures, &c., at once carry one back to the good old 'first family' days of Virginia."—John Nicolay, visiting Robert E. Lee's Arlington plantation home after it was seized by Federal troops, 1861

The treatment of slaves varied greatly among plantation owners. Some were strict to the point of brutality, administering severe punishment for the slightest infraction and running the home more by fear than respect. But for the most part, planters took relatively good care of their slaves, who were viewed as an expensive investment (a capable farmhand could cost more than $1,000 at auction). Punishment was doled out where appropriate, but minor infractions were often ignored. Many plantation owners also gave their slaves a small piece of land to farm for themselves and sometimes even paid them a small wage or allowance with which they could buy personal items. Of course, that's not to infer that the life of a slave was pleasant. Even under the best circumstances, slaves were still considered nothing more than property, and even the best-treated slave still dreamed of freedom.

Worse as the End Drew Near

As with small and midsize farms, many large plantations were hard hit as the Civil War went on. Even the wealthiest land baron had little purchasing power when all he had in the bank were worthless Confederate notes, and many planters found themselves scrimping to survive toward the end of the war. Plantation owners also faced the wrath of invading Union forces, many of whom saw the Southern plantation as the embodiment of Southern evil. It wasn't uncommon for Union forces to vandalize and even destroy plantation homes, steal personal belongings, set free the slaves, and harass or attack the owners if they were home.

Religion

Nineteenth-century America found itself in the midst of a religious upheaval. Prior to 1830, the majority of white Americans were of British heritage and Protestant in their beliefs. By 1830, however, the floodgates of immigration had been thrown wide open and tens of thousands of Irish and German immigrants made their way across the Atlantic. More than two-thirds of these new settlers were Catholic, a situation that greatly alarmed many Protestant Americans and resulted in an increase in nativist organizations. This anti-Catholic bias lasted for decades.

FACT

Some of the first abolitionists were the Quakers, who believed holding another man in servitude was a sin. In 1688, a group of Quakers made the first organized protest against slavery and the slave trade in Germantown, Pennsylvania. Many Southern Quakers migrated west rather than live in a slave-based society.

For the most part, Americans were a deeply religious people. The Protestant work ethic was alive and well during the Civil War era, and it was the rare individual in either the North or the South who didn't attend church regularly. In the North, the evil inherent in slavery was a popular subject, and abolitionist preachers used the pulpit to stir up antislavery sentiment. Southerners countered by quoting scripture they felt condoned slavery. Genesis 9:25-27, for example, was often used as justification for enslaving blacks. The passage quotes Noah, who has been angered by his son Ham, cursing all of Ham's descendants: "a slave shall he be to his brothers." According to the Bible, Ham fathered four sons, who gave rise to the southern tribes of the earth, including all of the people of Africa. Many Southerners also defended the institution with the argument that slavery was actually good for blacks because it enabled them to be converted to Christianity and thus go to heaven.

CHAPTER 20

Reconstruction and Remembrance

The seceded states had to be restored into the Union, and former slaves had to be acclimated to their new status as freed citizens. This was the work of Reconstruction, which lasted more than a decade. Its course was rocky and only imperfectly accomplished. The Civil War and its aftermath still have a firm grip on the American imagination, as evidenced by the numerous books, motion pictures, and television shows depicting or analyzing its many aspects.

Reconstruction

Reconstruction—the process of rebuilding the war-torn South—began shortly after the fall of the Confederacy and continued for approximately twelve years. The many policies enacted during this period by the U.S. Congress and Presidents Andrew Johnson and Ulysses S. Grant were designed to bring the seceded states back into the Union and aid displaced individuals, especially freed slaves, but many of the policies were also punitive. The Radical Republicans in Congress wanted to make sure the rebellious South was sufficiently penalized for putting the nation through four years of war and to ensure that such a thing would never happen again.

FACT

Civil rights for freed slaves was not an easy accomplishment. Many Southerners did all they could to keep blacks down following the war, often resorting to mayhem. And not all violence against blacks was at the hands of civilians. In New Orleans, forty-eight African Americans were killed when police viciously put down a peaceful demonstration promoting black suffrage.

Lincoln was eager to extend a compassionate hand to the South, despite the trials and tribulations it had wrought, and a December 1863 policy was one of his first endeavors in that direction. This policy offered a full pardon to any recanting Confederate who took an oath of allegiance to the United States and all of its laws and proclamations regarding the institution of slavery. The only exemptions to this offer of amnesty were Confederate government officials and high-ranking military officers.

In addition, the proclamation provided for the formation of a state government that would be recognized by the president when the number of persons taking the oath of allegiance reached 10 percent of the number of voters in 1860. Congress retained the right to decide whether to seat the senators and representatives elected from such states.

Lincoln based the proclamation on his unwavering belief that secession was illegal and thus all of the Southern states had remained in the Union. According to this view, the governments of the Southern states had

CHAPTER 20: RECONSTRUCTION AND REMEMBRANCE

temporarily been taken over by rebels, and the key role of Reconstruction was to return loyal officials to power. It was Lincoln's hope that the offer of amnesty would result in a snowball effect by which the leaders of the South would defect back to the Union and the seceded states would return one by one.

Congress Adds Its Weight

Many in Congress were fearful that Lincoln's early program, which was quite moderate, would leave intact the political and economic framework that made slavery a driving force in the South. Even though slaves had become free citizens as a result of the war, there was nothing to help them establish themselves as self-sufficient individuals. Rather than slaves in chains, they would simply become landless serfs forced to labor under nearly the same conditions. Many Congressmen believed Reconstruction should be more of a revolution in which the South was dismantled and rebuilt with more Northern sensibilities. Only then could freed slaves enjoy all of the benefits of citizenship, including the right to vote.

"With malice toward none, with charity for all . . . let us strive on to finish the work we are in, to bind up the nation's wounds . . . to do all which may achieve and cherish a just and a lasting peace among ourselves and with all nations."—Abraham Lincoln, in his second inaugural address, March 4, 1865

The first response to Lincoln's plan came from Radical Republicans in the form of the Wade-Davis Bill, which offered more stringent criteria for rejoining the Union. Lincoln killed the bill with a pocket veto, meaning he didn't sign or return the bill to Congress before it adjourned for the year. By the end of the war, Congress had passed the Thirteenth Amendment, which abolished slavery throughout the Union and gave Congress the power and authority to enforce abolition with the proper legislation. Shortly after the passage of the Thirteenth Amendment, Congress established the Freedman's Bureau, which was a federally funded agency designed to distribute food, clothing, and other provisions to impoverished freedmen and to oversee "all subjects" relating to their condition and treatment in the South.

President Andrew Johnson tried to continue Lincoln's moderate Reconstruction policies following Lincoln's assassination in April 1865. In May of that year, he granted amnesty and pardons, including the restoration of all property rights, except for slaves, to all former Confederates who took an oath of loyalty to the Union and accepted emancipation. Johnson also appointed provisional governors to lead the Southern states in drafting new constitutions that would allow them to rejoin the Union.

Johnson Limits Civil Rights

Johnson did not provide for the millions of slaves who suddenly found themselves free men and women. Johnson believed the Southern states should decide for themselves the future of freedmen, a shortsighted position that led to the institution of numerous Black Codes—state laws designed to keep African Americans out of politics.

Johnson tried to make the restoration of the Union as painless as possible by appointing men loyal to the Union to lead the readmitted states; however, Radical Republicans took a different tack. They felt that since the seceded states had been defeated in the war, they no longer had any rights and should be treated as conquered territories. In their eyes, black suffrage and equal rights were the most important goals of Reconstruction, followed by the rebuilding of the ravaged South.

Many Southern whites felt extreme anger and frustration at the abolition of slavery and often expressed their hatred for blacks with violence. Between 1865 and 1866, more than 5,000 African Americans were killed or severely beaten because of the color of their skin. So vehement was this racial hatred that the federal government quickly realized military control was needed to bring Southern blacks into the national mainstream.

1867: Harsher Reconstruction Policies

Johnson faced other problems as well. Many in Congress felt Reconstruction should be the responsibility of the legislative branch of government and Johnson had overstepped his authority as president in instituting certain Reconstruction policies. In order to maintain control, Congress enacted three Reconstruction Acts in 1867, which dramatically affected Johnson's moderate plans for the rebuilding of the war-ravaged South. The eleven Confederate states were divided into five military districts under commanders who had the authority to use the army to protect the lives and property of all citizens—especially blacks. New state constitutions were required to include a promise to ratify the Fourteenth Amendment, which granted citizenship to newly freed slaves and directed the federal government to protect citizens from arbitrary state actions, including Black Codes. Other conditions included a loyalty oath swearing allegiance to the Union and a ban that prohibited former Confederate leaders from holding political office.

"Now, therefore, I, Andrew Johnson, President of the United States, do hereby proclaim and declare that the insurrection which heretofore existed in the States of Georgia, South Carolina . . . and Florida is at an end and is henceforth to be so regarded."—President Johnson, announcing the end of the Civil War on April 2, 1866

Reconstructionist policies enacted by Congress achieved quite a bit, including the first public, tax-supported school systems in most Southern states. There were also strong attempts to broaden and strengthen the Southern economy through aid to railroads and other industries. Most important of all, blacks were finally given a voice in local, state, and federal government.

Carpetbaggers

Carpetbaggers were Northerners who moved to the South following the war to take advantage of the ensuing social and political turmoil. The disparaging name came from the luggage they typically carried, called carpetbags.

Carpetbaggers were feared and unwelcome by most Southerners because of the way they twisted issues and situations for personal financial gain. One common tactic was to use the chaos of Reconstruction to secure political positions, primarily on the shoulders of easily manipulated black voters. Once they were in office, carpetbaggers lined their pockets through graft and bribery with seldom a glance toward their constituencies.

But not all Northerners who moved to the South were immoral. Many kindhearted Northerners were eager to help the region get back on its feet. These included teachers, doctors, industrialists, clergymen, and agents of the Freedman's Bureau. In addition, a large number of Union soldiers who had been sent to the South during the war decided to settle there afterward because they fell in love with the natural beauty of the region. But even these innocent men and women were viewed with skepticism by Southerners of both races, and the term "carpetbagger" was used as a pejorative term for any Northerner for generations after the war.

African-American Contributions to Reconstruction

African Americans were not passive watchers during Reconstruction. Long denied the opportunity to learn how to read and write, old and young alike took advantage of teachers who set up schools to teach former slaves. Both the teachers and the pupils helped to set up schools of higher learning, colleges, and universities.

Many African Americans ran for and won public office. Two served in the U.S. Senate; twenty served in the U.S. House of Representatives. Both chambers worked to enact laws that guided Reconstruction. Others won seats at the state conventions that rewrote the state constitutions, ensuring civil rights for all citizens. Here and in state legislatures, African Americans helped write laws setting up tax-supported schools for both races, property rights for women, and more equitable taxation policies. The new laws also forbade imprisonment for debt and like measures.

Confederate Exiles

Failed rebels traditionally faced one of two fates: flight into exile or hanging. American Confederates had another choice: returning to their homes and living in the restored country. Nearly all of them did—but not all. Some could not stand the notion of life under a government they had fought against for so long; they headed off into exile instead. General John Breckinridge and naval commander John Wood fled to Cuba. So did a number of other ex-Rebels. Other generals sailed for Europe.

Missouri cavalry leader Jo Shelby would not surrender. He led his men through Texas toward the Rio Grande. Such notable Confederates as Generals Sterling Price, John Magruder, and Kirby Smith joined him; so did Texas governor Pendleton Murrah. Hundreds of disaffected civilians added to the growing column. Upon crossing into Mexico, Shelby and his cohorts sided with the French-supported Emperor Maximilian, who, sensing growing hostility from his subjects, thought it best not to enlist Anglo soldiers as mercenaries. But the emperor did offer the group of former Rebels a piece of land near Vera Cruz that they could live on. They called their settlement Carlota. After a few years, however, the French withdrew their troops from Mexico and Maximilian was executed. The heart went out of the exile colony and it dissolved.

An estimated 10,000 to 20,000 Confederates left the United States rather than live under its government. The number would have been higher had not Robert E. Lee urged his fellow Southerners to remain in their states and make lives as good citizens.

The most successful Confederate colonies were established in Brazil. Many Southerners favored Brazil because slavery was still legal there (it was abolished in 1888). The Brazilian government welcomed the Southerners, hoping they would establish cotton plantations and turn Brazil into a cotton-producing country. Thousands of former Rebels helped establish a handful of colonies. They and their descendents spoke English for decades, and they ran their own schools and churches. The exiles sent back for teachers and ministers to join them. Some of the descendents of these Confederate settlers became prominent Brazilian elected officials and businessmen. Today there are 350 members of Brazil's Fraternity of the Confederate Descendents.

For the most part, Confederate exiles drifted back to the United States after a few years. They could see there were no reprisals, and some had not been as prosperous in their new settlements as they had dreamed they would be.

The Official End of Slavery

The Thirteenth Amendment, ratified at the end of 1865, officially abolished slavery. It reads as follows:

> **Section 1**—*Neither slavery nor involuntary servitude, except as a punishment for crime whereof the party shall have been duly convicted, shall exist within the United States, or any place subject to their jurisdiction.*

> **Section 2**—*Congress shall have power to enforce this article by appropriate legislation.*

Its ratification freed approximately 4 million blacks who had not otherwise been freed over the course of the Civil War and ended the institution of forced servitude forever.

However, had things gone differently, the Thirteenth Amendment would have continued slavery rather than abolished it. In 1861, an amendment to that effect was proposed in a desperate attempt to avoid a civil war and keep the Union whole. It was supported by nearly half of the congressional Republicans and the vast majority of Democrats and had passed both the House and the Senate by the required two-thirds majority; however, the war erupted before the amendment could be ratified by three-quarters of the states.

Lincoln's Emancipation Proclamation officially made the abolition of slavery a goal of the war, but because it was a wartime edict, it freed only slaves from states in armed rebellion against the Union. There was a very good chance it wouldn't apply once the war was over, and many believed the Supreme Court would rule the proclamation unconstitutional.

In an attempt to end slavery in the United States once and for all, Lincoln laid the groundwork for a constitutional amendment abolishing the institution in 1864. The Democratic Party opposed ratification, even though Lincoln tried to sweeten the pot by promoting financial compensation from the federal government to all slaveholders. Despite objections from the Democrats, the Republican-dominated Senate quickly passed the proposed amendment in April by a vote of thirty-eight to six. The House voted on it twice before it finally passed in January 1865 by a vote of 119 to fifty-six.

Lincoln signed the amendment in a symbolic gesture the very next day, and eight states ratified it within a week. The passage of the Thirteenth Amendment was celebrated with a 100-gun salute from artillery batteries on Capitol Hill. It took eight months for the rest of the states to follow suit, and Lincoln did not live to see it ratified. The Thirteenth Amendment was officially ratified on December 18, 1865.

African Americans after the War

Southern blacks faced daunting challenges in the aftermath of the Civil War. Mainly illiterate and knowing little of the world beyond the location of their birth, they also faced a largely hostile white population who tended to blame many of their tribulations on black people. The federal government attempted to step in to ease the transition into citizenship for former slaves, but life in general remained harsh and threatening for African Americans.

The Freedman's Bureau

The Bureau of Refugees, Freedmen, and Abandoned Lands was established by Congress on March 4, 1865, in an attempt to aid the more than 4 million former slaves who lived in the South at the end of the Civil War. The Freedman's Bureau was initially intended to last for only one year, and it was hobbled by allegations of corruption as well as a lack of funds and manpower. However, it was still effective in helping the uneducated and poverty-stricken African Americans who suddenly found themselves without homes, jobs, or money. It ceased operation at the end of 1868.

The bureau's primary goal was to distribute food, clothing, fuel, and medical care to former slaves, as well as oversee their well-being and treatment. General Oliver O. Howard, a well-respected Civil War veteran, was chosen to head the bureau's 900 agents.

One of the agency's most difficult tasks was creating a judicial system that was fair to both blacks and whites. Not surprisingly, most Southerners weren't particularly eager to treat freed slaves fairly, so the bureau first established its own judicial authority with local agents, setting up temporary three-man courts to hear disputes.

QUESTION?

Why is Reconstruction said to have ended in 1877?
By 1877, most Southern states were pushing or had pushed Northern-supported governments out of power. The final straw came in the 1876 presidential election when the Republicans agreed to withdraw federal soldiers from the South in exchange for Southern support for contested electoral votes. The Republican candidate, Rutherford Hayes, became the nineteenth president, and Reconstruction efforts effectively ended.

The Freedman's Bureau also worked diligently to bring former slaves into a free labor economy. Plantations were still integral to the Southern economy, and the agency strove to bring African Americans into that work force with fair wages and the opportunity for advancement. One way in which that was accomplished was through the distribution of land that had been confiscated or abandoned during the war. The initial pledge was "forty acres and a mule" to every freed slave, but only about 2,000 freedmen in South Carolina and 1,500 freedmen in Georgia actually received the land as promised.

Another important concern was health care. The bureau tried to strengthen existing health care facilities and establish a series of health clinics. During its operation, the bureau helped nearly 500,000 freed slaves receive medical attention.

However, things were far from perfect in the New South. The region's economy continued to be dominated by agriculture, despite attempts to industrialize—a situation that would continue into the twentieth century—and many Southerners did all they could to keep African Americans from assuming their constitutionally guaranteed place in society. For example, many Southern states made it extremely difficult for blacks to vote by enacting deliberately prohibitive laws such as the poll tax. Most blacks also received far lower wages than white workers, which prevented them from buying land and otherwise becoming financially independent. Southern African Americans may not have been slaves any longer, but they were far from free. It wasn't until the civil rights movement of the 1960s that many of their invisible shackles were finally removed.

Black Codes

Black Codes were special laws passed by many Southern state governments early in Reconstruction to prevent former slaves from enjoying the benefits of their freedom. They restricted blacks' rights to buy, own, and sell property; make legally binding contracts; serve on juries; own weapons; and vote or run for political office. Black Codes also restricted African Americans from working in various professions, enforced apprenticeship prerequisites, required blacks to carry travel passes and proof of residence, and denied them their constitutional right to free assembly.

Margaret Mitchell's *Gone With the Wind* won the Pulitzer Prize for fiction in 1937 and has sold tens of millions of copies. It tells the story of a headstrong woman determined to survive the Civil War and Reconstruction, but it is criticized for its romantic view of Southern life and demeaning depiction of blacks both as slaves and freed persons.

Between 1866 and 1877, Congress tried to eliminate Black Codes by appointing Northern governors to head Southern states. However, after Reconstruction ended and politicians were replaced by Southerners, versions of Black Codes—known as Jim Crow laws after a popular minstrel song of the era—once again became commonplace.

The Civil War Timeline

1860

November 6
Abraham Lincoln is elected president

December 20
A state convention in South Carolina votes to secede from the Union

December 27
South Carolina troops seize Fort Moultrie and the federal arsenal in Charleston

1861

January 20
Florida, Alabama, Georgia, Mississippi, and Louisiana join South Carolina in seceding from the Union

January 29
Kansas is admitted to the Union as a free state

February 4
The six seceded states form a provisional government as the Confederate States of America (CSA)

February 9
Jefferson Davis is chosen president of the CSA by the Provisional Congress; Alexander Stephens is chosen as vice president

February 23

Texas secedes from the Union

March 4

Abraham Lincoln is inaugurated as the sixteenth president

March 16

The Confederate congress adopts a constitution similar to the U.S. Constitution but with one very important difference: it prohibits any law that interferes with slavery

April 12

South Carolina troops bombard Fort Sumter in Charleston Harbor; Major Robert Anderson surrenders the fort the next day

April 15

Lincoln proclaims a state of insurrection following the capture of Fort Sumter and calls for 75,000 volunteers to serve for three months

April 17

Virginia secedes from the Union

April 19

Union troops marching through Baltimore on their way to Washington, D.C., are attacked by Confederate sympathizers; twelve civilians and four soldiers die in the riot. That same day, Lincoln calls for a blockade of Southern ports.

May 6

Arkansas and Tennessee secede from the Union and join the Confederacy

May 13

Britain announces it will remain neutral regarding the Civil War and grants the Confederacy belligerent status

May 20

North Carolina secedes from the Union and joins the Confederacy

July 21

The First Battle of Manassas is fought; Union forces are routed

July 27

General George B. McClellan replaces General Irvin McDowell as head of the Army of the Potomac

August 10

Union commander Nathaniel S. Lyon is killed in the Battle of Wilson's Creek in Missouri, against Sterling Price and Benjamin McCulloch; Union general John Fremont later gains control of the strategic town of Cairo, where the Ohio and Mississippi rivers join

October 21

The Union is defeated at the Battle of Ball's Bluff, near Leesburg, Virginia

November 1

Lincoln retires General-in-Chief Winfield Scott and replaces him with General George B. McClellan

November 8

The *Trent* Affair occurs

1862

January 11

Edwin Stanton replaces Simon Cameron as Union secretary of war

February 16

Ulysses S. Grant takes Fort Donelson in Tennessee

February 21
The Battle at Valverde, in the New Mexico Territory, results in a Confederate victory

February 25
Nashville, Tennessee, falls to the Union without a fight

March 7–8
Confederate general Earl Van Dorn attempts to defeat Union forces at the Battle of Pea Ridge but is pushed back

March 9
The Union ironclad *Monitor* and Confederate ironclad *Virginia* engage in a duel at Hampton Roads, Virginia; the battle ends in a draw

March 11
Lincoln demotes McClellan from general-in-chief to commander of the Army of the Potomac

April 4
The Peninsular Campaign begins with a Union advance toward Yorktown, Virginia; Yorktown falls to the Union on May 4, and Williamsburg falls on May 5

April 6–7
The Battle of Shiloh results in a Confederate withdrawal from Pittsburg Landing, Tennessee.

April 7
Island No. 10 falls to Union land and naval forces, placing the Mississippi River under Union control all the way to Memphis

April 10
Lincoln signs a congressional resolution calling for gradual emancipation and the compensation of slave owners; slavery is also abolished in Washington, D.C.

April 25–May 1

The Battle of New Orleans

May 12

Natchez, Mississippi, also falls to the Union

June 1

Joseph Johnston is wounded in battle and is replaced by Robert E. Lee as leader of the Confederacy's Virginia forces

June 6

Union forces take Memphis, Tennessee

June 25–July 2

The Seven Days Battles results in a Union retreat and temporarily ends the Union threat to Richmond

June 30

The Union attempts to capture Tampa via gunboats, but Confederates refuse to surrender or retreat

July 20

Congress authorizes the acceptance of African Americans into military service and passes a second Confiscation Act that frees slaves belonging to all rebels

July 11

Lincoln names Henry Halleck as general-in-chief

August 28–30

The Second Battle of Manassas ends with a Union defeat; General John Pope, who led the Union forces, is replaced by McClellan

September 17

The Battle of Antietam in Maryland becomes the single bloodiest day of the war; though technically a draw, the battle forces Lee to abort his planned invasion of the North

September 27
The First Regiment Louisiana Native Guards becomes the first officially recognized black regiment

October 4
Union forces attack and occupy Galveston Harbor in Texas

October 8
The Battle of Perryville, Kentucky, stops a second Confederate invasion of the North

November 5
Lincoln dismisses McClellan a second time and replaces him with Ambrose Burnside

December 13
The Battle of Fredericksburg, Virginia, results in a Union rout with numerous casualties

December 31
The Battle of Murfreesboro, Tennessee begins; it ends inconclusively with a Confederate retreat on January 2, 1863

1863

January 1
Lincoln formerly issues the Emancipation Proclamation

January 1
Major General John Bankhead Magruder reclaims Galveston Harbor in Texas for the Confederacy

January 25
Lincoln replaces Ambrose Burnside with General Joseph Hooker as commander of the Army of the Potomac

March 3
Lincoln signs the first Conscription Act

May
The Bureau of Colored Troops is established by the U.S. War Department, signaling the active recruitment of blacks

May 1–4
The Battle of Chancellorsville, Virginia, results in a solid Confederate victory over Hooker's Army of the Potomac; the win is tempered by the loss of Thomas "Stonewall" Jackson

May 22
Grant attacks Vicksburg, Mississippi, and begins a lengthy siege of the city

June 22
West Virginia is admitted to the Union as a free state

June 27
Lincoln replaces Hooker with General George Meade as commander of the Army of the Potomac

July 1–3
The Battle of Gettysburg, Pennsylvania, results in a Union victory; Lee begins a retreat to Virginia and Meade fails to pursue him

July 4
Vicksburg finally surrenders to Grant after a lengthy siege, resulting in Union control of the Mississippi River

July 13–16
Crowds in several Northern cities riot in response to the Conscription Act

July 17
Jackson, Mississippi, is abandoned by Confederate troops

September 19–20

The Battle of Chickamauga, Georgia, results in a Union retreat to Chattanooga, Tennessee

October 3

Lincoln issues a proclamation making the last Thursday in November a national day of Thanksgiving

October 16

Lincoln appoints Grant commander of the united western armies

November 19

Lincoln delivers his famous Gettysburg Address

November 23–25

Grant comes to the rescue of Union-held Chattanooga, which had been besieged by Confederate forces; the Confederates later abandon Knoxville, bringing Tennessee under complete Union control

December 8

Lincoln offers amnesty to all Confederates willing to take an oath of allegiance

1864

January 19

Arkansas, a Union slave state, adopts a new antislavery constitution

February 3–14

General William Tecumseh Sherman captures Meridian, Mississippi, and begins his policy of "total warfare," destroying anything that could be used to aid the Confederacy

March 10

Grant is named commander of all the Union armies

April 12

Confederate soldiers under General Nathan Bedford Forrest capture Fort Pillow in Tennessee and slaughter hundreds of black soldiers in the aftermath

May 3

Grant, commanding 120,000 troops, begins his campaign to take the Confederate capital of Richmond

May 4

Sherman begins his march toward Atlanta with an army of 110,000 men

May 5–6

The Battle of the Wilderness ends in a draw between Grant and Lee

May 8–12

The Battle of Spotsylvania, Virginia, ends in a draw

May 15

General Jubal Early puts the brakes on a Union offensive by defeating Federal troops entering the Shenandoah Valley region of Virginia

June 1–3

The Battle of Cold Harbor, Virginia, results in a victory for Lee

June 7

The Republican Party nominates Lincoln for a second term as president despite growing public dissatisfaction with the way Lincoln has handled the war

June 15–18

Grant assaults Petersburg, Virginia, but is repelled by Lee; Grant lays siege to the city

June 27

The Battle of Kennesaw Mountain, Georgia, results in a Confederate victory over Sherman

July 14

General Early reaches the outskirts of Washington, D.C.; Early withdraws from the region when the Washington garrison receives reinforcements.

July 17

Jefferson Davis replaces Joseph Johnston who, with John B. Hood, was attempting to halt Sherman's assault on Atlanta

July 20–28

Hood attempts a direct assault on Sherman's army, resulting in high casualties

August 5

Mobile, Alabama, falls to Union admiral David Farragut, after the Battle of Mobile Bay

September 2

Sherman captures Atlanta

September 19–October 19

Union general Philip Sheridan drives Early from Virginia's Shenandoah Valley

October 13

Maryland adopts a new state constitution that abolishes slavery

October 23

30,000 men are engaged in the Battle of Westport, the greatest battle in Missouri; it is a Confederate defeat

October 25

Union cavalry defeat a Confederate force in Kansas during the Battle of Mine Creek

October 31

Nevada is admitted to the Union as the thirty-sixth state

November 8

Lincoln, buoyed by recent Union victories, is elected to a second term as president

November 16

Sherman begins his March to the Sea

November 30

The Battle of Franklin, Tennessee, proves a costly victory for Hood's Army of the Tennessee

December 15–17

The Battle of Nashville gives General George Thomas a solid Union victory

December 22

Sherman marches unopposed into Savannah, Georgia

1865

January 11

Missouri adopts a resolution abolishing slavery

January 15

Fort Fisher, which protects Wilmington, North Carolina, is captured by a combination of Union army and navy forces

January 31

The U.S. House of Representatives passes the Thirteenth Amendment abolishing slavery and goes to the states for ratification

February 1

Lincoln's home state of Illinois is the first to ratify the Thirteenth Amendment

February 22

Wilmington, North Carolina, is the last Confederate port to be taken by Union forces

March 3

Congress establishes the Bureau of Refugees, Freedmen, and Abandoned Lands to aid former slaves and white refugees

March 4

Lincoln is inaugurated for a second term

March 13

Davis signs a bill allowing blacks to join the Confederate army

April 1

The Battle of Five Forks, Virginia, results in a sound victory for the Union

April 2

Lee withdraws from Petersburg after ten months of fighting; he wires Davis that Richmond will soon fall

April 3

Union troops march into Petersburg and Richmond

April 6

The Army of Northern Virginia and the Army of the Potomac engage in their last battle at Sayler's Creek, Virginia

April 9

Confederate general Robert E. Lee formally surrenders to Union general Ulysses S. Grant at Appomattox Court House, Virginia

April 14

President Abraham Lincoln is shot by John Wilkes Booth; Lincoln dies the next morning

April 15

Vice President Andrew Johnson is sworn in as the nation's seventeenth president

April 18

Confederate general Joseph Johnston surrenders to General William Sherman, signaling the formal end to Confederate resistance

APPENDIX B

Resources

Websites

The Civil War/PBS
www.pbs.org/civilwar

The Trust
www.civilwar.org
The Civil War Trust is the largest battlefield preservation organization in the United States, and its website contains links to dozens of other Civil War-related sites, including the National Park Service Home Page (which includes separate pages for twenty-two Civil War battlefield sites, parks, and memorials), the United States Civil War Center, the Library of Congress American Memory Page, and the American Battlefield Protection Program.

The Valley of the Shadow Online Database (Virginia Center for Digital History)
http://valley.vcdh.virginia.edu
This website tells the story of the struggles of two communities, one Northern and one Southern. It includes primary documents from the Civil War era.

Books

A Companion to the Civil War and Reconstruction edited by Lacey Ford (Wiley-Blackwell)

A People's Contest: The Union and the Civil War 1861–1865 by Phillip Shaw Paludan (University Press of Kansas)

Battle Cry of Freedom: The Civil War Era by James M. McPherson (Ballantine Books)

Daughters of the Union by Nina Silber (Harvard University Press)

Don't Know Much about the Civil War by Kenneth C. Davis (William Morrow & Company)

Forever Free: The Story of Emancipation and Reconstruction by Eric Foner (Vintage Publications)

In the Presence of Mine Enemies: The Civil War in the Heart of America, 1859–1863 by Edward L. Ayers (W. W. Norton & Company)

Major Problems in the Civil War and Reconstruction, 2nd Edition edited by Michael Perman (Houghton Mifflin Company)

Mr. Lincoln's Camera Man: Mathew B. Brady, Revised 2nd Edition by Roy Meredith (Dover Publications)

Reconstruction: America's Unfinished Revolution, 1863–1877 by Eric Foner (Harper Perennial Modern Classics)

Scarlett Doesn't Live Here Anymore by Laura F. Edwards (University of Illinois Press)

The Civil War by Ken Burns (PBS Video)

The Civil War: A Narrative (3 Volume Set) by Shelby Foote (Vintage Books)

The Civil War: An Illustrated History by Geoffrey C. Ward, and Ric and Ken Burns (Knopf Publications)

The Civil War and Reconstruction: An Eyewitness History by Joe H. Kirchberger (Facts on File)

The Life of Johnny Reb: The Common Soldier of the Confederacy by Bell Irvin Wiley (Louisiana State University Press)

The Life of Billy Yank: The Common Soldier of the Union by Bell Irvin Wiley (Louisiana State University Press)

The Negro's Civil War by James M. McPherson (Ballantine Books)

Index

The EVERYTHING Series!

BUSINESS & PERSONAL FINANCE

Everything® Accounting Book
Everything® Budgeting Book, 2nd Ed.
Everything® Business Planning Book
Everything® Coaching and Mentoring Book, 2nd Ed.
Everything® Fundraising Book
Everything® Get Out of Debt Book
Everything® Grant Writing Book, 2nd Ed.
Everything® Guide to Buying Foreclosures
Everything® Guide to Fundraising, $15.95
Everything® Guide to Mortgages
Everything® Guide to Personal Finance for Single Mothers
Everything® Home-Based Business Book, 2nd Ed.
Everything® Homebuying Book, 3rd Ed., $15.95
Everything® Homeselling Book, 2nd Ed.
Everything® Human Resource Management Book
Everything® Improve Your Credit Book
Everything® Investing Book, 2nd Ed.
Everything® Landlording Book
Everything® Leadership Book, 2nd Ed.
Everything® Managing People Book, 2nd Ed.
Everything® Negotiating Book
Everything® Online Auctions Book
Everything® Online Business Book
Everything® Personal Finance Book
Everything® Personal Finance in Your 20s & 30s Book, 2nd Ed.
Everything® Personal Finance in Your 40s & 50s Book, $15.95
Everything® Project Management Book, 2nd Ed.
Everything® Real Estate Investing Book
Everything® Retirement Planning Book
Everything® Robert's Rules Book, $7.95
Everything® Selling Book
Everything® Start Your Own Business Book, 2nd Ed.
Everything® Wills & Estate Planning Book

COOKING

Everything® Barbecue Cookbook
Everything® Bartender's Book, 2nd Ed., $9.95
Everything® Calorie Counting Cookbook
Everything® Cheese Book
Everything® Chinese Cookbook
Everything® Classic Recipes Book
Everything® Cocktail Parties & Drinks Book
Everything® College Cookbook
Everything® Cooking for Baby and Toddler Book
Everything® Diabetes Cookbook
Everything® Easy Gourmet Cookbook
Everything® Fondue Cookbook
Everything® Food Allergy Cookbook, $15.95
Everything® Fondue Party Book
Everything® Gluten-Free Cookbook
Everything® Glycemic Index Cookbook
Everything® Grilling Cookbook
Everything® Healthy Cooking for Parties Book, $15.95
Everything® Holiday Cookbook
Everything® Indian Cookbook
Everything® Lactose-Free Cookbook
Everything® Low-Cholesterol Cookbook

Everything® Low-Fat High-Flavor Cookbook, 2nd Ed., $15.95
Everything® Low-Salt Cookbook
Everything® Meals for a Month Cookbook
Everything® Meals on a Budget Cookbook
Everything® Mediterranean Cookbook
Everything® Mexican Cookbook
Everything® No Trans Fat Cookbook
Everything® One-Pot Cookbook, 2nd Ed., $15.95
Everything® Organic Cooking for Baby & Toddler Book, $15.95
Everything® Pizza Cookbook
Everything® Quick Meals Cookbook, 2nd Ed., $15.95
Everything® Slow Cooker Cookbook
Everything® Slow Cooking for a Crowd Cookbook
Everything® Soup Cookbook
Everything® Stir-Fry Cookbook
Everything® Sugar-Free Cookbook
Everything® Tapas and Small Plates Cookbook
Everything® Tex-Mex Cookbook
Everything® Thai Cookbook
Everything® Vegetarian Cookbook
Everything® Whole-Grain, High-Fiber Cookbook
Everything® Wild Game Cookbook
Everything® Wine Book, 2nd Ed.

GAMES

Everything® 15-Minute Sudoku Book, $9.95
Everything® 30-Minute Sudoku Book, $9.95
Everything® Bible Crosswords Book, $9.95
Everything® Blackjack Strategy Book
Everything® Brain Strain Book, $9.95
Everything® Bridge Book
Everything® Card Games Book
Everything® Card Tricks Book, $9.95
Everything® Casino Gambling Book, 2nd Ed.
Everything® Chess Basics Book
Everything® Christmas Crosswords Book, $9.95
Everything® Craps Strategy Book
Everything® Crossword and Puzzle Book
Everything® Crosswords and Puzzles for Quote Lovers Book, $9.95
Everything® Crossword Challenge Book
Everything® Crosswords for the Beach Book, $9.95
Everything® Cryptic Crosswords Book, $9.95
Everything® Cryptograms Book, $9.95
Everything® Easy Crosswords Book
Everything® Easy Kakuro Book, $9.95
Everything® Easy Large-Print Crosswords Book
Everything® Games Book, 2nd Ed.
Everything® Giant Book of Crosswords
Everything® Giant Sudoku Book, $9.95
Everything® Giant Word Search Book
Everything® Kakuro Challenge Book, $9.95
Everything® Large-Print Crossword Challenge Book
Everything® Large-Print Crosswords Book
Everything® Large-Print Travel Crosswords Book
Everything® Lateral Thinking Puzzles Book, $9.95
Everything® Literary Crosswords Book, $9.95
Everything® Mazes Book
Everything® Memory Booster Puzzles Book, $9.95

Everything® Movie Crosswords Book, $9.95
Everything® Music Crosswords Book, $9.95
Everything® Online Poker Book
Everything® Pencil Puzzles Book, $9.95
Everything® Poker Strategy Book
Everything® Pool & Billiards Book
Everything® Puzzles for Commuters Book, $9.95
Everything® Puzzles for Dog Lovers Book, $9.95
Everything® Sports Crosswords Book, $9.95
Everything® Test Your IQ Book, $9.95
Everything® Texas Hold 'Em Book, $9.95
Everything® Travel Crosswords Book, $9.95
Everything® Travel Mazes Book, $9.95
Everything® Travel Word Search Book, $9.95
Everything® TV Crosswords Book, $9.95
Everything® Word Games Challenge Book
Everything® Word Scramble Book
Everything® Word Search Book

HEALTH

Everything® Alzheimer's Book
Everything® Diabetes Book
Everything® First Aid Book, $9.95
Everything® Green Living Book
Everything® Health Guide to Addiction and Recovery
Everything® Health Guide to Adult Bipolar Disorder
Everything® Health Guide to Arthritis
Everything® Health Guide to Controlling Anxiety
Everything® Health Guide to Depression
Everything® Health Guide to Diabetes, 2nd Ed.
Everything® Health Guide to Fibromyalgia
Everything® Health Guide to Menopause, 2nd Ed.
Everything® Health Guide to Migraines
Everything® Health Guide to Multiple Sclerosis
Everything® Health Guide to OCD
Everything® Health Guide to PMS
Everything® Health Guide to Postpartum Care
Everything® Health Guide to Thyroid Disease
Everything® Hypnosis Book
Everything® Low Cholesterol Book
Everything® Menopause Book
Everything® Nutrition Book
Everything® Reflexology Book
Everything® Stress Management Book
Everything® Superfoods Book, $15.95

HISTORY

Everything® American Government Book
Everything® American History Book, 2nd Ed.
Everything® American Revolution Book, $15.95
Everything® Civil War Book
Everything® Freemasons Book
Everything® Irish History & Heritage Book
Everything® World War II Book, 2nd Ed.

HOBBIES

Everything® Candlemaking Book
Everything® Cartooning Book
Everything® Coin Collecting Book
Everything® Digital Photography Book, 2nd Ed.

Everything® Drawing Book
Everything® Family Tree Book, 2nd Ed.
Everything® Guide to Online Genealogy, $15.95
Everything® Knitting Book
Everything® Knots Book
Everything® Photography Book
Everything® Quilting Book
Everything® Sewing Book
Everything® Soapmaking Book, 2nd Ed.
Everything® Woodworking Book

HOME IMPROVEMENT

Everything® Feng Shui Book
Everything® Feng Shui Decluttering Book, $9.95
Everything® Fix-It Book
Everything® Green Living Book
Everything® Home Decorating Book
Everything® Home Storage Solutions Book
Everything® Homebuilding Book
Everything® Organize Your Home Book, 2nd Ed.

KIDS' BOOKS

All titles are $7.95

Everything® Fairy Tales Book, $14.95
Everything® Kids' Animal Puzzle & Activity Book
Everything® Kids' Astronomy Book
Everything® Kids' Baseball Book, 5th Ed.
Everything® Kids' Bible Trivia Book
Everything® Kids' Bugs Book
Everything® Kids' Cars and Trucks Puzzle and Activity Book
Everything® Kids' Christmas Puzzle & Activity Book
Everything® Kids' Connect the Dots
     Puzzle and Activity Book
Everything® Kids' Cookbook, 2nd Ed.
Everything® Kids' Crazy Puzzles Book
Everything® Kids' Dinosaurs Book
Everything® Kids' Dragons Puzzle and Activity Book
Everything® Kids' Environment Book $7.95
Everything® Kids' Fairies Puzzle and Activity Book
Everything® Kids' First Spanish Puzzle and Activity Book
Everything® Kids' Football Book
Everything® Kids' Geography Book
Everything® Kids' Gross Cookbook
Everything® Kids' Gross Hidden Pictures Book
Everything® Kids' Gross Jokes Book
Everything® Kids' Gross Mazes Book
Everything® Kids' Gross Puzzle & Activity Book
Everything® Kids' Halloween Puzzle & Activity Book
Everything® Kids' Hanukkah Puzzle and Activity Book
Everything® Kids' Hidden Pictures Book
Everything® Kids' Horses Book
Everything® Kids' Joke Book
Everything® Kids' Knock Knock Book
Everything® Kids' Learning French Book
Everything® Kids' Learning Spanish Book
Everything® Kids' Magical Science Experiments Book
Everything® Kids' Math Puzzles Book
Everything® Kids' Mazes Book
Everything® Kids' Money Book, 2nd Ed.
Everything® Kids' Mummies, Pharaoh's, and Pyramids
     Puzzle and Activity Book
Everything® Kids' Nature Book
Everything® Kids' Pirates Puzzle and Activity Book
Everything® Kids' Presidents Book
Everything® Kids' Princess Puzzle and Activity Book
Everything® Kids' Puzzle Book

Everything® Kids' Racecars Puzzle and Activity Book
Everything® Kids' Riddles & Brain Teasers Book
Everything® Kids' Science Experiments Book
Everything® Kids' Sharks Book
Everything® Kids' Soccer Book
Everything® Kids' Spelling Book
Everything® Kids' Spies Puzzle and Activity Book
Everything® Kids' States Book
Everything® Kids' Travel Activity Book
Everything® Kids' Word Search Puzzle and Activity Book

LANGUAGE

Everything® Conversational Japanese Book with CD, $19.95
Everything® French Grammar Book
Everything® French Phrase Book, $9.95
Everything® French Verb Book, $9.95
Everything® German Phrase Book, $9.95
Everything® German Practice Book with CD, $19.95
Everything® Inglés Book
Everything® Intermediate Spanish Book with CD, $19.95
Everything® Italian Phrase Book, $9.95
Everything® Italian Practice Book with CD, $19.95
Everything® Learning Brazilian Portuguese Book with CD, $19.95
Everything® Learning French Book with CD, 2nd Ed., $19.95
Everything® Learning German Book
Everything® Learning Italian Book
Everything® Learning Latin Book
Everything® Learning Russian Book with CD, $19.95
Everything® Learning Spanish Book
Everything® Learning Spanish Book with CD, 2nd Ed., $19.95
Everything® Russian Practice Book with CD, $19.95
Everything® Sign Language Book, $15.95
Everything® Spanish Grammar Book
Everything® Spanish Phrase Book, $9.95
Everything® Spanish Practice Book with CD, $19.95
Everything® Spanish Verb Book, $9.95
Everything® Speaking Mandarin Chinese Book with CD, $19.95

MUSIC

Everything® Bass Guitar Book with CD, $19.95
Everything® Drums Book with CD, $19.95
Everything® Guitar Book with CD, 2nd Ed., $19.95
Everything® Guitar Chords Book with CD, $19.95
Everything® Guitar Scales Book with CD, $19.95
Everything® Harmonica Book with CD, $15.95
Everything® Home Recording Book
Everything® Music Theory Book with CD, $19.95
Everything® Reading Music Book with CD, $19.95
Everything® Rock & Blues Guitar Book with CD, $19.95
Everything® Rock & Blues Piano Book with CD, $19.95
Everything® Rock Drums Book with CD, $19.95
Everything® Singing Book with CD, $19.95
Everything® Songwriting Book

NEW AGE

Everything® Astrology Book, 2nd Ed.
Everything® Birthday Personology Book
Everything® Celtic Wisdom Book, $15.95
Everything® Dreams Book, 2nd Ed.
Everything® Law of Attraction Book, $15.95
Everything® Love Signs Book, $9.95
Everything® Love Spells Book, $9.95
Everything® Palmistry Book
Everything® Psychic Book
Everything® Reiki Book

Everything® Sex Signs Book, $9.95
Everything® Spells & Charms Book, 2nd Ed.
Everything® Tarot Book, 2nd Ed.
Everything® Toltec Wisdom Book
Everything® Wicca & Witchcraft Book, 2nd Ed.

PARENTING

Everything® Baby Names Book, 2nd Ed.
Everything® Baby Shower Book, 2nd Ed.
Everything® Baby Sign Language Book with DVD
Everything® Baby's First Year Book
Everything® Birthing Book
Everything® Breastfeeding Book
Everything® Father-to-Be Book
Everything® Father's First Year Book
Everything® Get Ready for Baby Book, 2nd Ed.
Everything® Get Your Baby to Sleep Book, $9.95
Everything® Getting Pregnant Book
Everything® Guide to Pregnancy Over 35
Everything® Guide to Raising a One-Year-Old
Everything® Guide to Raising a Two-Year-Old
Everything® Guide to Raising Adolescent Boys
Everything® Guide to Raising Adolescent Girls
Everything® Mother's First Year Book
Everything® Parent's Guide to Childhood Illnesses
Everything® Parent's Guide to Children and Divorce
Everything® Parent's Guide to Children with ADD/ADHD
Everything® Parent's Guide to Children with Asperger's
     Syndrome
Everything® Parent's Guide to Children with Anxiety
Everything® Parent's Guide to Children with Asthma
Everything® Parent's Guide to Children with Autism
Everything® Parent's Guide to Children with Bipolar Disorder
Everything® Parent's Guide to Children with Depression
Everything® Parent's Guide to Children with Dyslexia
Everything® Parent's Guide to Children with Juvenile Diabetes
Everything® Parent's Guide to Children with OCD
Everything® Parent's Guide to Positive Discipline
Everything® Parent's Guide to Raising Boys
Everything® Parent's Guide to Raising Girls
Everything® Parent's Guide to Raising Siblings
Everything® Parent's Guide to Raising Your
     Adopted Child
Everything® Parent's Guide to Sensory Integration Disorder
Everything® Parent's Guide to Tantrums
Everything® Parent's Guide to the Strong-Willed Child
Everything® Parenting a Teenager Book
Everything® Potty Training Book, $9.95
Everything® Pregnancy Book, 3rd Ed.
Everything® Pregnancy Fitness Book
Everything® Pregnancy Nutrition Book
Everything® Pregnancy Organizer, 2nd Ed., $16.95
Everything® Toddler Activities Book
Everything® Toddler Book
Everything® Tween Book
Everything® Twins, Triplets, and More Book

PETS

Everything® Aquarium Book
Everything® Boxer Book
Everything® Cat Book, 2nd Ed.
Everything® Chihuahua Book
Everything® Cooking for Dogs Book
Everything® Dachshund Book
Everything® Dog Book, 2nd Ed.
Everything® Dog Grooming Book

Everything® Dog Obedience Book
Everything® Dog Owner's Organizer, $16.95
Everything® Dog Training and Tricks Book
Everything® German Shepherd Book
Everything® Golden Retriever Book
Everything® Horse Book, 2nd Ed., $15.95
Everything® Horse Care Book
Everything® Horseback Riding Book
Everything® Labrador Retriever Book
Everything® Poodle Book
Everything® Pug Book
Everything® Puppy Book
Everything® Small Dogs Book
Everything® Tropical Fish Book
Everything® Yorkshire Terrier Book

REFERENCE

Everything® American Presidents Book
Everything® Blogging Book
Everything® Build Your Vocabulary Book, $9.95
Everything® Car Care Book
Everything® Classical Mythology Book
Everything® Da Vinci Book
Everything® Einstein Book
Everything® Enneagram Book
Everything® Etiquette Book, 2nd Ed.
Everything® Family Christmas Book, $15.95
Everything® Guide to C. S. Lewis & Narnia
Everything® Guide to Divorce, 2nd Ed., $15.95
Everything® Guide to Edgar Allan Poe
Everything® Guide to Understanding Philosophy
Everything® Inventions and Patents Book
Everything® Jacqueline Kennedy Onassis Book
Everything® John F. Kennedy Book
Everything® Mafia Book
Everything® Martin Luther King Jr. Book
Everything® Pirates Book
Everything® Private Investigation Book
Everything® Psychology Book
Everything® Public Speaking Book, $9.95
Everything® Shakespeare Book, 2nd Ed.

RELIGION

Everything® Angels Book
Everything® Bible Book
Everything® Bible Study Book with CD, $19.95
Everything® Buddhism Book
Everything® Catholicism Book
Everything® Christianity Book
Everything® Gnostic Gospels Book
Everything® Hinduism Book, $15.95
Everything® History of the Bible Book
Everything® Jesus Book
Everything® Jewish History & Heritage Book
Everything® Judaism Book
Everything® Kabbalah Book
Everything® Koran Book
Everything® Mary Book
Everything® Mary Magdalene Book
Everything® Prayer Book

Everything® Saints Book, 2nd Ed.
Everything® Torah Book
Everything® Understanding Islam Book
Everything® Women of the Bible Book
Everything® World's Religions Book

SCHOOL & CAREERS

Everything® Career Tests Book
Everything® College Major Test Book
Everything® College Survival Book, 2nd Ed.
Everything® Cover Letter Book, 2nd Ed.
Everything® Filmmaking Book
Everything® Get-a-Job Book, 2nd Ed.
Everything® Guide to Being a Paralegal
Everything® Guide to Being a Personal Trainer
Everything® Guide to Being a Real Estate Agent
Everything® Guide to Being a Sales Rep
Everything® Guide to Being an Event Planner
Everything® Guide to Careers in Health Care
Everything® Guide to Careers in Law Enforcement
Everything® Guide to Government Jobs
Everything® Guide to Starting and Running a Catering
   Business
Everything® Guide to Starting and Running a Restaurant
**Everything® Guide to Starting and Running
   a Retail Store**
Everything® Job Interview Book, 2nd Ed.
Everything® New Nurse Book
Everything® New Teacher Book
Everything® Paying for College Book
Everything® Practice Interview Book
Everything® Resume Book, 3rd Ed.
Everything® Study Book

SELF-HELP

Everything® Body Language Book
Everything® Dating Book, 2nd Ed.
Everything® Great Sex Book
**Everything® Guide to Caring for Aging Parents,
   $15.95**
Everything® Self-Esteem Book
Everything® Self-Hypnosis Book, $9.95
Everything® Tantric Sex Book

SPORTS & FITNESS

Everything® Easy Fitness Book
Everything® Fishing Book
Everything® Guide to Weight Training, $15.95
Everything® Krav Maga for Fitness Book
Everything® Running Book, 2nd Ed.
Everything® Triathlon Training Book, $15.95

TRAVEL

Everything® Family Guide to Coastal Florida
Everything® Family Guide to Cruise Vacations
Everything® Family Guide to Hawaii
Everything® Family Guide to Las Vegas, 2nd Ed.
Everything® Family Guide to Mexico
Everything® Family Guide to New England, 2nd Ed.

Everything® Family Guide to New York City, 3rd Ed.
**Everything® Family Guide to Northern California
   and Lake Tahoe**
Everything® Family Guide to RV Travel & Campgrounds
Everything® Family Guide to the Caribbean
Everything® Family Guide to the Disneyland® Resort, California
   Adventure® Universal Studios®, and the Anaheim
   Area, 2nd Ed.
Everything® Family Guide to the Walt Disney World Resort®,
   Universal Studios®, and Greater Orlando, 5th Ed.
Everything® Family Guide to Timeshares
Everything® Family Guide to Washington D.C., 2nd Ed.

WEDDINGS

Everything® Bachelorette Party Book, $9.95
Everything® Bridesmaid Book, $9.95
Everything® Destination Wedding Book
Everything® Father of the Bride Book, $9.95
Everything® Green Wedding Book, $15.95
Everything® Groom Book, $9.95
Everything® Jewish Wedding Book, 2nd Ed., $15.95
Everything® Mother of the Bride Book, $9.95
Everything® Outdoor Wedding Book
Everything® Wedding Book, 3rd Ed.
Everything® Wedding Checklist, $9.95
Everything® Wedding Etiquette Book, $9.95
Everything® Wedding Organizer, 2nd Ed., $16.95
Everything® Wedding Shower Book, $9.95
Everything® Wedding Vows Book, 3rd Ed., $9.95
Everything® Wedding Workout Book
Everything® Weddings on a Budget Book, 2nd Ed., $9.95

WRITING

Everything® Creative Writing Book
Everything® Get Published Book, 2nd Ed.
Everything® Grammar and Style Book, 2nd Ed.
Everything® Guide to Magazine Writing
Everything® Guide to Writing a Book Proposal
Everything® Guide to Writing a Novel
Everything® Guide to Writing Children's Books
Everything® Guide to Writing Copy
Everything® Guide to Writing Graphic Novels
Everything® Guide to Writing Research Papers
Everything® Guide to Writing a Romance Novel, $15.95
Everything® Improve Your Writing Book, 2nd Ed.
Everything® Writing Poetry Book